COMMON SENSE CHRISTIAN LIVING

Books by Edith Schaeffer

L'Abri
Hidden Art
Christianity is Jewish
What is a Family?
A Way of Seeing
Affliction
Everyone Can Know (with Francis Schaeffer)
Lifelines
The Tapestry

COMMON SENSE CHRISTIAN LIVING

by
Edith Schaeffer

THOMAS NELSON PUBLISHERS
NASHVILLE • CAMDEN • NEW YORK

Published in Nashville, Tennessee, by Thomas Nelson, Inc. and distributed in Canada by Lawson Falle, Ltd., Cambridge, Ontario.

Printed in the United States of America.

Unless otherwise indicated, the Scripture quotations in this book are from the New King James Version. Copyright © 1979, 1980, 1982, Thomas Nelson, Inc., Publishers.

Scripture quotations noted NIV are from the Holy Bible: New International Version. Copyright © 1978 by the New York International Bible Society. Used by permission of Zondervan Bible Publishers.

Scripture quotations noted KJV are from the King James Version of the Bible.

Library of Congress Cataloging in Publication Data

Schaeffer, Edith.
  Common sense Christian living.

  1. Christian life—1960-   I. Title.
BV4501.2.S282   1983   248.4   83-8263
ISBN 0-8407-5280-6

Dedication

I'd like to dedicate this book to those who taught me what common sense Christian living is all about! I began learning as a child, and of course my parents and Chinese amah and my sister Elsa especially influenced me, along with my sister Janet, and the wider family. Then came along Fran, when I was seventeen, and from then on he influenced my thinking and actions, ideas and practical life.

It is hard to dissect the "when" and the "where" of one's learning. But my children have taught me a great deal about common sense Christian living that I would not have known had they not been a part of my life, as they grew and dispersed ideas, and as they became my friends with their own personalities and diverse points of view. Then, along came three sons-in-law and one daughter-in-law, each of whom had their part in opening my "eyes of understanding" to new facets of Christian living. Now fourteen grandchildren are making their contribution to my growing understanding, and one grandson-in-law.

Therefore, this book is dedicated to those whose lives are a part of mine, including the wider circle of the family, who have been . . . and are . . . the human factor in my continuing process of learning—for I am still learning! These people are the *human* factor in all our learning, although, for those of us who know Him, the understanding the Lord gives cannot be measured in any way.

Contents

Film

The film version of *Common Sense Christian Living* is available from Franky Schaeffer V Productions, P.O. Box 909, Los Gatos, CA 95031. This magnificent five-episode film brings all the warmth and personality of Edith Schaeffer herself to the audience. In an intimate lecture and discussion group setting, with a small gathering of people, Edith Schaeffer presents, in person, the ideas contained in this book.

The series is in 16mm color. Each episode is 30 minutes long. The titles of the episodes are:

I and II—Continuity in the Family
III and IV—What Is Real Spirituality?
and V—What Is Prayer?

Within those episodes is covered the content presented in this book.

For information, please write to Franky Schaeffer V Productions or call 408/356-6677.

Acknowledgements

So many people in every area of life, in every creative work that is made—from bridges to newspapers, from meal preparation to the bringing forth of a book—are never "acknowledged" at all. Appreciation that is felt is so frequently not expressed.

I would like to acknowledge that after writing a book there are many people involved in the final product . . . and one would have to list *all* the people working in publishing, printing, sales, advertising, and in bookstores to cover the reality of who makes it possible for books to be on our shelves or in our hands as we settle down beside a fire to read on a cold and windy night!

I can't begin to list everyone fairly who had something to do with the bringing out of this book, but—THANK YOU—you know who you are.

Thank you, Franky, for pushing for the film series and taking the weight with Jim to gather a crew and do all the work of filming so that the book would have something to "accompany" . . . as it would be written to fill out what could not be included in the films.

Thank you, Anne, for inviting an audience, and thank you, each one of you in the audience, for being so open with your questions and asking not only your own honest questions, but ones which will be a help to other people.

Thank you, Rochester L'Abri workers, Diane, Libby, and Lloyd, for your help during the pressed times of filming and writing.

Thank you, husband Fran, for bearing with me through another "book-pregnancy" of my eating-sleeping-waking-in-the-night period of bringing forth another book.

Thank you, Mary Lou, for your unhesitating willingness to step in and do the rereading and editing I was unable to do at that particular moment . . . thereby saving a month of time for the publishing date.

Thank you, Mike, Gail, Jim, and other L'Abri workers, for pitching in to do a variety of things when needed. And—thank you again, each one of my children and grandchildren, for helping me to know and live the contents—at least to a degree! I am still learning. We don't learn to live . . . all on our own . . . anymore than we can produce a finished product all on our own.

Thank you, Ray Cioni, for a beautiful cover. . . . You have chosen a blend of colors to "frame" Mary Cassatt's painting that will blend into the homes of many people as it sits on their coffee tables. That painting you chose, Ray, gives a window into what a glimpse of common sense Christian living has consisted of through centuries. Thank you for such a vivid glimpse, which speaks both gently and strongly at the same time.

Thank you, Sam Moore, Larry Stone, and all who comprise Thomas Nelson Publishers at this time of history, . . . for launching this book!

Foreword

WHEN YOU SEE THE film *Common Sense Christian Living*, you will be able to slip into the library of Plummer House in Rochester, Minnesota, and join the thirty people, invited by Anne Brown, one of our L'Abri workers in Rochester, who came for five evenings to listen to my lectures and to ask their very real questions. Perhaps the honest questions of this cross section of people will be your questions too. There were as many men as women. There were married couples and single people. There were doctors, nurses, schoolteachers, pastors, IBM engineers, a stockbroker, mothers and homemakers, a bookstore owner, a roadbuilder.

This filming, done by Franky Schaeffer V Productions, will enable you to be a part of the audience at any time, in your own home, or church, or camp, or retreat, as thoroughly as if you had been sitting in Plummer House. However, although these periods of time are intensive, five half-hours are not sufficient to give as much as this book can give as you sit in front of a fire, or curl up in bed, or study at your desk, or sit in a lawn chair in the sun to read and think. The book also adds material for study and discussion with friends, your family, or a study group.

This book does not try to cover everything that pertains to Christian life, nor does it try to be a handbook for Christian living.

It does deal with what it means to live on the basis of constantly realizing that all of life is to be our spiritual life. We are to rejoice that as we create beauty as architects or gardeners, as farmers or cooks, we are doing what God made human beings capable of doing. We are made in the image of the Creator, to be able to have ideas, choose among them, and be creative in a tremendous diversity of ways.

We are not to live our lives in compartments labeled "spiritual" and "secular," as if our scrubbing the floors, pruning the trees, adding a porch to the house, playing ball with our children, preparing a meal for friends, inventing a new kind of camera or wagon, or running for town council, are neutral things, and that only going to church, praying, or reading our Bibles are Christian portions of our living.

We need to look straight at the questions of what it means to be compassionate to those in doubt or despair, and how to deal with our own ups and downs. We need to realize that what we *are*, what our family life demonstrates to onlookers, is of as much importance—and often more so—than what we *say* as we teach, lecture, preach, or sing in our Christian church activities.

I believe that what is *in* this book is of intense importance and is often in danger of being left *out* of our understanding of what Christian living is meant to be! The New Testament is, of course, our handbook of what the Lord expects of us in our period of time in the land of the living, before we go to be with Him through death or before we are in our new bodies at the Resurrection. This book is not an attempt to cover every area of that which is to make up our Christian lives. Of course we are to search for a Bible-believing church in order to have communion with other believers, and to be "gathered together" week by week. Of course there is importance in carefully studying the Bible and asking for God's help in our growing understanding. Of course there is to be a constant struggle against whatever our own weaknesses are, and the temptations that so easily hit us.

History has gone through a great many periods, with the prevalent temptations, evils, or issues frequently ignored by the Christians of that immediate period. At each period of history it was important that some Christians urged others to wake up and recognize they were being blind to some things and falling into rationalizing that which was wrong in that period. Read Revelation 2 and 3 to be reminded of this. God searches the hearts and minds of His people in generation after generation. We are to be careful not to be fooled by Satan's lies that surround us in our immediate moment of history. We need to help each other be alert and to examine the dangers of tolerating things we are not to tolerate.

We are to be among the ones in all the stream of history who "overcame him by the blood of the Lamb" (Rev. 12:11). To the church in Pergamos (see Rev. 2), the warning was given concerning the temptation to be enticed by those who held to the teaching of Balaam. They were to watch out, and to overcome the temptations to eat food sacrificed to idols and to take part in sexual immorality. The church at Sardis was admonished to wake up. A deadness had crept in. "Be watchful, and strengthen the things which remain, that are ready to die, for I have not found your works perfect before God" (Rev. 3:2).

The slave trade needed active opposition in one period of history. William Wilberforce (1759–1833) lived a life of true common sense Christianity as he sacrificed other people's good opinions of him and courageously pioneered in fighting the whole matter of slavery in his day. A true spiritual life was being lived by people in another period of history as they fought the introduction of the opium trade in China, when certain English people put money above any consideration of the preciousness of human life. Hitler was born in 1889, and somewhere along the path of history Christians in Germany were in need of waking up to the issues of their day. They needed to get involved with issues that might not have seemed spiritual by their definition, but which indeed should have been a part of their priorities in Christian living.

From the time of God's people at any point of history recorded in the Old Testament, to the time of the early church, on up to our time in history, there have been admonitions concerning the need to be aware of righting wrongs, of being salt to preserve a rotting culture, rotting in one way or another.

This book will deal with some of the practical issues of today as they affect each one of us, our families, our friends, our churches, our neighbors, and our country. It also will be practical in very down-to-earth areas of everyday life.

It is a book for our own moment of history as we face the things that are confusing in our rapidly changing culture. Our children and grandchildren need us to have as much understanding as is possible of the things they face day by day. If we are teachers of other people's children, or are nurses and doctors caring for bewildered people who have been abused physically, intellectually, or emotionally because of new waves of immorality or changing standards, we *need* to be ready to face today's battles, today's variety of Satan's attacks, today's "issues" affecting the people among whom we live and work . . . not yesterday's issues, not the "issues" of ten or fifty years ago!

This book deals with some of the things we need to be concerned about in our *Common Sense Christian Living*—TODAY!

CHAPTER ONE

Introduction

HOW DID YOU DECIDE to write this book? is the question that comes so frequently concerning each book. This time I will try to answer before you begin to read! Franky, our film-maker son, had asked me to let him and his partner Jim make a film called *Common Sense Christian Living*, which would be of my lecturing to some people and answering their questions. Looking back, it still seems amazing to me that the time and place fit together for Franky and Jim, for the people in the audience, for the film crew of nine men, for the particularly lovely library to be free those nights in Plummer House, in Rochester, Minnesota. There were so many factors that had to fit together that we realize it was not just "good planning," humanly speaking.

The film was professionally made with the lighting arranged to come through rice paper-covered windows to give a soft, natural light. It was the first time I had done such a thing, and it was not an easy task for Franky to direct his mother in the making of a film. For me it was scary to think I might spoil miles of film or do the wrong thing!

However, I can honestly say that those were very "real" evenings. It was not long before I forgot the cameras and became intensely absorbed in communicating what I felt needed to be understood by the people I was talking to, including Franky and Jim and the crew as well as the audience.

This book has been written to give you the content of the lectures, and the questions and answers given those evenings. The book contains the very real questions that mattered to very real people. They were their own questions, not prompted nor handed out on a paper. Actually the book and the film should go together hand in hand. The film should be shown in your home, your church, a camp, a retreat, during a conference, for a luncheon, for a Bible study evening, and so on. Each person who sees the film should have the book to read. The book is much more full: all that is contained in the book would have taken too long for you to have on film. Anyway, a book can fill out or complete some of the thoughts that were started on film.

This book does not try to cover everything in life, nor does it try to be a complete handbook for Christian living. It is made up of intimate talks together, with some portions answering as honestly as possible some direct questions . . . which may be your questions too.

Very much has been left *out* of the book. What is *in* the book, I believe, is of intense importance, and is in danger of being left out of our lives. This is not simply a repeating of the usual outline, because I believe we need to consider what is so often left out of a lot of teaching or understanding about Christian living.

What Is Common Sense?

"She has a Ph.D. in archeology, but out on the dig she simply doesn't show any common sense." "That brown-haired nurse is worth all the others because of her obvious supply of common sense . . . just plain common sense." "That high-school graduate I had this summer to help with my dairy farm is going to make a good vet—he has so much common sense."

Common sense—what is it?

It is common sense to quickly take the baby off the changing table or bed and put him or her on the floor in a safe spot before answering the telephone. It is common sense to recognize signs of hunger, or a dry throat, and to supply children, guests, or family with something to fill that physical need.

Is common sense simply an old-fashioned term that has no place in today's highly trained, highly specialized, highly analyzed, self-introspective society? Do people have so much "know-how," so many "how-to" books, so many charts and lists, tests and goals that the need of common sense has been pushed out of our minds, and the phrase has been pushed out of our vocabulary? Or do you and I say to each other just as frequently as our great-grandparents did, "*Please* use your common sense!"

It is interesting to look at definitions of *common sense* and *sense*.

Webster's Compact Dictionary[1] gives a very compact definition: "common sense, ordinary good judgment." And in this small dictionary, the third definition under *sense* is "intuition regarding a situation."

In the larger *Webster's New Collegiate Dictionary*[2] we find the first definition of *common sense* is: "sound and prudent but often unsophisticated judgment." Turning to the word *sense* in that same dictionary we come across definition 6a: "capacity for effective application of the powers of the mind as a basis for action or response: INTELLIGENCE b: sound mental capacity and understanding typically marked by shrewdness and practicality." And a line or two farther down comes: "SENSE, COMMON SENSE, GUMPTION, JUDGEMENT, WISDOM, . . . ability to reach intelligent conclusions."

These are definitions to get your pencil out and underline!

The *Doubleday Roget's Thesaurus*[3] gives a list of words that will be useful while we are thinking of definitions to help our basic understanding. The following list of synonyms accompanies *common sense:*

reason	plausibility
logic	coherence
judgment	clear-headedness
intelligence	lucidity
mother wit	consistency
rationality	intelligibility
sanity	

Before we plunge into what all this means when we add the words *Christian living*, we should underline other lists from both the dictionary and the thesaurus that give us a definition of the *opposite*. What does *senseless* mean? We need to recognize that the negative of *sense* or *common sense* needs words that hit us so strongly that we do not have a vague, misty, foggy, blurred idea of what the antithesis of *sense* consists of.

First, Webster's definition of *senseless:* "destitute of, deficient

---

[1]Walter C. Kidney, ed., *Nelson's New Compact Webster's Dictionary* (Nashville, Tenn.: Thomas Nelson Publishers, 1978).

[2]*Webster's New Collegiate Dictionary* (Springfield, Mass.: G. & C. Merriam Company, 1979).

[3]Sidney Landau and Ronald Bogus, eds., *Doubleday Roget's Thesaurus* (New York: Doubleday, 1977).

in, or contrary to sense: as a: UNCONSCIOUS b: FOOLISH, STUPID c:
MEANINGLESS, PURPOSELESS."

Second, the list of synonyms from *Roget's Thesaurus* for *sense-less:*

foolish	purposeless
insane	idiotic
stupid	brainless
silly	emptyheaded
nonsensical	scatterbrained
irrational	mad
meaningless	crazy

In today's confusion of voices throwing words at us concerning life, we need to sit still and quietly sort out the ideas and influences so that we can keep from being swept away by a tidal wave of that which is false. Happily, there is truth. Truth exists, and truth makes sense. The exciting thing is that because truth makes sense, when we come to find truth and to base our lives on it, then there is a practical possibility of doing what Webster defines as *sense.* There is a practical possibility of our finding a capacity that continues to grow, a "capacity for effective application of the powers of the mind as a basis for action or response."

DULL?

No, exciting!

When we come to answer questions and discuss what common sense Christian living is all about, we are not talking about hanging our minds on a hook outside the door and coming into a room filled with emotion and some airy fairy kind of spiritual atmosphere where thinking is taboo and where the words *common sense* seem ill chosen. We are talking about the opposite of foolish, meaningless, stupid, and purposeless—the total opposite.

When we come to know truth is true, in our minds, a basis is now there within us. Each of us who comes to this moment of clarity has a basis for action and response. We can have response to the God we know exists, and we can begin to see actions in our everyday lives that correspond to Him, and to His creation. Purpose and meaning take shape! Little by little we come to discover the wonder of how complete the Christian life is. Little by little we come to discover some small measure of what it means to live in the light of who we are as made in the image of the Creator, to live in the midst of His creation—free to make limited discoveries until finally when Christ returns we are released from all hindrances to making the tremendous discoveries ahead of us, discoveries of perfection! As we live in the Creator's creation we are to be different after we come to know the Creator Himself and come to recognize the marvel of having His help in creativity which He made us capable of . . . not by a fluke but by careful design.

Common sense Christian living leaves no place for compartments, for boxes labeled "spiritual life," "business life," "family life," "sick leave," "entertainment," "vacations," "studying," "physical exercise," "gardening," "painting," "hobbies," "time spent with children," or "Christian work." The title encompasses all of life—the mundane and the exotic, the tragedies and the thrills, the afflictions and the surprises of joy.

Common sense Christian living includes the drudgeries—the unchanging preparation of three meals a day, or delivering newspapers, or plowing fields, or putting fifty-seven pieces in the proper places as the wide belt passes you in a car factory, or facing the complicated decisions of an executive, or teaching a class of thirty fifth-graders. It also includes the sudden bursts of creative ideas, composing music, or a poem, or a garden, or a table arrangement for supper, realizing that such things are not meaningless, stupid, purposeless, and foolish simply because we are in a world where all the news is of war, and more war and more destruction and suffering.

The Bible is full of contrasts between fools and wise people, between foolishness and wisdom. Rather than going on simply with human definitions of *sense* and *senselessness*, of *wisdom* and *foolishness*, we can look next at God's differentiation, or definition of the wide differences among people as they honestly seek truth, and later live in some measure on the basis of truth, or turn their backs on truth and live on the basis of an assortment of lies.

> The fool has said in his heart,
> "There is no God."
> They are corrupt,
> They have done abominable works,
> There is none who does good.
>
> The LORD looks down from heaven upon the children of men,
> To see if there are any who understand, who seek God.
>
> Ps. 14:1–2

The use of "fool" here is not name-calling; it is the accurate description given by the Creator, the perfect, everlasting God, of any human being who says—not just with throat and lips, but inwardly with all of the completeness of the person—"There is no God." In the New Testament in the Book of Luke there is the parable of the Rich Fool—another kind of fool. You perhaps remember the story Jesus told to teach a strong, important lesson. He told of a very rich man who didn't know what to do with all his excess of crops. He decided to tear down his barns, build larger ones and store up enough to live a life of ease.

> "'And I will say to my soul, "Soul, you have many goods laid up for many years; take your ease; eat, drink and be merry."' But God said to him, 'You fool! This very night your soul will be required of you; then whose will those things be which you have provided?' So is he who lays up treasure for himself, and is not rich toward God."
>
> Luke 12:19–21

Here is a second kind of person God calls a fool. This is not someone who does not believe in the existence of God, but a person who has put success in material things in the place of what is called "richness toward God." There *is* a richness to be discovered that is not foolish. This opposite kind of richness is something we need to know about, Jesus goes on to say, as He points out that life is more than food, and the body more than clothes. In the next paragraph Jesus puts a spotlight on the reality of what will take place if the balance is right. He does not say material possessions are not needed, or are not good. Speaking of material things He says: "'For all these things the nations of the world seek after, and your Father knows that you need these things. But seek the kingdom of God, and all these things shall be added to you'" (Luke 12:30–31).

The fool says, "There is no God," or, "If there is a God I am taking care of myself first." The astounding evidence the precise universe gives of God's existence is accepted by the attributes of a human being labeled "sense" or "wisdom." The fantastic logic of the fact that if this God who created the universe exists is that it is foolish, inane, nonsensical, irrational to turn one's ears away from His directions as to how to live.

In the New Testament in the Book of Romans, a big searchlight is turned on to human beings who have foolishly turned away from the truth and reality of God's existence, and are living accordingly. Imagine a large stage with a scene being enacted before you such as is described in Romans. Imagine the accompanying music and costumes, the lighting and special effects. In today's world it would not take much imagining, as TV sets bring this kind of scene into the home only too often, and people are plunged into a vivid demonstration of what God is talking about, day after day.

However, it isn't even necessary to look at a play, a film, or a discotheque to be immersed in example after example of all that God gives us through Paul's description in Romans—*Newsweek* and *Time* magazines, the daily newspaper, and news broadcasts give sufficient evidence that the Book of Romans is indeed up-to-date.

Read the whole first chapter of Romans for yourself, but I want to quote a few lines here:

> . . . because, although they knew God, they did not glorify Him as God, nor were thankful, but became futile in their thoughts, and their *foolish* hearts were darkened. Professing to be *wise,* they became *fools* and changed the glory of the incorruptible God into an image made like corruptible man—and birds and four-footed beasts and creeping things. Therefore God also gave them up to uncleanness, in the lusts of their hearts, to dishonor their bodies among themselves, who exchanged the truth of God for the lie, and worshiped and served the creature rather than the Creator . . .
> Rom. 1:21–25, emphasis added

What a swap! A whole life based on a lie, with truth thrown away. What a swap! Millions of lives based on lies, millions of human beings following the examples of others who have exchanged the truth of God for a lie. Millions of devastated lives, torn to pieces emotionally, psychologically, and physically following that which leads to meaninglessness and purposelessness in every area of life.

> For this reason God gave them up to vile passions. For even their women exchanged the natural use for what is against nature. Likewise also the men, leaving the natural use of the woman, burned in their lust for one another, men with men committing what is shameful, and receiving in themselves the penalty of their error which was due. Rom. 1:26–27

Our newspapers and television news are full of flying banners and marching human beings flaunting their determination to continue exchanging the truth of God for a lie in actions and lifestyles that bring a variety of physical results in their own bodies, in addition to results affecting many other people. A "penalty" often doesn't need to be handed out formally, but it follows with frightening swiftness as the news is full of scandal stories that would fit in to what was written two thousand years ago in warning.

Do the words *sound and prudent* in any way describe the diversity of ways in which human beings can make decisions to swap even looking for truth with settling down to live on the basis of "the big lie" in its different forms? Remember that Webster's first definition of *common sense* is "sound and prudent but often unsophisticated judgment."

Do people who do not believe God exists, or who do not yet know God exists ever have what could be called "common sense"? Yes. I believe many do, and I want to talk about that later. However, millions of people today are living in the category being described here—a category that would fit "terrorists" of a variety of kinds, living in a cross section of neighborhoods across the world.

> And even as they did not like to retain God in their knowledge, God gave them over to a debased mind, to do those things which are not fitting; being filled with all unrighteousness, sexual immorality, wickedness, covetousness, maliciousness, full of envy, murder, strife, deceit, evil-mindedness; they are whisperers, back-biters, haters of God, violent, proud, boasters, inventors of evil things, disobedient to parents, undiscerning, untrustworthy, unloving, unforgiving, unmerciful; who, . . . not only do the same but also approve of those who practice them.   Rom. 1:28–32

Terrorists attack governments and attempt to upset any existing order. I've used the word *terrorist* to describe those who would attack the true order of the universe God made and the reality of who and what human beings really are. People are swapping their own fulfillment in order to attempt to be something human beings were not made to be. The environment that will allow the growth and development of truly human human beings has been polluted, and we are aware of twisted, deformed emotions and understanding, as well as actions.

We who want to live in the light of the existence of God, and who want to lead balanced lives on the basis of the truth of what exists and also of who we are, need to be aware that the atmosphere or environment has been polluted and that we need some kind of discernment, perhaps seen as a "gas mask," to sift ideas and understanding so that we don't become either warped or stifled.

We need to consider what "sense" rather than "senselessness" has to do with our own day-by-day living, what "wisdom" rather than "foolishness" has to do with our own day-by-day thinking. We *are* in the world in this point in history. We do not yet live in heaven. We have to consider our need for growing understanding, for constant help from God, as well as our need of being helpful to the world around us. What does it mean to be "salt" in a world that is filled with decay? What does it mean to be "light" when the world is becoming darker?

Do we give approval to those who practice murder, strife, deceit, evil, and so on through the list in Romans 1? Do we give approval by drawing up our drawbridge, so to speak, and retreating into our own castle fortress, not interfering at all with that which is considered "not the business of a Christian"? Interweaving the quote from the New Testament with that which God said through Isaiah helps us to see that human beings have continually used their freedom of choice to choose that which throws them into the category of fools rather than the wise. Choice has been used through the centuries to choose a lie rather than truth, right back to the first choice in the Garden of Eden for death rather than life. It isn't a lack of evidence of truth's existence that has brought about the misery among human beings, but the continual deluge of human choice hitting history like a tidal wave at times, and like an eroding stream at others. People who operate on the basis of lies concerning the universe and also concerning who they are as human beings, are wise only in their own eyes, so God says in Romans 1:22: "Professing to be wise, they became fools. . . ."

Isaiah gave that information brilliantly centuries ago as God gave him the message people needed to hear then. And we still need it in this moment of history.

> Woe to those who draw iniquity with cords of vanity,
> And sin as if with a cart rope;
> That say, "Let Him make speed,
>   and hasten his work
> That we may see it. . . ."
>
> Woe to those who call evil good, and good evil,
> Who put darkness for light, and light for darkness,
> Who put bitter for sweet, and sweet for bitter!
>
> Woe to those who are wise in their own eyes,
> And prudent in their own sight!
>
> Is. 5:18–21

Earlier in this chapter of Isaiah the people have been described as similar to the ones in the quotations from Romans. These are people God speaks to in judgment because their whole interest is in adding house to house, field to field, as well as in having drinking parties.

> But they do not regard the work of the LORD,
> Nor consider the operation of His hands.
> Therefore my people have gone into captivity,
> Because they have no knowledge.
>
> Is. 5:12–13

This deeper dilemma of human beings needs to be faced before we can deal with what common sense Christian living could mean to a child of the living God, to someone who has become His child through understanding that He does exist and that He has provided a door, an entrance, to Himself through the Messiah, so long shown to be the Way.

We live in a polluted atmosphere. We breathe the same air as everyone else in our cities, valleys, factory areas, or even mountains and seasides. The sun shines on us with its drought-producing fierceness at times, and the floods come to our doors. We are affected by the physical, material, historic surroundings in which we live.

We also are bombarded by a diversity of ideas and enticements that are polluted by "lie" rather than truth. One of the biggest lies is that there is no truth, that no absolute exists at all. That lie continues to bring forth a stream of changed lifestyles, changed laws, changed educational standards, changed behavior standards, shifting morals, and constantly differing "measuring sticks" for checking up on ourselves.

What is the answer? To shut ourselves up in a glass cage with nonpolluted air streaming in and sterile food somehow delivered without contact with the world?

It seems to me that our common sense should help us here to see that Christians should live as whole beings on the basis of what they have been created to be in the reality of the geography lived in, and the time of history lived in—on the basis of the very opposite of being a fool. That is, Christians should live on the basis of the wisdom of God which is available to us.

There is a blur around us, a mixture that confuses us. We need to care about not just muddling on and trying to live in separate compartments. We need to strive for wholeness in a practical way, hour by hour and day by day, that there might be the reality that is meant to be in me and in you.

> Therefore the LORD said:
> ". . . these people draw near to Me with their mouths

And honor Me with their lips,
But have removed their hearts far from Me,
And their fear toward Me
    is taught by the commandment of men.

Is. 29:13

Does life seem so senseless that talking about common sense sounds idiotic? Is there no source from which help can come when we despair of any meaning? Again we go to what the Lord says:

Surely you have things turned around!
Shall the potter be esteemed as the clay;
For shall the thing made say of him who made it,
"He did not make me"?
Or shall the thing formed say of him who formed it,
"He has no understanding"?

Is. 29:16

The chairs are on the ceiling; the ship is upside down in the ocean! We are surrounded by people turning things, ideas, philosophies, theories, upside down and saying not only that the potter did not make them, but that there is no potter . . . the clay formed itself into a pot by chance! We must not be affected by "seasickness" in the "upside-downness" around us; rather, we must recognize that there is "sense," and that we can live in the light of that sense.

It is really because human beings are created beings, not beings shaped by pure chance, that there is a natural understanding of the narrower meaning of common sense. *It is because the truth of the universe makes sense that we can understand something of the preciseness of the order of the cosmos in the wider meaning of sense.*

How is it that we can talk about common sense in the smaller things and expect human beings to recognize that it is a natural thing to anticipate the possibility of a tragic fall and therefore to remove the baby from a high unprotected table before answering the telephone? It is because we are communicating to people with the capacity of imagining what might happen if such a fall took place. It is because we are communicating to human beings with a capacity for understanding, a capacity for intelligence and judgment. Human beings have been created with a capacity for common sense which is meant to be encouraged and trained, not dismissed and ignored.

CHAPTER TWO

———————— ❧ ————————

Despair Makes Sense!

THE INVENTIVE, CREATIVE MIND of human beings is something people have because of being made in the image of God—to have ideas, to think, to choose, to be creative, as well as to be capable of love, communication, and understanding.

Are human minds capable of making sound judgments with plain common sense? Of course we would all say "yes" to that question. There is "educated sense" and "common sense." There is highly prejudiced "sense" influenced by phrases such as, "All scholars say" or "All intelligent educated people know. . . ." A mind really *open* to what makes sense, to what fits in with reality, to what fits in with history even in our own short period of experience in living, is a rare thing!

If we are going to talk about common sense Christian *living*, we need to begin by realizing that this living deals not just with religious things, but with every corner of life, and that the living we are talking about is to be lived with every part of our makeup. We have minds which God made us to have. These minds are involved in the understanding of the things God urges us to understand. When we consider truth, we must not hang our minds on a hook and walk into a room where only emotions are to be involved. That act would not make any sense at all!

As we picture a family made up of a variety of ages of children, sons and daughters, including cousins perhaps, aunts and uncles, and grandparents, reading a psalm together in midsummer or during a snow storm, we are picturing specific individuals with very different personalities and a wide variety of questions. There are more or less curious ones, more or less interested ones, happy-go-lucky ones, and very serious, fearful, or unhappy and depressed ones. The people in your family and mine differ as much as the weather during the year—bright sunshine, wild winds and sleet against the windows, soft snow falling, or early spring pussywillow buds bursting. There are moods that differ as well as personalities that differ. It is impossible to idealize what an hour of conversation will be like. One cannot plan real responses. Spontaneous reactions or sudden doubts do not follow a study guide.

You and your children, your larger family, or your friends, should utilize common sense in the way theories *do* or *do not* fit the facts or the observations. Don't just hand out a list of phrases and dogmas with only ridicule for any other position. Have a thoughtful attitude, and keep up—to some degree, at any rate—with what is being put forth in today's world as being "superior" to God's Word that has come down through the centuries.

Perhaps you are reading through the Book of Psalms together as a family—maybe at bedtime, at a meal if the family can be together, or one day a week at a picnic, or during Sunday tea by the fireplace. When you come to Psalm 19, pause after the first four verses:

> The heavens declare the glory of God;
> And the firmament shows His handiwork.
> Day unto day utters speech,
> And night unto night reveals knowledge.
> There is no speech or language
> Where their voice is not heard.
> Their line has gone out through all the earth,
> And their words to the end of the world.
>
> Ps. 19:1–4

How powerful! God is saying that when we look up at the stars, the moon, the planets, the cloud formations, when we watch the sunset or the sunrise, we are not only supposed to be seeing something, we are to be discovering something as clear as written or spoken words. Do you realize what this is telling us? The marvel of what we can see with our eyes from day to day in the skies, as well as with telescopes, is like seeing words, language . . . a universal language that doesn't need translation. We are supposed to be recognizing the fantastic greatness of our God, the Creator of all that. Then we are to go on remembering that the heavens are only a small part of the intricacies of the whole universe.

"Let's go outside, or stick our heads out of the window a minute, and *look.*" Conversation may spring up outside and continue as you come in, until you feel you should go on and finish the psalm together. But there should be no break between this time and the reading of your evening story (whatever book you are in at the moment, such as *Little Men, Little House on the Prairie,* or *Robinson Crusoe*). This time must be a natural flow of life, a part of living together for however long this present combination of people have together, intertwining the reading of lovely books, awe about nature, consideration of each other's interests, and discussion of God's Word. No moment is frozen: children grow, people change, and history moves on.

When you get to Psalm 96, you should all remember and point out that God's creation is *constantly* His signature, constantly something we should listen to as well as look at. By "listen to" I do not mean that we are to hear an audible voice, but we are to "hear" in the way we do when we read a book. We read the Bible and "hear God's Word" clearly from *Him* and not intercepted, and we read His creation and stop to recognize how clearly He has spoken.

> For the LORD is great and greatly to be praised;
> He is to be feared above all gods.
> For all the gods of the peoples are idols,
> But the LORD made the heavens.
>
> Ps. 96:4–5

As your family talks together, you should often bring something to read aloud that enables *thinking* to begin at an early age, and continue growing. "Listen," you may say, "you know, scientists have been teaching for a long time that all the universe just came about by chance, and that there is no God to have had ideas and to have created everything. Of course, the first scientists did believe God existed and that they were discovering things about His creation. But for a long time, scientists have been saying they are sure everything happened by chance. They don't believe anyone back then decided what to do, thought about something in the future, or made a decision that would affect history—it was always just 'chance.'"

I recently read something that sounds unbelievable, which you could use at this point. It was sent to me from Ranald in Greatham L'Abri, from the English newspaper, *The Observer,* Sunday, February 28, 1982. (You may have read it in *Newsweek,* March

1, 1982.) Read carefully the book reviews of Dr. Crick's book, from which these quotes come:

> An atheist, he [Dr. Crick] writes, "An honest man, armed with all the knowledge available to us now, could only state that in some sense, the origin of life appears at the moment to be almost a miracle, so many are the conditions which would have had to be satisfied to get it going."

> He believes that organic soups may have formed on a million planets in our galaxy alone, and that it may have been on another planet, with more favorable conditions, that life began.

> He adds that if that happened soon enough after the birth of the universe, at least two billion years ago, that life would have been able to generate an advance civilization early enough to spread life to the infant Earth.

> Such civilization could have sent out unmanned probes to stars near by and found that chemical soups existed on other planets. Knowing that they were doomed either by a short-term catastrophe or in the long run when their sun died, they could have decided to spread life to at least one of them.

> If that did happen, Dr. Crick goes on, they would probably have sent out bacteria by guided rockets. Billions of them could be fitted into a space ship and they could probably be deep frozen for the ten thousand years it would take the rocket to arrive on target.

> The civilization would probably send several types of bacteria in each space ship to maximize their chances of survival on an alien planet.

> Dr. Crick, who advances his theory with suitable tentativeness, spoke to *The Observer* about the theory last week.

> He said that he was floating the theory as an hypothesis but was by no means committed to it. It was the sort of theory that one "puts in the bottom drawer to see how the evidence goes." . . .

> Sir Fred Hoyle [a British astronomer] told *The Observer* that he welcomed Prof. Crick's book. "He has clearly decided that the standard theory of the origin of life doesn't work. It is very nice to find someone of Crick's quality who has gone through the arguments and come to the same conclusion."

Don't you think you and your family, you and some other children or younger people, you and your friends, or you alone with yourself, could have quite a discussion as to the faith needed to believe such a theory?

The thoughts that came to my own mind were something like this: Humanism is a deep-seated faith in chance, a mindless,

Did Noah's Ark bring first life to Earth?

by GEOFFREY LEAN, our Environment Correspondent

LIFE came to Earth in an interstellar Noah's Ark, sent out by a doomed civilisation elsewhere in the galaxy, suggests a book published last week.

Science fiction and pseudo-scientific books with similar theories are common enough. What makes this one remarkable is that it is a serious work by one of the foremost scientists of the age.

Its author is Professor Francis Crick, who shared a Nobel Prize in 1962 for what another Nobel prize-winner has called 'the greatest achievement in science of the twentieth-century.' With an American scientist, James Watson, he worked out the structure of the genetic material DNA, discovering the key to the reproduction of all living things.

With this book ('Life Itself; Its Origin and Nature,' (Macdonald, £6.95), the 65-year-old Dr Crick joins a small band of scientists who assert that life could have arrived on Earth from space.

Sir Fred Hoyle, the controversial British astronomer, also believes that life could have had an extraterrestrial origin, but Professor Crick scathly dimisses his theories.

The orthodox view is that life started spontaneously in a rich chemical bouillon in the waters of the young Earth over three and a half billion years ago.

Laboratory experiments have created such a soup by mimicking the conditions of the time, mixing methane, ammonia, hydrogen and carbon dioxide (thought to make up the early atmosphere) with water, and subjecting them to electric shocks to simulate flashes of lightning a n d bombardment with ultraviolet light.

But although those experiments have rapidly created important building blocks of proteins, no one has succeeded in making a living cell or anything like one. Scientists assume that over hundreds of millions of years life did indeed evolve in that way, but its origin remains the greatest scientific mystery.

Dr Crick, who is now a professor at the Salk Institute for Biological Studies in California, says it is not easy to see how life could have started in that way.

An atheist, he writes: ' An honest man, armed with all the knowledge available to us now, could only state that in some sense, the origin of life appears at the moment to be almost a miracle so many are the conditions which would have had to be satisfied to get it going.'

He believes that organic soups may have formed on a million planets in our galaxy alone, and that it may have been on another planet, with more favourable conditions, that life began.

He adds that if that happened soon enough after the birth of the universe, at least ten billion years ago, that life would have been able to generate an advance civilisation early enough to spread life to the infant Earth.

Such civilisation could have sent out unmanned probes to stars near by and found that chemical soups existed on other planets. Knowing that they were doomed either by a short-term catastrophe or in the long run when their sun died, they could have decided to spread life to at least one of them.

If that did happen, Dr Crick goes on, they would probably have sent out bacteria by guided rockets. Billions of them could be fitted into a space ship and they could probably be deep

PROFESSOR CRICK by Levine

frozen for the ten thousand years it would take the rocket to arrive on target.

The civilisation would probably send several types of bacteria in each space ship to maximise their chances of survival on an alien planet.

Dr Crick, who advances his theory with suitable tentativeness, spoke to THE OBSERVER about the theory last week.

He said that he was floating the theory as an hypothesis but was by no means committed to it. It was the sort of theory that one ' puts in a bottom drawer to see how the evidence goes.'

He pointed out that more than 20 years ago the ' big bang ' theory of the origin of the universe ' sounded fanciful and rather religious.' But in time t h e evidence mounted to vindicate it.

Sir Fred Hoyle told THE OBSERVER that he welcomed Prof Crick's book. ' He has clearly decided the standard theory of the origin of life doesn't work. It is very nice to find someone of Crick's quality who has gone through the arguments and come to the same conclusion.'

Reprinted with permission from the London *Observer*.

meaningless trust in accidents of history. Out of this spring life-styles based on championing causes that destroy each other, and a screaming for freedom and choice while putting prison bars around true freedom and true choice.

It is not a matter of facts against faith. Children should understand this as soon as possible. Faith is needed to believe that back there—"billions of years ago" by the scientists' own dating—a civilization was fearing extinction.

Where did they come from?

Where did their fear come from?

A wonderful contrast has been revealed to human beings explaining the form of the universe and the origin of life: it was all created by a living, infinite, eternal, personal God.

Don't apologize for the alternative teaching that God created the heavens and the earth. Point out that it makes more sense to believe that ideas, thoughts, and decisions existed before particles. Point out that God reveals the answer the scientists grope for in trying to explain the "almost miracle" of life. God, infinite and eternal, is able to produce the conditions that sustain life on this earth. The miracle of life is His miracle.

Be sure to read Isaiah 45:18–19:

> For thus says the Lord,
> Who created the heavens,
> Who is God;
> Who formed the earth and made it,
> Who has established it,
> Who did not create it in vain,
> Who formed it to be inhabited:
> "I am the Lord, and there is no other.
> I have not spoken in secret,
> In a dark place of the earth;
> I did not say to the seed of Jacob,
> 'Seek Me in vain.'
> I, the Lord, speak righteousness,
> I declare things that are right."

What a gorgeous piece of information concerning God's creation of the earth! "[He] did not create it in vain, who formed it to be inhabited." Talk about meditating on God's Word! You could spend hours looking at a flower, a tree, grass, or birds flying past, the sea surging in scalloped patterns on the sand, the mountains cutting their silhouettes into the evening sky, remembering that "[He] did not create it in vain who formed it to be inhabited." He created the conditions that would sustain life!

SCIENCE

A Life-Giving Comet?

Probing the origins of life on earth, a biologist and an astronomer have performed the improbable feat of reinventing religion. Conventional science has invoked the workings of chemistry over almost limitless time to bring the order of life out of the planet's primitive chaos. But life seems to have begun rather quickly: the more scientists have looked, the further back they have found signs of life; the earliest fossil cells, about 3.6 billion years old, are almost as old as the solar system itself. Pondering such mysteries, Nobel Prize-winning biologist Francis Crick and Sir Fred Hoyle, the distinguished astronomer, have independently strata laid down about the time of the extinction show extraordinarily high concentrations of the element iridium. Iridium is very rare on earth but quite abundant in asteroids. The concentrations, Alvarez calculates, point to an asteroid 10 kilometers across, much bigger than any that has landed in historical time. The dust thrown up by such an impact might have blocked the sun long enough to kill marine plankton, cutting off the ocean's food chain at its source. The shading effect of the dust might also have lowered the earth's temperature dramatically, killing large animals such as the dinosaurs. Alternately, in a scenario by geologist cules of life; in his new book, "Life Itself," he points out that, with minor exceptions, the genetic code is the same for all living creatures that have been tested, suggesting a single source for all life on earth.

Hoyle's thinking on the origins of life has gone through several stages. In a recent lecture, he outlined a theory that was not unlike Crick's. But in his 1978 book, "Lifecloud" (written with Chandra Wickramasinghe), he suggested that primitive living cells originated in comets and were "seeded" on earth early in its history. In "Lifecloud" he also pointed out that earthly organisms are strangely out of tune with conditions in the rest of our solar system; the wavelengths of light that chlorophyll uses most efficiently, for example, are not those in which the sun's spectrum is concentrated. Such speculation outside the mainstream of science has led Hoyle to exactly the view that seemed self-evident in the Middle Ages: that life did not arise spontaneously on earth. According to this theory, the origins of life are inherently unknowable, or at best a problem for the scientists far out in space where it did arise.

JERRY ADLER with JOHN CAREY

Bettmann Archive

Nineteenth-century vision of a deadly comet: 'Seeding' the young earth

supposed a *deus ex galaxia* to explain the sudden appearance of life on earth: the "seeding" of space by intelligent beings from distant corners of the universe.

Crick and Hoyle may have the most far-out hypothesis, but they are not alone in asking whether life on earth was made possible—or at least influenced—by objects from the far reaches of the solar system. Astrophysicist Armand Delsemme of the University of Toledo believes that the stuff of living things—including hydrogen, carbon and oxygen—came from comets, which brought gas and organic material to a lifeless, airless earth 4 billion years ago. And Berkeley geologist Walter Alvarez has suggested that an enormous asteroid may have wiped out all the dinosaurs, and numerous lesser animals, in the Cretaceous extinction 65 million years ago.

Geologic evidence for such an asteroid is quite strong. At 26 sites around the globe, Cesare Emiliani, an asteroid might have struck the ocean and vaporized so much water that a greenhouse effect *raised* the earth's temperature. This theory has a certain advantage: since the ocean floor is continuously destroyed and created anew, the crater from such a shock might no longer exist, which would account for the embarrassing fact that it has not been found.

Colonies: If a crater is ever discovered, it may help settle the issue, and there is hope that more precise geological data will illuminate the Alvarez hypothesis. But it is hard to imagine any experiments that could put Crick's and Hoyle's ideas to the test. How, for instance, can one investigate Crick's hypothesis that a higher civilization in another solar system, fearing extinction as its sun began to die, colonized earth with spaceships filled with frozen bacteria? Crick's interest in what he calls "directed panspermia" rests on peculiarities in mole-

Yes, you have something to say concerning the truth and the *sense* truth makes. It is possible to understand why people are in despair if they are trying to base their lives on a lie, and have not recognized that there even is a truth, let alone what that truth is.

Remember whenever you are discouraged about the blindness of someone you may be talking to that Jesus, who is described in the Book of John as being always with God the Father, was not believed by those to whom He explained truth. "He was in the world, and the world was made through Him, and the world did not know Him. He came to His own, and His own did not receive Him" (John 1:10–11).

If people through centuries have not recognized the creation as being made by God, and if people looking into the eyes of Jesus, the Son of God, did not recognize Him as the Creator or the Messiah, then why should we be discouraged when some people turn away without recognizing the truth when we speak about it, in our limited way of explaining things?

We must realize that the Bible itself includes the Book of Ecclesiastes to show that "black writing"—that is, poetry, songs, or prose written out of utter despair—is sensible *if God does not exist.* If we live in a universe that came into being by chance, if there is no hope of life after death, then indeed everything is meaningless, senseless, and purposeless.

> "Meaningless! Meaningless!"
> says the Teacher.
> "Utterly meaningless!
> Everything is meaningless".
> Eccl. 1:1 NIV

Without God, the generations are an endless cycle of repetition. God is fair in verbalizing the dark side of truth to many generations. It makes sense that there is no sense—without God. People have been given the negative as well as the positive concerning truth. However, since God *does* exist, the bulk of the Bible is concerned with explaining the truth of His existence and telling what has happened when people have turned away from Him.

Constantly throughout history, the opportunity of finding truth and wisdom and understanding is made known by word of mouth, as well as by the word of God—the Bible. There is not an elite to whom a secret formula has been given. The compassion of God, His invitation to come to Him, His fantastically costly sacrifice for our salvation, His promises to be with those who come to Him for help and not to forsake them, have been rejected, spurned, scorned, disbelieved, turned away from—not in one generation, but in centuries of generations! Leaders and prophets have been raised in one time of history after another. Noah was giving valid truth and warning, but people laughed at him. Jeremiah spoke not only of the wrath of God, but of His compassion.

The deliberate choice to live a meaningless and purposeless life as painlessly as possible, even trying to lengthen the span of living without meaning, has been passed down to children time after time in history. The impact of these choices to turn away from the truth of God's existence and His offer to give understanding to those who seek Him is like the deep sound of an intonation that reverberates over miles of space. *No* is a choice. The invention of a diversity of "free thinking" that is free from the boundaries of what really exists (i.e., God and creation, or the work of His hands) brings about the bondage of an endless variety of tyrannies.

You and I may be able to have patience with the masses of people who turn away from God, from the truth of the universe, and from themselves. We may even have patience with groups of such people who live near us, and with whom we have social or working relationships. We may look at the variety of ways people portray meaninglessness, and as we look at a film, play, TV, or read the papers, have a kind of patience as well as compassion for such people. But too often, you and I are in danger of having *no* patience at all with the people who mean the most to us if they turn away from God. We are apt to completely discount the seriousness of their doubts, and to feel there is no honesty in their search.

We don't live in the pages of a book. Neither you nor I can turn a page, start another paragraph, and spend only ten minutes in contemplating life without God—and then calmly, or arrogantly, expect our family members and friends to start another and alternative page at the same time!

It is totally unfair to expect everyone close to us to agree exactly with our own convictions, and to come to a certainty of the sense truth makes with the exact same speed we have come. People are individual human beings, not carbon copies of one another in any respect.

When God commands us strongly and clearly to love not only our friends and family but even our enemies, that love is meant to be demonstrated in practical ways. We will go into many aspects of this area of our lives later in this book, but at this point we must face the reality that true love recognizes honest sadness and despair.

To end a discussion with anger at any child or adult who has not taken a "sensible position" after we have presented or read something we felt to be convincing is to miss a precious opportunity of demonstrating love and compassion. To shout slogans concerning Christianity as you slam the door is not to demonstrate patience, nor is it to take doubt and despair seriously.

We must respect despair. We must respect the thoughts and feelings of anyone who lives believing that there is no God, no meaning, no purpose in continuing to live in history.

By "respect" I mean we should treat seriously any human being who is thinking along the lines of "accidents, illnesses, war, old age, death, inventions turning into bigger destruction . . . why?" Whether it is your nine-year-old or your teen-ager saying such things, common sense should make you snap to attention and realize that this is a valid depression about the world. Don't just snatch the person into a "sterile" room, pushing everything else out of sight and sound, and recite church creeds to that one.

First listen. Then listen some more. If the words of rock music on the lips of friends or blaring forth from the record player are bothering that child, listen to the words together. Show true sympathy for the person who wrote them. Take it on its face value as to honesty, and talk over the fact that given this person's "base" for life (that no God exists), then of course he or she would be right. Point out the fact that so often God is being sworn at, but even *that* is dishonest. If there is no God, how can one swear at Him or blame Him? How empty is a universe with no one at home to blame!

Perhaps the young person has seen the recent program (*Nova,* Public TV) screaming that God is dead, screaming in heartbreaking songs about the meaninglessness of the merry-go-round of life. If you are talking to someone about this dark, ugly look at life, point out the absolutely ridiculous ending of the program of three people singing about how love could change the world! Where is this love to stem from? Why would any people suddenly be different and act differently? The ending of that production is similar to Crick's talking about how that imaginary civilization "probably would have sent several types of bacteria in each space ship to maximize the chances of survival on an alien planet."

We need to take time to listen, however. We need to ask for help from God to keep quiet, if we are His children. At times, keeping quiet is as important as speaking. How to make truth known is a delicate affair. Yes, truth is unchanging, but people are individuals who differ, and the focus of the binoculars one twists to get rid of blur must be adjusted to fit the eyes of each individual. In the same way, eyes of understanding need the "binoculars" adjusted in order for the sudden reality to come into focus and the glad cry to burst forth: "Oh I see; I do see. It is true. It is really true."

The number of teen-age suicides is increasing in America. This is true in other countries too. One or another kind of false view of life has been accepted by these very teen-agers. In Japan, success at exams is so important that children have committed suicide because of failing exams or making low grades. The focus has been twisted as to what makes life hopeless or full of meaning.

Drugs and alcohol blur the reality of life in any form and slow up any search for truth. Many who have been drawn to drugs and alcohol as a way of life are so fuzzy that committing suicide is a short step to escape withdrawal pain or some other sudden fear. Other teen-agers, however, really take a look at the world through all the sources of information they can get and decide it isn't worth going on.

Often a child with a physical disability who could be helped vastly if helped early enough is neglected even by affluent parents because that disability simply will not be accepted by the parents. There is an ignoring of symptoms that is utterly selfish and egotistical on the part of parents or other family members. This also can be true with emotional or intellectual needs.

Togetherness is a tremendous need on the part of each family member. How can we possibly know if a search is going on, an honest search for truth and answers to life, if we push aside the shy, awkward, hesitant attempts of a child or young person to communicate with us? If an unsympathetic reception is given to questions or doubts or fears expressed, if a harsh response is given to voicing the quotes of cynical writers or artists or actors, if a laugh is the response to a sadness about the lostness of some clown or some philosopher, then the shy personality simply runs back into the woods like a startled deer, or flies away to another bush like a frightened butterfly. Togetherness, friendship, trust, open conversation, and respect have to grow a very small bit at a time. Common sense is meant to come rushing to our aid here.

But doesn't one ask for God's help? Yes, of course, God's help. But we need to remember that this young person in need is only walking the same path we or someone in our family did only twenty years or so ago. We need to ask God to help us respond with *human* response on the level of the person's need.

Common sense causes someone towering over a small child to get down beside the child, kneeling or sitting on the floor to be at eye level with that small person, and then to listen and respond. Getting on an eye level and listening with respect for the distress that is also there is a matter of praying for help in the use of imagination and common sense. Of course we need God's help in both understanding and in meeting a need in another person, but that help does not take us up into a cloud floating above the reality of what is going on . . . on Tuesday the sixth of October . . . when you stand in your kitchen facing your own flesh and blood who is filled with rebellion or dismay or confusion or some sort of a true search for truth. You and I are not God; we are weak and unable to deal perfectly with the needs of other human beings, whether they are two or twelve or twenty-two. However, we have no other possibility of practicing compassion than in situations where compassion is needed.

So often people think of compassion as a *feeling* that places them above other less sensitive people. The feeling of sorrow, agony, or deep hurt for a variety of kinds of suffering, a variety of kinds of deprivation calls for action for two reasons. Reality of compassion can only take place when an *action* is taken to help someone—with food, clothing, a place to live, bandages, or an operation, as far as physical needs go. Reality of compassion for the despairing people of the world, the people who are trying to live without God and who see life as worthless and meaningless, also calls for some sort of action.

Too many people are concerned about the suffering in distant lands without recognizing or doing anything about the suffering of their own children or teen-agers who are struggling for answers to questions that are extremely important to the one asking them. We've long heard the old saying, "Charity begins at home." This is true in many ways. Of course, it is not supposed to stop at home. That is only the beginning! However, we could add to that old-fashioned and often flip saying, another one—without the flipness, please—"True compassion starts at home." True compassion—for those who are writing the cynical and despairing books, for those who are putting on the plays that portray life as a grotesque merry-go-round, for those who blare forth the songs of hopelessness, for those who ask the questions in music or poetry that they state are unanswerable—must begin with listening to your own teen-ager, or one who is in your neighborhood who finds in those books, plays, or music an expression of his own despair.

People who do not believe in God want to blame Him for lack of compassion. Unhappily, even some who do believe in God echo this criticism of God's not caring with love and compassion for the human beings He created. Even while people are screaming for "choice" in the wildest manner, they want God to stop all human choice where it hurts their plans. Such inconsistency and such demands are dictating to God (if indeed He exists) to stop war and allow tyranny to go unchecked while at the same time asking God to give freedom to millions to kill their own children before they can be born to live *any* kind of life. Criticism of God's compassion often stems from human beings who have utopian plans, but who fail to recognize that the world has no superhuman beings who could carry out such plans. History ought to teach us that individuals must change before the living and working together of these individuals can change!

Human beings are so cruel to other human beings. The scornful skepticism that realistic thinkers express about life comes from looking throughout history at all the wars, uprisings, changing governments, tyranny in various forms, and violence. They see cruelty not only between nations and, within countries, between brothers, but they see the cruelty against wives and children battered physically or in other ways for generation after generation. In the midst of all this history, a minority or remnant has passed truth down so that it may always be found.

How is the compassion of God shown? God does not ignore the reality of those who search with honesty and sincerity for truth, for Himself, when they have before turned away from Him and even have worshiped idols. In the Book of Deuteronomy God, speaking to the people of Israel, reminds them of how He brought them out of slavery in Egypt, and tells them about the land He is giving them. However, the warning is very strong. The holy, just, perfect God says He will not allow people to worship false gods of false religions, idols made with men's hands, without consequences following that kind of evil. He speaks of scattering His people among the nations if they turn away from Him, and there, in those other nations, they will worship "man-made gods of wood and stone, which cannot see or hear or eat or smell" (Deut. 4:28 NIV).

It is in this dark context, then—after Hebrew children and grandchildren have turned away from God into heathen worship that included the killing of one's own children in sacrifice to false gods, a detestable practice that God hated—that God gave this compassionate promise.

> "But from there you will seek the LORD your God, and you will find Him if you seek Him with all your heart and with all your soul. When you are in distress, and all these things come upon you in the latter days, when you turn to the LORD your God and obey His voice (for the LORD your God is a merciful God), He will not forsake you nor destroy you, nor forget the covenant of your fathers which He swore to them."
> Deut. 4:29–31

When you thrill with the love of God expressed in that wonderful tenor solo from Mendelssohn's *Elijah*, "If with all thine heart ye truly seek me, ye shall surely find Me—thus saith the Lord—thus saith the Lord," remember that God is speaking to that whole nation in a time of their turning away deliberately.

That invitation to seek Him with all one's heart and soul is widened to all human beings, not just to the Jews. Jeremiah gives the Lord's call and promise to the captives in Jeremiah 29:12–14:

> "Then you will call upon Me and go and pray to Me, and I will listen to you. And you will seek Me and find Me, when you search for Me with all your heart. I will be found by you . . . and I will bring you back. . . ."

Yes, evil and wickedness will be judged and punished. Yes, we have a just and holy God. But the God of compassion has opened the way for sinful human beings to turn away from the horror that their own and others' sin has produced from century to century. There is a possibility of turning back to God and, through His Son, the long-promised Lamb, becoming a son of God, a child of the Master of the universe!

This is the God of the Old Testament, whom so many people turn from as harsh and unloving, trying to divide God's Word falsely. Such an idea is without understanding of how wonderfully God unfolds His love in the Old Testament. As we face the contempt and mockery of those who, young or old, would declare that God does not exist and then go on to blaspheme Him; as we stand in front of someone who is surrounded by others who have drawn him or her into slippery places where doubts of the existence of a perfect God of love make it seem impossible to even begin a search for truth—then is when we need to reread and then read again God's own declarations.

God is the God of wisdom—sense—and He invites people to look for wisdom and understanding, not just to have a religious feeling that some seeker may consider out of reach. If you think I am simply writing my own thoughts, turn to Proverbs in the Old Testament and read:

> My son, if you receive my words,
> And treasure my commands within you,
> So that you incline your ear to wisdom,
> And apply your heart to understanding;
> Yes, if you cry out for discernment,
> And lift up your voice for understanding,
> If you seek her as silver,
> And search for her as for hidden treasures;
> Then you will understand the fear of the LORD,
> And find the knowledge of God.
> For the LORD gives wisdom;
> From His mouth come knowledge and understanding.
>
> Prov. 2:1–6

We can't look into another person's mind and see honesty and sincerity there. We can't read a person's deep motives and find wholehearted, genuine desire for truth there. But God can. God is able to evaluate the true search and to describe it as one that is as thorough as a person looking for silver or for hidden treasure. God is able to hear and interpret the real and earnest "cry" or "call" to Him for true insight. God is pleased when a human being wants the reality of understanding. Reread that Proverbs passage and thank God that "from His mouth come knowledge and understanding." He has given the Bible to make it possible to preserve, during all the changes of history, that which *will* give wisdom and knowledge and understanding to the seeking human being.

Senseless, meaningless lives stumbling in dark places, hearing a jumble of conflicting voices, constantly pressing for a nonexistent utopia? Yes, people in such a state may have leftover bits of what human beings were created with when they were given thinking, choosing, loving, communicating, and common sense. The Fall spoiled the world *and* human beings, and nothing has been perfect since. But there are leftover bits of health, beauty, intelligence, creativity, skills, talents, and inventiveness as well as common sense. As the rain falls on the just and the unjust, so various qualities are found in people whether they are among those who have found truth or not. God speaks to people in such a state of darkness, with a direct message over and over again.

> "'As I live,' declares the LORD God, 'I have no pleasure in the death of the wicked, but that the wicked turn from his way and live. Turn, turn from your evil ways! For why should you die, O house of Israel?'"
>
> Ezek. 33:11

Yes, the common sense to put salt on icy steps, to put a feverish child to bed and call a doctor, to smother a small fat fire on the stove with cool calm, to leave a note for a wife or husband when called away unexpectedly, to be thoughtful about a child's birthday, and to visit a grandmother in the hospital, may be found in atheists, agnostics, and those who follow false gods and bow to idols. But the deepest kind of sense found in someone who does not know the true and living God is that sense which stirs up a search for truth. In the deepest dark of the night, such a one should be calling out, "Oh God, if there is a God, help me to be sincere in my search for You." God honors such a reality of seeking and promises the finding of the rare treasure of truth.

However, for those who crowd into churches and Christian services, who sit in front of Christian TV programs, who flock to rallies or meetings of various kinds and say all the right words, there is a warning in this same chapter of Ezekiel. It comes at the end of the chapter, where God is explaining to the prophet that outward appearances are *not* evidence of what is taking place inside the whole person.

> "As for you, son of man, the children of your people are talking about you beside the walls and in the doors of the houses; and they speak to one another, everyone saying to his brother, 'Please come and hear what the word is that comes from the LORD.' So they come to you as people do, they sit before you as My people, and they hear your words, but they do not do them; for with their mouth they show much love, but their hearts pursue their own gain. Indeed, you are to them as a very lovely song of one who has a pleasant voice and can play well on an instrument; for they hear your words, but they do not do them."
>
> Ezek. 33:30–32

How many of us are not putting into practice what the truth, translated into everyday, ordinary lives, should be causing us to do? How many *never* put into practice in their home lives, lives in business or in the field, in the dentist's office or the hospital surgery, in the factory or the butcher shop, as a fisherman or a salesman, that which would make it clear to God Himself that Christianity to us is not simply a "love song" and a kind of entertainment, or a special stop for refreshment in the midst of other refreshment? How many listen to Christian services today as if they were love songs for entertainment in the same way the people did in Ezekiel's day when they were listening to God's direct words? What actions can we point to, can you point to, which prove to God Himself that we are not simply hearing words and music and expressing devotion with our mouths, but that we are actually putting the words into practice?

Common sense Christian living is recognizing in some way, a step at a time, how we can put into practice (as Ezekiel puts it) that which we say we believe. The Book of James makes this extremely strong in saying that only in our actions can we show that we do not simply have a "dead faith."

Life without God. Senseless? Meaningless? Full of despair? Yes.

But . . . life mouthing "God-words,"
    life bowing the head but not the heart,
    life lived as if God and His Word did not exist, while
        chattering phrases out of hymns or Bible verses,
    is also senseless!

Such life is directly contrary to the directions, the commands, and the careful admonitions of the Bible.

It is common sense for the professing Christian to listen to God's Word and to practice it!

Perfectly? No, not until Jesus comes back.

But as in practicing tennis, the piano, gardening, exercises, or any other thing in life, practicing God's Word brings about visible changes!

Over a period of time!

Line upon line!

Moment by moment.

CHAPTER THREE

Continuity in the Bible

RECENTLY SOMEONE SAID TO me, "You can't use that word *continuity*. The American people won't understand what you are talking about."

My reaction was too strong, I know. I spit out, "You know why? Because all they know is brokenness and change in relationships! All they are given are patterns of brokenness and shifting goals as well as standards! It isn't that the *word* is at fault—it's that the concept has been largely lost."

My emotions were too heated, I realize, but in thinking over the importance of understanding not just a word, but the whole concept, it seemed to me that a very careful definition should be given and a very careful study made of the deep underlying truth that *we have been created to understand continuity*!

"To understand a *word*? How silly!" someone may say. And the answer would be, "Language is meant to express ideas as well as facts, concepts as well as attitudes. With language we can describe something of who we were made to be. With language we can describe something of who God is, and what He has unfolded to us of truth. Words are important."

However, to barge on and stubbornly use a word without careful definition, especially a word so essential to our own understanding of life as this one, would be like putting a hungry baby's bottle too high for his hand to touch, or a child's apple on the other side of a screen, or a hospital patient's lunch on a table too far from the bed to reach. It is worse than not serving any food at all. My hope is that not only will the word *continuity* be thoroughly understood by more people, but that lives will be lived differently, and that a new generation will understand what continuity can mean in their own families.

First, let me pull out *Webster's Dictionary* and *Roget's Thesaurus* again. Webster's will give us definitions and the thesaurus will give us synonyms—both of which will spark some thinking, a bit like ice water splashed on our minds to wake us up!

We'll look at the verb *to continue,* the noun *continuity,* and the adjective *continuous.* Something in your life and mine will hit us in the midst of the definitions! This is not a spelling class nor a basic English lesson, but an explanation of what we are in danger of losing—life.

Webster's gives the following definitions for *continue:* "1: to maintain without interruption a condition, course, or action 2: to remain in existence: ENDURE 3: to remain in a place or condition: STAY 1 a: to carry on or keep up: MAINTAIN."

For *continuity* the dictionary says: "1 a: uninterrupted connection, succession, or union b: persistence without essential change c: uninterrupted duration in time 2: something that has, exhibits, or provides continuity: as a: a script or scenario in the performing arts b: transitional spoken or musical matter especially for a radio or television program c: the story and dialogue of a comic strip 3: the property characteristic of a continual function."

Under *continuous* we find: "Marked by uninterrupted extension in space, time, or sequence."

Whether people know it or not, they couldn't be alive physically without the continuity of crops that grow with spring planting and autumn harvesting, or the continuity of springs in the earth that provide water! We think of rain, sunshine, natural fertilizers that continuously supply the needs of fish and animal life, as well as human life. Perhaps radio is your field, and you know something about continuous radio waves that make it possible to send music and words through the air. The universe has been made with a continuity that life counts upon in a staggering totality.

But let's look at the synonyms that the thesaurus gives for both the positive and the negative of these words. I'm going to put them in two columns so that we can recognize the opposite, or antithesis, rapidly and then take time to contemplate something in the area of what is going on in our own history!

Synonyms for continue	*Antonyms of continue*
maintain	retract
preserve	terminate
last	cut short

persist	end
remain	leave off
go on	finish
keep on	desist
endure	cease
persevere	give up
hold out	fail
stick at	
pursue	
abide	
stay	
tolerate	

Now look at what Roget's Thesaurus says about the noun *continuity* and its opposites.

Synonyms for continuity	*Antonyms of continuity*
continuation	cessation
extension	stoppage
continuance	interruption
coherence	termination
persistence	suspension
duration	
progression	
prolongation	
perpetuation	
succession	
endurance	
sequence	

Don't chills go up and down your spine when you think of how few human beings know the reality day-by-day, through the years, of all the things continuity is made up of, and how many know so much about relationships, citizenships, and even life itself "ceasing," "stopping," "being interrupted," or being "terminated"? Many people have never been told that they have not ever seen continuity, let alone experienced it because of human choice. The saddest thing about human beings is the blindness that has been increased by pollution of a diversity of kinds, blindness that blots out what is missing. We all need to know what it is that we are missing.

But do let's finish defining the words, with the adjective form and also the adverb form, to tie it up a bit more completely before we go on.

Synonyms for the adjective continuous	*Antonyms of continuous*
connected	discontinuous
extended	interrupted
prolonged	suspended
unbroken	broken
entire	sporadic
whole	divided
continuing	
uninterrupted	
unchanging	
intact	
undivided	
endless	

Synonyms for the adverb continually	*Antonyms of continually*
repeatedly	occasionally
constantly	irregularly
eternally	fitfully
forever	randomly
always	spasmodically
ceaselessly	sometimes
endless	

With these words defined by other words, we can press on and come to a startling appreciation of the continuity God has given us in the Bible concerning Himself, the truth of what exists, and how it affects us. We can also uncover more concerning the conflicts that tear people apart, that confuse us inside ourselves at times. What continuity is all about and why human beings have a natural hunger for continuity in their lives is something we all need to understand increasingly throughout our lives. By *words* and by the *examples* of our actions and choices, we need to make known the preciousness of continuity to our contemporaries, as well as to our children, grandchildren, and so on. If we drop the ball, who is going to pick it up? We are in a relay race, whether we want to be or not, and truth is either being handed on or it is being dropped. Other human beings can be affected if some are careless or apathetic "runners"!

I wish you could join us at this moment in the L'Abri chapel, looking out over the Rhone valley below and the Alps above, their peaks majestically touching the blue sky high above the rolling mountains and villages perched between the barren rocks and the lush valley, on the higher flower-filled meadows. To look out at this view of a portion of God's handiwork and to hear a blend of voices earnestly singing, "Immortal, invisible, God only wise . . ." with the Flentrop organ, made by the hands of Flentrop, one of God's created human beings, is far more than "seeing with eyes" the view, and "hearing with ears" the music, more even than joining in with one's own voice, no matter how marvelous or how cracked, to praise this God. The "far more" is suddenly realizing that the God being sung about in such words truly is *eternal*. The hymn comes from 1 Timothy 1:17: "Now to the King eternal, immortal, invisible, to God who alone is wise, be honor and glory forever and ever. Amen." God is eternal. The words "forever and ever" would mean nothing without the existence of a truly eternal God. God is our hope for continuity in life, and for—oh, staggering thought!—continuity in eternity. We are talking about words like *unchanging, always, forever, unbroken,* and *eternal* having *meaning*.

We are talking about such words making sense!

We are talking about where the comfort of *hope* comes from.

Maybe you saw the funeral of the Earl of Mountbatten, as it was filmed by BBC in order for a wider number of people to be in that great cathedral by way of eyes and ears. The sudden cutting off of the life of Prince Charles' beloved great-uncle is a tragic reminder of the opposite of "continuity" being "cessation, termination, interruption" as a continual part of history.

As that fabulous organ was joined by trumpeters and the wonderful music poured forth, there came the time for the singing of Lord Mountbatten's favorite hymn. I'm sure that this was his favorite hymn at every stage of his career in the Royal Navy. Admirals and seamen, captains and the youngest recruits have sung this hymn on board ships, in tiny seaman's chapels in many a harbor, wherever believers from the Navy, the Marines, or the Merchant seamen of the United States, Britain, Canada, or other countries have gathered to worship.

Masculine voices boom out, and feminine ones now soar above them as women have joined the Navy or the Marines.

> Eternal Father, strong to save,
> Whose arm doth bind the restless wave,
> Who bid'st the mighty ocean deep
> Its own appointed limits keep:
> Oh hear us when we cry to Thee
> For those in peril on the sea.

What a comfort this hymn has been to people going off to sea to face an incredible variety of dangers—dangers from enemy weapons, from human mistakes, from the storms at sea, from illness, fevers, epidemics, or thirst.

"Oh hear us when we cry to Thee,/For those in peril on the sea." How many close families, relatives, and friends of sailors have sung this as a deep cry to the Eternal God! Whether sung to the accompaniment of the greatest of organs such as in Westminster Abbey or the pump organ in some tiny chapel, whether sung in the voice of a leading opera singer or in the off-tune voice of a tone deaf person, it does not matter; it is addressed not to people, but to God. God Himself is being addressed. It is a prayer. "Eternal Father . . ."

God is eternal. He has always been eternal. There has been no interruption to His being eternal. King David sang to this same God with psalms we still sing now, psalms that are a comfort to those who go down to the sea, as people have done for centuries.

> Praise is awaiting You, O God, in Zion;
> And to You the vow shall be performed.
> O You who hear prayer,
> To You all flesh will come. . . .
> By awesome deeds in righteousness You will answer us,
> O God of our salvation,
> You who are the confidence of all the ends of the earth,
> And of the far-off seas;
> Who established the mountains by His strength,
> Being clothed with power;
> You who still the noise of the seas,
> The noise of their waves,
> And the tumult of the peoples.
> They also who dwell in the farthest parts are afraid of Your signs;
> You make the outgoings of the morning and evening rejoice.
>
> Ps. 65:1–2,5–8

Before Moses' death, when he was pronouncing a blessing upon the Israelites, he called upon the unchanging, immortal, living God, who is the same throughout all time and who was singled out from all the false gods of manmade religions surrounding them:

> "There is no one like the God of Jeshurun,
> Who rides the heavens to help you,
> And in His excellency on the clouds.
> The eternal God is your refuge,
> And underneath are the everlasting arms. . . .
> [He is] the shield of your help"
>
> Deut. 33:26–27,29

Moses was calling upon God, whom he knew so well (over a long period of time and through a wide diversity of circumstances) to be the God of continuity, the God who would keep His promises, the God of justice as well as compassion.

You are getting impatient to ask questions.

"But what about Lord Mountbatten? That horribly senseless bomb of the IRA terriorist blew up his little boat, and both he and his young nephew died on the sea in the end. How does that, and all the deaths and injuries through countless years of sea battles, figure in with all that prayer to the 'Eternal Father, strong to save'?"

"What about all the ugliness of history?"

"What about cruelty, suffering, and death? How does that make sense with the existence of a compassionate God?"

Picture all those who have sung fervently with all their hearts, "Oh hear us when we cry to Thee,/For those in peril on the sea." Why didn't they all give up entirely when the perils multiplied?

We might ask why another Jew, many years after Moses, did not give up when his perils multiplied. The King James translation of the Bible uses the word *perils* to tell of all the dangers Paul faced in his travels to speak and make truth known. Why didn't he give up? One would think it didn't make sense. One might think common sense would have made Paul retire and live a more protected life, rather than urging others to continue and "endure to the end." In this context, please read a quotation from 2 Corinthians:

> Thrice was I beaten with rods,
> once was I stoned,
> thrice I suffered shipwreck,

a night and a day I have been in the deep;
In journeyings often,
in perils of waters,
in perils of robbers,
in perils by mine own countrymen,
in perils by the heathen,
in perils in the city,
in perils in the wilderness,
in perils in the sea,
in perils among false brethren;
In weariness and painfulness,
in watchings often,
in hunger and thirst,
in fastings often,
in cold and nakedness.

2 Cor. 11:25–27 KJV

What *sense* does it make to cry to God, the eternal One, the all-powerful Creator?

Eternal Father, strong to save,
Whose arm doth bind the restless wave,
Who bid'st the mighty ocean deep
Its own appointed limits keep:
O hear us when we cry to Thee
For those in peril on the sea.

Who could explain the sense it makes? Who can answer the "why"?

Job was one who struggled with these questions in the fog and darkness of all his deluge of disasters. God answered Job with a flow of counterquestions, only a short number of which are quoted here. (To read it all in context, read Job 38—40.)

Then the LORD answered Job out of the whirlwind, and said: . . .

"Where were you when I laid the foundations of the earth?
Tell Me, if you have understanding.
Who determined its measurements? Surely you know!
Or who stretched the line upon it?
To what were its foundations fastened?
Or who laid its cornerstone,
When the morning stars sang together,
And all the sons of God shouted for joy?

"Or who shut in the sea with doors,
When it burst forth and issued from the womb,
When I made the clouds its garment,

And thick darkness its swaddling band;
When I fixed My limit for it,
And set bars and doors;
When I said, 'This far you may come, but no farther,
And here your proud waves must stop!'?"

Job 38:1,4–11

A few verses later God questions with sarcasm Job's knowledge of light and darkness, adding, "Do you know it, because you were born then,/Or because the number of your days is great?" (Job 38:21).

The Eternal God speaks to each one of us, who lives fifty, sixty, seventy, eighty, ninety, one hundred years. He asks us to use our sense, the sense He gave us, to consider the length of "forever," to contemplate "eternity," to recognize that we need to acquire our information from someone who has lived longer than we have, who knows more than we can discover in our small speck of a lifetime, compared with the eons upon eons of time we talk about. Do we know something, anything, because we have lived so many years?

God goes on to ask who it is that commands nature? Or earth? Or outer space?

"Can you bind the cluster of the Pleiades,
Or loose the belt of Orion?
Can you bring out Mazzaroth in its seasons?
Or can you guide the Great Bear with its cubs?
Do you know the ordinances of the heavens?
Can you set their dominion over the earth?"

Job 38:31–33

Later, God asks Job who gave human beings their intelligence. God asks the basic question of where thinking and understanding have come from. This is the question that scientists like Dr. Crick struggle with when they say that the origin of life is "almost a miracle" because there are "so many conditions that have to be satisfied to get it going." And he is only speaking of "life" . . . not even going into the amazing factor of the human brain, abstract thinking, verbalized communication, and one mind understanding the complex communication given from another mind! God asks Job, "Who has put wisdom in the mind? Or who has given understanding to the heart?" (Job 38:36).

At the beginning of Chapter 40 the Lord asks Job a final question that binds up all the others. We need to let God ask us this question in the quietness of a walk on the beach, along a country road, in a city park, on a mountain trail, or at the end of a climb, sitting on a rock. We need to let God ask us this question when we are lying in a bed ill, or sitting in a wheelchair, or if we are in a concentration camp behind barbed wire.

Moreover the LORD answered Job, and said:

> "Shall the one who contends with the Almighty correct Him?
> He who rebukes God, let him answer it." . . .

Then the LORD answered Job out of the whirlwind, and said:

> "Now prepare yourself like a man;
> I will question you,
> and you shall answer Me:
>
> "Would you indeed annul My judgment?
> Would you condemn Me that you may be justified?"
>
> Job 40:1–2,6–8

The Creator is communicating to Job, and also to you and me. The Eternal God made human beings to have minds capable of understanding fantastically diverse things, to have hearts (or complete personalities made up of emotions, sensitivities, and responses to a complicated variety of things) capable of something called wisdom, sense, and recognition of justice and values beyond what the mind can acquire and store as knowledge. The Eternal God alone can give us what He knows we need to satisfy our questions of:

"Where did it come from—both the continuity and the flaws?"

"What is the matter with the history of human beings, that a poet could write as he looked at the beauty of nature, 'Where every prospect pleases, and only man is vile'?"

"How can I explain the greatness of human beings and at the same time the cruelty of human beings?"

"If it has all come by chance, why can't the computer give an answer?"

It makes sense that if indeed God created human beings in His image to be able to think, choose, and communicate, then He would communicate to these human beings and point out to them what they could not discover for themselves. The communications of God were positive as He explained to Adam that it was not good for him to have to live and work alone. God had put Adam into the landscaped garden He had planted and planned. He had explained the freedom Adam was to have in caring for this fabulous land and in eating the variety of things that were growing.

It was a positive explanation that God made to Adam and Eve as He brought them together and told them clearly that this was to be the basic relationship of life . . . so basic that the children who would be born would one day leave father and mother to cleave to their wives and husbands. That first man and his wife were very marvelously instructed that this lifelong relationship was going to be unaffected by the children growing up, and that as a man went to be with his wife, it was leaving of the centrality of being with his parents, putting his wife first in consideration. All this has been recorded for us to know about.

What else did the stupendous sunset walks and talks consist of as far as subject matter goes? As Adam and Eve walked and talked with God in the cool of the day, there is a strong probability that they asked questions. God was communicating with His finite people, the human beings He had made to be able to listen to and understand His communication. They were not thrown out on their own, to sink or swim in the universe so full of fabulous discoveries to be made.

There was such an endless amount and variety of raw materials out of which to create all that was possible for them to create— whether musical instruments or houses, whether sculpture or gardens, whether modes of travel or studies of animals—all possibilities were there within these two human beings, male and female with wonderful differences yet blending likenesses. Unity and diversity! There they were!

The Bible is a very concise book, with complete continuity and containing all we need to know to understand the basic questions of life. It gives us the history we could not know, had not God chosen to reveal it to us. It gives us an account that "makes sense." It goes on to tell us as much about what God expects of us as we can handle. It also pulls back a curtain on the giant stage of the future, for a brief moment, so that we may glimpse something of the wonder of what is ahead. We are not left with a fear that nothing will ever change. We are promised that perfection is something we are yet to experience.

The continuity of God's communication to human beings as it is unfolded in the Bible makes it crystal clear that the brokenness and separation that spoiled that early walking and talking with God came at a specific historic moment. God made people to be able to have a continuity of truth and a relationship with Himself that would not have had to be broken. Continuity is a part of who human beings are.

One negative command was made concerning the fruit of that one tree in the garden, "you shall not eat, for in the day that you eat of it you shall surely die" (Gen. 2:17). That command gave the key to the possibility of unbroken continuity of relationship with God, with each other on a human level, and with an unchanging body.

Have you heard it said, "The minute you are born, you begin to die," speaking of the aging process? It is an uncomfortable statement! We don't like accidents, illnesses, weaknesses, or loss of sight, hearing, taste, or movement in any degree. Whatever you may say about "becoming old gracefully," the desire to run, swim, kick high, ski like the wind continues past the physical high point in any person's life who has been accustomed to physical freedom. But the minute Adam and Eve were created they did not begin to die! They were given a condition that, had it been believed and fulfilled, would have been the finding of the fountain of life. No fences were put about the world and all its possibilities—only around the one fruit of the one tree.

God's word to Adam and Eve was a positive introduction to freedoms and creativity and fulfillment. God's word also included that which had to be believed to be obeyed. It was the place where the contrast between the truth and a lie was first observed by human beings. Lucifer came to accuse God of lying. Lucifer was attacking God, fighting back to try to destroy the trust of these first two human beings.

He continues to do the exact same thing today. "Hath God said . . . ?" (Gen. 3:1 KJV) was his question to Eve. "Hath God said . . . ?" is Lucifer's question to non-Christian and Christian alike. In the area of throwing out *all* of God's Word and being agnostic, it is Lucifer's question to the unbeliever. In the area of throwing out *part* of God's Word, and living on the basis of watered-down, edited bits and pieces of God's Word, it is Lucifer's question to professing believers. "Hath God said . . . ?"

Lucifer, who had been the highest of God's created angels (who also were creatures of choice, not puppets) had made his choice to rebel and to gather as many other rebels as he could among the angels, and then turn to gathering men and women. He succeeded in twisting Eve's desire for *more* than she already had been given to the point of her taking action. Eve chose to believe that God had lied and that Satan had told the truth. And she acted upon that belief. Adam did the identically same thing.

Remember James has pointed out that faith without works is dead. Eve and Adam showed forth completely and without question by their actions that they doubted God's word. This was not something in the area of an inward struggle and a search for an answer; this was a strong and completely observable action. This was a choice deliberately made and then acted upon.

They chose what God had said would bring them death because they expected to be choosing happiness beyond that which God had given them. They chose that which resulted in all the horrors of the world because of a greedy desire for more than they had in the Garden of Eden's freedom. They chose to break the continuity of their close relationship with God by exhibiting a confidence and trust in Satan. They chose to do that which they immediately felt compelled to try to hide, rather than an open freedom to look for God's closeness. Brokenness and separation came immediately.

To not understand the Fall has nothing to do with not understanding theology. To not understand the Fall is to not understand where all the thorns, thirst, sickness, cruelty, wars, and death come from. Death is the separation of the person from that person's own body. God did not create us to be separated from our bodies. Bodies are good things! Bodies are amazingly complicated and wonderful. When God created the universe with all its intricacies, plant life and sea life, animal life and then human beings, it was *all* good and perfect. It has been spoiled, devastated, wrecked, and is therefore not normal but very abnormal . . . since "normal" was what everything was before the Fall.

Did Lucifer, Satan, win hands down? Has God been defeated?

What happened right after that terrible choice was made? Did Adam and Eve drop dead immediately? No, what happened was that they began to experience the truth of what God had spoken into their ears. Their bodies were not separated from their whole persons, but immediately they experienced

> separation from God,
> separation from the garden,
> separation in their relationship with each other (each
>   blamed the other in their first fight),
> separation psychologically (a shade of schizophrenia

would have set in, along with the kind of thing we mean when we say, "The minute you are born, you begin to die").

This was that minute for Adam and Eve, and for all the rest of the people who have been born since, as *their* chromosomes began all the "generations"! The genes no longer would pass down everlasting life, but physical as well as spiritual death.

God immediately made clear that Lucifer was going to be defeated. God made known right away that He had a plan whereby there could be a restoration of this brokenness, a re-establishing of communication, a final victory over death.

As the very opposite of continuity had started, as Adam and Eve's period of time in the Garden of Eden was to come to an end, as the freedom of communicating with God face to face was to be suspended—all the words which are the antithesis, or opposite of continuity—came into full force, not as *words* but as *happenings*. Let's go back to our word list and look it over in the context of the Fall.

There was *cessation* of those wonderful walks with God, rather than *continuation*. There was a *stoppage* of the lifestyle in that perfect garden rather than an *extension* of time there. There was *termination* of perfection rather than a *preservation* of that possibility in life. There was a *failure* to trust God exhibited in the choice, rather than an *abiding* faith. Brokenness in every form was now introduced to history and to all of the created world, rather than a *continuing* wholeness that could have gone on unchangingly forever.

But before God sadly turned Adam and Eve out of the garden (and we know of the sadness as we read that God is not willing that any should perish, and of the Messiah's weeping over Jerusalem—see Matt. 18:14; 23:37-39), He introduced them to a brand new thing. He introduced them to *hope*!

Hope had not been needed before because perfect fulfillment was within reach day by day. Now brokenness, separation from God and from the garden, psychological struggles and questions within ("Why did *I* do such a thing?"), and accusations ("Why did *you* do such a thing?") gave birth to depression, despair, cynicism, unhappiness, frustration, doubts, irritations, dissatisfaction, dismay. All these feelings must have been overwhelming as they flooded into those two people who had never had anything but perfect feelings before. No guilt had ever been known in their conversation or in their experience.

Now what?

God did not put them out until *hope* was given to them. Hope was spoken of as a possible concept as they left to begin life in an abnormal world, changing now to have *many* negative things as well as the separation they were to know. The hope was given verbally as a promise was made, and was given as a strong demonstration that they would not forget. In Genesis 3:15 God said to the serpent, which was the form Lucifer took when he talked to Eve and Adam:

> "And I will put enmity
> Between you and the woman,
> And between your seed and her Seed;
> He shall bruise your head,
> And you shall bruise His heel."

Someone was coming to be born of a woman who would have victory over what Satan had just accomplished. There was *hope* that there would be a victory over Satan and the results of the choice so recently made. This was the first promise of the coming Messiah, recognized because the continuity of the rest of God's Word is so vivid that it cannot be mistaken. Adam and Eve did not leave the garden without being given hope ahead. In some way the seed of a woman was going to do something that would change the dark picture. A plan was hinted at. God had a plan for restoration at some future moment. This was a verbalized promise Adam and Eve could pass down to their children and grandchildren and great-grandchildren.

Before Adam and Eve left the Garden of Eden, God made something else clear. The new feeling of guilt and shame, not known before, had caused Adam and Eve to sew fig leaves together to hide their nakedness from God. Before they left the garden "Also for Adam and his wife the LORD God made tunics of skin, and clothed them" (Gen. 3:21).

What did the word *die* mean as far as experience went? Adam and Eve did not drop dead, nor did they see a human being separated from his body until Cain killed Abel. But before human death took place, they were shown that nothing could cover them now that they had sinned—disobeyed, declared they did not believe God—without death taking place. An animal had to die that they could be covered. It was an illustration, as well as an introduction to all that was ahead.

The fabric of the Bible is woven with unmistakable threads of continuity which bring understanding of the centrally important truths to the diverse minds of human beings who have read or heard these truths over all periods of history and in every geographic location in the world. The Bible is not a book of broken bits and pieces, isolated stories and parables that make a collection of religious tales. The Bible presents true truth, truth that is unchanging, truth that fits in with what exists, truth that answers the questions of life.

How spectacular is God's utter fairness in communicating to the human beings who had turned away from His truth to the lie of Satan! How wonderfully awesome is the *hope* that God set forth without delay to those two who must have known depression after their tragically wrong choice.

Choice had been given. Results had been pointed out clearly. Justice demanded that the Holy God should allow the death that had been chosen to continue without termination.

However, the love of the God who is love, the compassion of the perfectly compassionate God, expressed itself in immediately setting forth hope.

The ninth chapter of Hebrews makes it clear that never has there been a time when remission for sin has been offered without the shedding of blood. Adam and Eve saw the animals die and felt the skins covering their sudden shame in the same kinetic, forceful way that Abraham saw the ram die in Isaac's place. Yes, Abraham understood far more by that time, but the continuity of people coming to God on the basis of the blood of a lamb, looking forward to the One who would be the Lamb of God, really started in the Garden of Eden with the strong hint given in Genesis 3:15.

I wish that right here, between one paragraph and another, I could insert the whole book I have written called *Christianity Is Jewish*. This bird's-eye view of the Bible follows the unfolding of the truth concerning the centrality of *the lamb* throughout the Bible. The continuity of the Bible is fabulous. From beginning to end, God has unfolded His plan of redemption and restoration for torn, fallen, unfulfilled, suffering, sinful people. Throughout all the eons of history people have understood, turned back to God, believed, and accepted the truth and reality of the sacrifice made for human beings by the Second Person of the Trinity, the Son of God, the Lamb of God, the Messiah, the Lord Jesus Christ.

What about before the Messiah came? The way back to God was looking forward to the coming of the promised Messiah, taking an action to demonstrate that belief in God's promises. The children of Israel put blood on their doorposts that night in Egypt, believing that as the lamb had been killed and the blood had been applied according to God's instructions through Moses, their first-born would be safe. The angel of death would pass over the house if the blood had been applied, showing that the people inside had believed God's instructions to be accurate and true.

The celebration of the Passover for many years was always to look back to that historic moment of deliverance in Egypt, and to look forward to the Messiah who would come to make deliverance assured for all who believed on Him. The historic time arrived, and the long-promised Seed of the woman was born in Bethlehem. The Messiah died on Mount Moriah where, some centuries before, Abraham had stood looking forward with eyes of faith. Abraham was seeing, feeling, and touching his son Isaac who had been taken off the altar, with a ram dying as the substitute, but Abraham had a measure of understanding as to what the remission of sin was all about.

Abraham and Isaac had been given a glorious confirmation of the continuity they already knew a lot about, as they faithfully worshiped God by bringing a lamb, time after time. Hope was rekindled continually as God unfolded truth throughout the centuries, through His prophets, to be recorded in His Word.

"Behold the Lamb of God," John the Baptist said of Jesus, as He came to be baptized. God the Father spoke at that time, "This is My beloved Son, in whom I am well pleased" (Matt. 3:17). The Holy Spirit descended like a dove. Crystal clear for eyes to see, ears to hear, and accurate reporters, with the additional accuracy of the inspiration of God, to report.

Continuity was not broken in the Bible. Isaiah described the death of the coming Messiah so clearly (see Is. 53), speaking of the lamb being brought to the slaughter, that no one could miss what was being said in direct connection with all that had gone before, as well as with all that was to come. The word was to be passed down by word of mouth from father to son, from mother to children, from grandparents to grandchildren. God cautioned people to keep the continuity of *knowing* truth and *understanding* truth alive, that hope might be offered to *every* generation in a world so very much spoiled and affected by the abnormality that followed the Fall.

In the Book of Acts, Paul makes it crystal clear to the Jews that "That promise which was made to the fathers . . . God has fulfilled . . . for us their children, in that He has raised up Jesus" (Acts 13:32–33). In other words, Paul is saying, "Can't you see the continuity? Can't you see how it all fits in?"

Later, Paul gives Timothy a charge concerning Timothy's ministry. After telling him to preach and instruct with great patience, Paul adds, "They will turn their ears away from the truth, and be turned aside to fables" (2 Tim. 4:4). Not only is the continuity of the *one* way to come to God unchanging, but the continuity of turning away from God is always the same. It is a turning from truth to lies, a turning away from truth to myths. It is the putting of the bitter in place of the sweet, and of evil in place of good. It is not a neutrality, but a substitution of the wrong for the right. The continuity of that *exchange* is emphasized throughout the Word of God.

God has always given fair warning and adequate explanation.

Why is it that the believing children of the living God can have hope in the midst of a world of suffering that continues to touch and hurt them? How is it that Paul could write such a list of afflictions and then urge us to keep on? Where is the comfort of singing about the Eternal God and the "hope of all the ends of the earth"? How can there be comfort and hope in the midst of ugliness, tyranny, affliction, sabotage, and terrorism of a terrible variety? The reality of hope comes in the understanding of the reality of the historic Fall and the subsequent history of an abnormal world. In light of this, there are two things for us each to review in our minds as well as our feelings.

First, Adam and Eve did not drop dead the minute they sinned, although death was to be a result of that sin.

Second, no person who has ever come to God through His appointed way, looking forward to the coming of the Lamb or back to His death on the cross, has been instantaneously transferred to heaven, nor to perfection in body, mind, or any other part of life!

Just as God's promise of death to Adam and Eve took place as separation from Himself, from the perfect garden, from their own psychological perfection and other things they had known, and much later from their bodies—so the promise of God to each one who has come to Him through the Lamb takes place in first of all being restored to God in communication, with the wall of separation removed, and in being restored partially in other areas of life. *The perfection is ahead.* The hope is to be a hope based on believing God has spoken the truth concerning what is ahead of us. The hope is to be a hope that gives us glimpses of joy as we dwell on the promises with certainty that God is trustworthy.

> Oh God, our help in ages past,
> Our hope for years to come,
> Be Thou our guide while life shall last,
> And our eternal home!

God is utterly fair. He gave a very complete book for us to read and reread.

It is possible to read the Bible with no human help and have the marvel of the continuity and wonder of truth become crystal clear. My husband, Francis Schaeffer (as I wrote in detail in my book *The Tapestry*), thought he had found the answers to all his philosophic questions in the Bible as the very first person ever to do so! He accepted the Lamb as His Savior without human help while he was only seventeen years old.

Dr. Hans Rookmaaker, a leading art critic and former professor of art history in the Free University of Amsterdam, had nothing but the Bible to read during his imprisonment in solitary confinement during the war (he was Dutch, being held by Germans). It was during that reading that he saw the marvel of the answers . . . the continuity . . . the truth . . . the awesome wonder that the key was there in the Bible. It made sense. It gave the answers that nothing else did. He believed, there in the prison. Neither prison bars, in Hans Rookmaaker's case, nor theologically liberal preaching, in Francis Schaeffer's could shut out the clarity of the light which is the Truth. Truth can penetrate a great variety of darknesses! Hope.

God is not ashamed to be called our God in times of distress, depression, despair, shipwrecks, sudden attacks of terrorists, cancer, fire, airplane crashes, because He knows there is an unbroken continuity ahead of us. He has made us to be fulfilled by continuity, and He is preparing that for us. "Therefore God is not ashamed to be called their God, for He has prepared a city for them" (Heb. 11:16). The city is certain. God has promised it is being prepared. In the midst of the abnormal world, in the midst of the cause-and-effect history, in the midst of horrors of so many sorts that pour forth from the daily news, we have a book to read—God's unchanging book, which gives adequate explanation and a certain and sure hope.

Jesus said He was going to prepare a place for us, and promised by word of mouth in an audible voice heard in the disciples' ears, "I will come again and receive you to Myself . . ." (John 14:3).

Jesus was going to die after that, and despair was going to hit those same disciples. He had given them a hope to cling to when that despair would hit. Hope had been given to Adam and Eve before they left perfection to live in the flow of historic results from their sinful choice. A solution had been given that would never change. But the fulfillment of that solution did not take place in Adam and Eve's lifetime.

The Lamb, the Messiah, had been so long looked forward to as a hope. His death and the onslaught of persecution and troubles that hit the believers after His ascension must have thrown many of them into times of impatience for His return; despair as to whether they could hang on, depression as to what "enduring to the end" was going to mean.

The period of history some people wish they could have lived in is the period when these people imagine they would have had such a thrill at being able to see and touch Jesus, the promised Messiah, the Lamb of God. Yes, marvelous. But to live amidst the ongoing history of continued thorns, thirst, illness, death of loved ones, prison, beatings, shipwreck, and so on would have been a great contrast. Anyone who thinks that *that* contrast would be easier than the things we face today, lacks common sense or insight!

Paul wrote to the Thessalonians about very mundane, everyday life, about things like working hard with their own hands, minding their own business, and loving each other. Then he said, "But I do not want you to be ignorant, brethren, concerning those who have fallen asleep [that is, died], lest you sorrow as others who have no *hope*" (1 Thess. 4:13, emphasis added). It is the same hope held out, the hope that never changes, the hope of one day being in the midst of a restored situation, a restored world where the final victory has effect for ever and ever and ever. There is not only a continuity in the Bible of the Lamb as the one way to possessing a sure hope, but there is a continuity of *hope* being given to each human being who will believe God, so that he or she may have immediate comfort.

> For the Lord Himself will descend from heaven with a shout, with the voice of an archangel, and with the trumpet of God. And the dead in Christ will rise first. Then we who are alive and remain shall be caught up together with them in the clouds to meet the

Lord in the air. And thus we shall always be with the Lord. There-fore comfort one another with these words.

1 Thess. 4:16–18

Continuity in the Bible?

Oh yes, there is continuity. The justice of the perfect God is met, in that sin is not forgiven without a price. The price is so great that only the Son of God Himself could pay for it with His own life, as He died on the cross. The love of God meets His justice at that same place and time!

The continuity of the Bible is so perfect that when hope is held out to Adam and Eve concerning the woman's Seed, who would one day have victory over Satan, that hope goes out through the gates of the garden with them to be taught to their children. Abel clearly understood and worshiped with the lamb, with hope.

The very last chapter of the Bible begins with "And he showed me a pure river of water of life, clear as crystal, proceeding from the throne of God and of the Lamb" (Rev. 22:1). No mistaking the identity of truth here. God lightens the city and the Lamb is the light. Here the Lord God Almighty and the Lamb are the temple. Here—where there will be no more curse, no more sorrow, no more tears—will be the throne of God and the Lamb.

An emphasis is made that all this is *true*. A warning is given at the end, as in the beginning. The warning at the end of the Bible is that nothing is to be taken away from this book, and nothing is to be added. The continuity of truth is not to be added to nor sub-tracted from. God's Word is truth. No wonder it is attacked by the enemy!

And finally the time will approach for the last enemy to be destroyed—which is death itself—and for the resurrection to take place. The Bible's last words are: "He who testifies to these things says, 'Surely I am coming quickly.' Amen. Even so, come, Lord Jesus! The grace of our Lord Jesus Christ be with you all. Amen" (Rev. 22:20–21).

How superbly complete is God's absolute base for our lives!

CHAPTER FOUR

Continuity in Life

MORE THAN TWENTY YEARS ago, a ten-year-old girl said to our daughter Debby, "When I grow up, you know what I'm going to do?"

"What?" asked Debby.

"I'm going to stay married to my first husband for ten years, then I'll marry a lot of different men for short times."

This was a child staying in a Swiss boarding school while her parents went through their current divorce. She was calmly stating her ideals. To stay married to one man, then to marry a succession of men sounded to her like quite a natural goal in life, similar to traveling and trying different climates for short periods. Why not? She obviously had not been taught by example or careful explanation how priceless continuity is and how valuable and central it is to a balanced human life.

This little girl is in her thirties by now. One wonders whether her dreams have come true, and how satisfying her attempts to taste happiness have been. Thousands and thousands of people have never discovered what a lasting human relationship is like, some because of having had all their relatives and friends killed in war, or drowned or starved in a disaster. Some refugees have been torn, time after time, from every relationship. Other people are as ignorant of the value of lasting human relationships and how to treasure and protect them as poverty-stricken people would be if they might happen upon some rare china, using the Spode cups to mix paint or weed killer.

To live from birth in a refugee camp in tents of flapping fabric, or in makeshift shacks made of bits and pieces of any available material, and never to know that the words *home, village, country, school,* or *community* have any other shades of meaning beyond

64

what has been experienced in that refugee camp is to be ignorant of what some other people in the world think of as "normal life." To be deprived by circumstances of growing up in a family that feels a part of several generations because of old photo albums, yellowed letters, stories passed down, or personal contact with grandparents and great expectations for the youngest generation ahead, is to be so ignorant of the experiences of the continuity of family relationships as to be unable to picture a "normal life."

Whether we are talking about the refugees of Cambodia, the Near East, or Somalia, or children who live in broken homes, going to school with other children from broken homes, getting explanations of life from those who believe there are no absolutes, no patterns, no norms of any kind, no permanency of ideals, no patterns for the shape of dreams—in both kinds of deprived childhoods there are two tragic problems in the area of dreams for the future.

First, the dreams are likely to be shaped by the only reality known, as the ten-year-old girl's were, or the dreams might be of a better tent in another refugee camp with more food and water!

Second, the dreams are also likely to be so unrealistically of perfection that the dreamed-of "perfect life" would have to be lived with perfect people (who do not exist), in a perfect town or village (which does not exist), in a perfect country (which does not exist), and governed by unfailingly wise and perfect people in government (who do not exist). The dreams of utopia—whether dreamed by children concerning a mate, a home, a place to live, or a country to live in, or dreamed by young adults concerning what a relationship should be like and what a breakfast conversation should consist of, or dreamed by management concerning what labor should be like, or labor as to what management should be like, or dreamed by Parliament or the House of Representatives concerning what the prime minister or the president should be like, or by the prime minister or the president as to what Parliament or the House should be like—are so often unrealistic.

But, the problem is that people are always sure that all that needs to be done is to change to the choice of another person, or people, and *then* all will be perfect. The problem is that agnostics, or secular humanists, or people in the midst of a variety of false philosophies or religions, do not know about the Fall and have no explanation as to what is wrong with the world or the people in it. And very often, believers in God's existence, those who *say* they base their lives on His Word, do not recognize the central place of the Fall in their own practical lives. We who are believing Christians are *still* imperfect. We live with imperfect people at home, in our work, and in our churches, as well as in the world!

Is there a common sense factor in Christian life as it relates to continuity being a practical possibility? Is continuity an airy fairy, unthinkable, absurd concept? Is it so unattainable as to be cruel to even talk about it at all? What about people who are half way through life and because of their own, or other people's choices, have had nothing but brokenness?

In many circles in today's history, expectation of continuity in relationships is almost unheard of. "I really don't think *any* marriage can last, do you?" is a common question expecting only the answer, "Oh, of course not." The concept of continuity is misunderstood as being a barrier to personal freedom and happiness.

Relationships are thought of as only for really short periods of time. The popular opinion of a relationship, expressed in all the media, is that it is something that should provide "fulfillment," "satisfaction," "happiness," "enjoyment," "pleasure," "understanding," "contentment." How quickly must all these positive things take place in a relationship? In the "NOW"? All too often, the immediate moment's desire or hunger tempts us all to make an incredible exchange. The possibility of everything that continuity has to offer for generations, as well as for a lifetime, is kicked aside for the *now* of an immediate or imagined satisfaction.

Do you remember Esau's choice?

> Now Jacob cooked a stew; and Esau came in from the field, and he was weary. And Esau said to Jacob, "Please feed me with that same red stew, for I am weary." Therefore his name was called Edom. But Jacob said, "Sell me your birthright as of this day." And Esau said, "Look, I am about to die; so what profit shall this birthright be to me?" Then Jacob said, "Swear to me as of this day." So he swore to him, and sold his birthright to Jacob. And Jacob gave Esau bread and stew of lentils; then he ate and drank, arose, and went his way. Thus Esau despised his birthright.
>
> Gen. 25:29–34

Esau sold his birthright which meant affecting other human beings for generations to come! He sold a continuity of life and events—threw away a precious possibility of a different life for himself and his children and children's children, right down to the descendants of Esau today! Repercussions, consequences, ripples in history still going on today, were effected by Esau's choice at that time. Human beings are not pebbles that fall into the water and cause no ripple; our choices cause unending ripples. Esau chose to satisfy his immediate hunger as the fumes from a red lentil stew hit his nostrils! What an exchange for a birthright!

But, day after day, thousands of people choose a totally selfish search for personal happiness, some form of immediate fulfillment, freedom to "do what feels good" or to kick anyone who might get in the way, exchanging *continuity* for one's self and for one's children and grandchildren for a terrific variety of that "mess of pottage." What "mess of pottage" has tempted you, or me, and how can we see things clearly in the light of the whole of history, rather than in the immediate now?

Pressures are terrible at certain crisis moments of life, converging with the force of the winds that come together in what is known as "the wind shear factor." Such pressures can rip apart a relationship like the winds can rip apart a plane in the air! We each have a varying amount of selfishness that is a pressure from within. Pressures come from without on the part of people who find their pleasure in other people's failures as a form of self-justification for failures in their own lives. When selfishness hits hard, wiping out all thought of future results in history and the effects on a wide circle of people, and when friends whisper in your ear, "You deserve freedom . . . you deserve a higher salary . . . you are too good to take any more of this. . . ." Then the "wind shear pressure" builds up! As a Christian you have another pressure added, since our accuser has not yet been cast down (see Rev. 12:10).

Satan is attacking God as he accuses each Christian of loving something far more than God, and so in every case Satan is eager to see us put self first at any cost! That "at any cost" includes the cost of disregarding our opportunity to show the Lord in this present life the reality of our love and trust of Him in practical ways.

Someone might ask here, "Hey, aren't you mixing things up? What has the continuity of a marriage relationship, or family relationship, or other human relationships to do with our relationship with God? Isn't there a wall of division here that puts these two parts of our lives into different rooms with no connection?"

As we go on, the answer will be given. In brief, however, our understanding of what is involved in working at continuity in human relationships and our understanding of what is involved in working at *our* side of our relationship with God have a lot in common. There is a blending and exchange of the lessons learned. We grow in understanding as time goes on. We grow in the understanding of what God made us to be capable of in the area of continuity on a finite level during the limited confines of one lifetime. We also grow in the understanding of what is ahead of us in both continuity of an eternal relationship with God and with other perfect human beings in heaven!

When we hear statistics of the ratio of divorces to marriages, we must realize that many, many people have never been a part of relationships that last a long time. Children are growing up in an atmosphere in which temporary relationships are the "normal" way of life. The dividing of a child's time between "a weekend with father" and "weekdays with mother" is more confusing than simply the broken unity of the together names "Mother and Father." The breaking up of the name "Mom and Dad," which is a couplet that spells solidity, a solid home to which to return after physical or mental travel, is confusion enough. But the confusion is compounded when the short weekend with father includes another woman whom the child is supposed to "relate to, Dear." And the multiplication of confusion comes in the man that now has taken Father's place with Mother, and the added grandparents, sisters, and brothers who have *no* blood ties, and new babies that are half-brothers or half-sisters. No wonder a little boy of seven in such a situation sighed deeply and exclaimed, "I can't wait until I grow up and can have a home of my own!"

Why is it that relationships are being gloomily regarded as something that can not ever go on and on? Is it a twisted understanding of what a human being is capable of? Is it a lack of knowing that there is *anything* in the universe that continues? Is it a loss of observing any two people or a family working at the upheavals that come day after day in their living under the same roof with a feeling that there *is* something worth working for?

The capability of human beings having lasting relationships that span several generations has been shoved aside, not believed possible, not prepared for, not expected to be demonstrated! Relationships that go on through unpleasant incidents—disagreements of a variety of sorts, difficulties big and little, hurt feelings, unfair treatment of each other, unthoughtfulness, forgetfulness, silence and lack of communication for a period, moods, and sudden anger—are considered to be archaic, old-fashioned and something to be scorned . . . not something that can be worked on and improved.

There is an oft-repeated statement these days: "Children are better off if their parents divorce because a home where there are fights and constant disagreements is very bad for them." Period!

What is ignored all too often is the fact that children discuss with other children the signs of an impending divorce and what terrifies them, and brings tears in the night, is the fear that the fights they are overhearing mean a split is on its way. No one of any age feels comfortable when people are shouting at each other, but there is a measure of comfort in being assured that although this disagreement may *sound* fierce, there *will* be a solution. One of the two who are arguing will have enough imagination and ingenuity to work out a solution concerning the day off or the vacation about which there is such a difference of opinion! Is the soup burned? A resourceful cook will hurry and make a substitute without continuing the argument that, "it can't be tasted." Children need to see *solutions* take place, not only as a reassuring factor in their present home lives, but as an example for the future.

Children need to be able to say to other children, "Well, my mother and dad get a little upset at times. One or the other gets very angry at other times. But they do love each other really, and they love us, and they have lots of imagination and many ideas as to how to make it all up and do something pleasant together after the fight is over!" Sadly, very few children today have seen the pattern of living *through* differences, coming out the other side of them, of someone's apologizing to someone else—or both apologizing—and then one of the two having a brainstorm about going for a picnic, eating supper in front of the fire, having watermelon out under the lilac bushes, playing a game after supper, reading two chapters of the current book while nibbling on popcorn, or getting out a map and planning a "someday kind of a vacation." And very, *very* few children have friends who can tell them how it works!

Facing the reality of being imperfect—explaining to children that the family is made up of a number of imperfect people of different ages, living together under often difficult circumstances—puts things into a different perspective. There is a desperate need for patterns of how to cope, not just seminars on the subject. There is a need of seeing a compromise work out in a real-life situation. There is great value in *hearing* someone keep quiet, or in *watching* patience work! The skill of changing the subject without doing so obnoxiously needs to be observed. Children need to recognize how mother prepares ahead of time to relieve strain. "Daddy wanted this done before he came home, so let's surprise him. You cut up the bananas and this grapefruit and a piece of watermelon into squares this size. And I'll finish this letter I said I'd type for him [or sew the button on the shirt, or whatever]."

In today's world mother may be at the office and dad may be preparing dinner. If so, he must be the one to be sensitive enough to realize the children are hot and cranky and need a relaxing time in a bubble bath before mother gets home. Perhaps the children are low on blood sugar and need a scrambled egg on toast points, a glass of milk, and a fruit yogurt before daddy (or mommy) gets home. It's not a bad idea to point out, "People get cranky and unreasonable sometimes just because they are hungry. Human beings are so complicated!" This is the school for human relationships: the home, the family!

Faithfulness, dependability, reliability, steadiness, trustworthiness, ability to understand and get along with other people are qualities looked for among businessmen, farmers, educators, government officials, and so on down through the list of possible careers. From where are these and other qualities that lead to treating other people as human beings to come? When children or adults hear a constant barrage of "I want my rights"; "I want happiness"; "I want to do my thing"; "I want to go out and get what I deserve in life"; "I want to be fulfilled"; "I want the perfect relationship," they are constantly being taken into the area of daydreams. Selfish, egotistical daydreams? Yes, but putting that aside for the moment, the daydreams are utopian in one way or another. Perfection does not exist. There are no perfect people or perfect situations. Your or my "rights" collide head on with another person's "rights."

In the search for what does *not* exist, what could be a growing, changing situation, with continuity as a framework for growth, is smashed into pieces. Think of continuity as a trellis for a vine. Gradually the plant puts out tendrils that cling to the trellis and take its shape. The ivy or the flowing vine needs years to become what it can be on *that trellis*. To transfer it to another garden sets it back, or kills it altogether. The vine can take storms and blights, or the baby pulling at it, or a child cutting parts of it, if it has care in replanting, fertilizing, and watering. In this picture, the same trellis is the continuity, a familiar framework.

No illustration is perfect. But we need to understand that the insistence on having what does not exist and the insistence of smashing through all that human beings really *are*, to try to find fulfillment in what they are *not*, bring sorrow. Esau was not very satisfied with the memory of that red lentil stew. Hunger came again. A birthright such as he gave up was intended to be passed down from generation to generation. He had smashed his own *true* rights by grabbing for something in search for a temporary fulfillment. The shout for rights is so loud, and the beat of the drums is so in rhythm with that shout, that common sense is drowned out! Common sense is meant to help us think through the waves of anger or temptation. It helps us realize that we are in danger of losing what is priceless, that which is not worth swapping for a bowl of lentil soup.

There is a factor in our relationship with God that is totally different from our relationship with husband or wife, mother or father, children, sisters or brothers, cousins, aunts, grandparents, friends, fellow workers, neighbors, church members, and so on. That factor is that God is perfect. Our Heavenly Father, our Friend and Shepherd; our Intercessor Jesus Christ; our Comforter the Holy Spirit are each perfect!

God's side of His relationship with us is absolutely perfect. He is so tremendous in His infiniteness and His diversity, that we will never get to the end of coming to know Him. But the gradual progress of knowing God will never be on the same level as knowing a finite, limited ever-changing human being. God tells us that He does not change. He will be tomorrow as He was yesterday. We can depend on Him to be faithful, reliable, trustworthy. He has said He understands us. We are told that the promises He made centuries ago are just as true today—not just true in the academic sense of truth, but true to you and me personally. His truth makes a difference to our present lives, as well as to our part and place in eternity.

Let's consider for a moment our relationship with God, and the factors needed to make it a growing reality, since our side of that relationship is imperfect. Continuity of any relationship needs verbalized expression of love and trust, as well as actions that show forth love in a variety of practical ways day by day.

God has carefully given us His Word, which expresses His love clearly, so that we can reassure ourselves constantly as we read. When we read, "God so loved the world" (John 3:16), it is not meant to be impersonal, but it is in reality a precious verbalization to each of us personally. God carefully expresses His love so that there is no shadow of doubt. We are meant to take His Word as true to us personally and actually bask in His verbalized love. When we read in Jeremiah 31:3, "Yes, I have loved you with an everlasting love;/Therefore with lovingkindness I have drawn you," we are meant to respond not only inwardly, but also with a verbalized response. When we read in 1 John 4:10, "In this is love, not that we loved God, but that He loved us and sent His Son to be the propitiation for our sins," we are meant to accept that love as if we were reading God's letter written just to us, each one personally. God has carried out His love in action, in the most perfect way. But He also has verbalized His love in words we may read over and over again, sing, hear in our own brains. For this reason, we are meant to read the Bible frequently so that we may have the communication of the continuity of God's love in the midst of a broken world full of hate.

Just so, we need the help of verbalizing our love for God over and over again. Words have an effect upon us. The words coming out of our own mouths influence us! Never forget that. We affect ourselves, we influence ourselves by the things we say with our tongues which then enter our own ears. The phrases and words may form in our brains, but as we speak aloud there comes an underlining, making them stand out in our own thinking and understanding. Human beings are affected by what they hear spoken in their own voices! We can consciously and deliberately reject ideas or words that are suddenly in our minds and deliberately *not* say these things, turning away from them. Speaking and declaring repetitively, *not with a mindless kind of repetition,* but with serious consideration, can affect us amazingly.

How can I help my love for God my Father, Jesus my Savior and Lord, the Holy Spirit my Comforter, to become more real, to grow with a consistent growth? One necessary means of growth is verbalization of that love and trust in thoughtful and constant words. Our own ears need to hear our own voices telling God we love and appreciate Him. Our own minds need to think of the endless reasons why we love God, but those reasons need to be put into words and spoken.

"I will bless the LORD at all times; His praise shall continually be in my mouth" (Ps. 34:1) is translated "I will extol the LORD at all times; his praise will always be on my lips" in the New International Version. This psalm of David's should be enlarged upon over and over again with fresh words of our own: "Oh Lord, right now I want to wipe out complaining thoughts and words from my mind. I need Your help to make real and true my praise of You. As

I sort out these clothes to wash, I thank you that you have provided a cleansing for me. I thank you for washing me and making me clean in your eyes. I do want to praise You, O God, with a praise that will bring joy to You, and I want my love to grow during my short lifetime. Please don't let me waste the time that I have to praise You with my lips. As I tell You I do really love You, may these words be acceptable to You because they are more real to me day by day. O Lord, I love You. Please help my lack of love, and open my eyes to my blind spots in this area."

Constantly during the day we need to verbalize to the Lord our expressions of love, dwelling on the reasons for that love, whether it is the titanic reason of His providing eternal life, or the recognition of the wonder of His design of the first snowdrop or violet found in the woods in spring.

> My soul shall be satisfied as with marrow and fatness,
> And my mouth shall praise You with joyful lips.
> When I remember You on my bed,
> I meditate on You in the night watches.
>
> Ps. 63:5–6

With David, we, in our own century, our moment of history, are to verbalize with our lips our satisfaction with our compassionate and wonderful God. In the night when we lie awake, when it is easy to fret or become full of fears, we are to think about God and meditate upon His goodness to His children. We are to trust Him by verbalizing that trust and to love Him by expressing that love. This expression of love can be combined with crying for His help in a moment of trouble and deep need. Our lack of understanding of our circumstances, fears, and distresses does *not* cancel out the possibility of expressing love. The expression does not have to be false because we are in physical pain or in the middle of a shock. The very verbalized recognition of the continuity of our love for God . . . in the imperfect manner of our human love, coupled with acknowledging that we appreciate His verbalized assurance of His love for us . . . helps us in the very "eye of the storm," time after time in life. "Whenever I am afraid,/ I will trust in You" (Ps. 56:3) is not just David's declaration to God. It must be our spoken declaration too.

In our human relationships, we need to practice verbalizing our love for each other. Husband and wife need to hear each other's expressions of love with a flow of continuity. If you find it hard to speak, then write that love into a poem or ditty or note to stick under the pillow, or in the pocket of the other person. Do not just do it for a birthday, but on an ordinary rainy day! "I love you" should ring in the ears of the other person, after he has hung up the telephone. The sound of the spoken words is a help to the ears, mind, and emotions of the one speaking them. The very words remind the speaker, as well as the hearer, of the reality of what has happened in past weeks, months, years. Memories of what caused that love to take place, to grow, to be real at other moments in history come flooding back. Spoken words can cause negative or positive incidents in the continuity of relationships. We influence reality by our spoken words.

Another dimension of the expression of love is the sexual relationship. It is meant to be a communication. However at any time in life, even when the "fires burn low" the physical touching of each other in response, the holding of hands when walking along in silence, communicate a great variety of things. Love or joy, appreciation or sympathy, agreement or impatience, "let's go" or "let's stay" can all be expressed with a squeeze of the hands . . . with no words spoken. It is true too that eyes can communicate nonverbally, as well as can gestures. But the words "I love you" are still important—growing even more important as life goes on and we grow older.

Does this mean that two people in any relationship in life can simply say, "I love you" without any feeling of love? Giving even a trivial reason for having an appreciation of something about that other person right at that moment helps.

"I love you."

"Why?"

"Oh, I love the way your hair looks right now since you washed it . . . so shiny and squeaky clean."

Trivial? No, practical, and sensible, and the stuff of response!

Are we all, then, to be capable of giving a "soft answer" when the crystal water pitcher, hot out of the dishwasher, is filled with ice water and cracks? Are we to be *so* controlled and calm that we think up a lovely thing to say when mud is brought in on the freshly cleaned rug, or the toast is burned, or the chicken is turned into charcoal in an oven left too high during church? Can we look at shirts, underwear, handkerchiefs, and a teacloth all shades of pink because red socks were put into the load of wash and washed at too high a temperature, and say an appreciative word about the good sponge cake from last week? When bills come in and one person has overspent, or the tax money has been used for another purpose, does the strain drain away immediately to provide a pleasant exchange of ideas with *no* unpleasant words?

In other words, can we give a nice little list of sentences that are to be mechanically recited at the appropriate times? The answer to all these questions is a resounding *no*. As human beings we are imperfect, sinful, affected by the Fall, affected by our own weaknesses and the quirks of our own individual personalities. We are not like each other, and we cannot predict our own flare-ups, let alone those of others. We are also affected by physical stresses such as coming down with the flu, or by low blood pressure, or by a drop in blood sugar, or by a headache, or by just plain fatigue. We get angry, furious, upset, or simply irritated, and we blurt out something that then stirs up a quick retort on the part of the other person. Back and forth words fly. However, there are some ground rules to be resolved early in married life, concerning relationships with our children and others. I feel that allowing ourselves (and I include myself in that) to say harsh things to each other *beyond a certain point,* is very, very dangerous. It will affect getting things back together again and going on in our continued relationship and our growing love. Because we know someone very well, we can say things that are so cutting, and hurt so thoroughly at the most tender spots that the memory of these sentences penetrates like a surgeon's knife.

You know each other—you and your friends, your spouse, your parents, your children, your grandparents, or your aunts and uncles. You know the most vulnerable spot, the Achilles' heel of another person's emotional and psychological make-up. You know what makes that person feel uncertain, inadequate, or unimportant. You know exactly how to pull that person down. Therefore in the middle of a disagreement, a knockdown, drag-out fight, you know that there are certain subjects and certain inadequacies in the other person that, if you talked about them, would produce a drastic effect. That effect would be *so* drastic that it would harm that person emotionally and cut him down so that it would be a long time before confidence could be built up, even if you said, "Sorry."

After that kind of a diatribe, sarcasm, accusation, or tongue lashing, the "sorry" would bring inward doubts: *Did he or she or the children or grandmother really feel that way about me? Was it anger, or just the true opinions bursting forth?* At that point it is hard to get things together again. The extremely important thing to sort out early in a relationship is what things are off limits. The first requirement is to acknowledge that indeed there *are* things off limits.

Some people are sensitive about a physical handicap, a difference in family background, a lack of formal education or natural talent, a tendency to make repeated mistakes whether in speech or in choices, or a family background that makes the person embarrassed. There could be many examples that would be totally opposite from each other in what would hurt if thrown in a person's face. When the decision is made, and the choice has been voiced "for better or for worse," these peculiarities in each other's sensitivities—what I call off-limit areas—should be indelibly written in each other's memories, to be avoided when the flare-ups come!

Continuity is to be expected—and preparation for continuity is necessary when we realize that in any relationship between two imperfect people, there will be imperfect situations, imperfect conversations, and imperfect arguments! We must not think the relationship has to come to an end because we have shouted unkind words or whispered blame and accusations in big or little situations. However, in the midst of this practical preparation for coping with and weathering difficulties, it is very necessary to try to decide what will be always off limits. I know this is possible because after forty-seven years of married life, both Fran and I have maintained our own personal decisions not ever to throw certain accusations at each other. This does not say we have not hurt each other many times, but simply that there is possibility of establishing a line for one's self and stopping at that line.

Although God is perfect and does not make mistakes, human beings are even prone to go off limits in making judgments of God's perfect compassion, love, goodness and wisdom and criticizing God or declaring that God has done something He has *not* done at all.

As God's children, through having accepted Christ's work for us, accusations are definitely always off limits. As we stand before the Creator of the universe, the all-wise, perfectly holy, mighty God, who made us in His image, who upholds the universe, who understands all things, who has shown His compassion in providing a way for us to come to Him through the Messiah, the Lamb . . . how dare we shake our fist in His face? How dare we question God and say, "Why did you do this to me?"

Jesus was angry at the results of the Fall as He stood before the tomb of Lazarus. As my husband has so often said, "Jesus could be angry at death and abnormality and not be angry at

Himself as God." Death is a result of the Fall. Death is that which Satan has brought into history. We can be angry at a person when we are caught in the awful results of cause-and-effect history following the Fall, or following attacks of Satan, or following human choices of one kind or another—but that person is never God. We may not understand our tragic situation. We may not feel we can face life after a terrible shock. We may not feel that we know how to cope in the midst of a war, or avalanche, or earthquake, or famine. But it is always off limits to blame God. We are not to run away from God, shaking our fist at Him and screaming. We are to run *to* Him when we are shaking with grief or trembling with fear.

He is our refuge and strength; a very *present* help in trouble. Our help is to come from Him as we run into the shelter of His arms, away from the noise of the battle, or the storm. He has promised us comfort, and we need to climb on His lap as a weeping, hurt child, not to kick at Him.

We can look into His Word and see what He has said we are to do when we face a hard moment. We can come with appreciation of that Word and thank Him even as we search for His verbalization to us for the moment of need. He has prepared a verbalized careful explanation to fit our various times of need.

In the very midst of the most difficult times filled with anxiety, God has given us *His* pattern for the continuity of our relationship with Him. He does not leave us without explanation of what to do.

> Rejoice in the Lord always. Again I will say, rejoice! Let your gentleness be known to all men. The Lord is at hand. Be anxious for nothing, but in everything by prayer and supplication, with thanksgiving, let your requests be made known to God; and the peace of God, which surpasses all understanding, will guard your hearts and minds through Christ Jesus.
>
> Phil. 4:4–7

There is value, of course, in being honest and not plastic in our rejoicing. But God has made it clear that the path to praising and loving Him in an anxious time is through reviewing what He has done in the past. "With thanksgiving" (v. 6) refers to a reality of reviewing what one is thankful for. As these instances and realities are verbalized, the immediate need can be measured by the wonder of who God is, and what He has done in the past. But it is after the requests have been made and with trust as to God's wisdom in dealing with those requests, that the peace that passes all understanding flows in. It is not automatic—God sets forth conditions which help us to have such a reality.

Of course any words can be said with falseness. Do you try to analyze whether you really love God or love another person *before* you ever say the words, "I love you"? We are so pulled in to self-analysis today that we are in danger of being like the thousand-legger. Do you know the old story of the thousand-legger bug? Someone said to the bug, "You've got to learn how to put one foot in front of the other." When the poor bug tried to sort out the complicated process which had been so natural before, it fell on its back with its thousand legs in the air! So ended its walking naturally!

Self-analysis and introspection can be so harmful. It can be like pulling off the wings of a butterfly to see how they were fastened. The analyzing of what is meant by "I love you" while trying to analyze all of one's feelings can be really horrible. That kind of so called "honesty" is not always helpful.

You may say, "What in the world are you talking about? Aren't we supposed to be honest in all our statements and always speak the truth?"

I would reply, "Let us be really very careful as to whether we are rationalizing our motives for making hurtful criticism." We have been told that the tongue is the most dangerous portion of our whole body. James 3:5-12 warns us of the slippery traps into which we can fall when we use our tongue in criticism to tear down relationships, and cause destruction in the church or other groupings in life, right up to the country's government. "Honesty" is often used as a cloak to cover up a spiteful lashing out at someone close to us, or in a wider circle.

Human beings can tear down the person they have promised to love and cherish for life simply in order to free themselves for another person to whom they have consciously or unconsciously been attracted. When God says that the human heart is deceitful, it is a warning to each of us that we are to be careful not to deceive ourselves. An old pastor I used to love to hear preach frequently said, "What is deep in the well of the heart comes up in the bucket of the mouth." The deceit starts in the heart, and spills forth in a rush of rationalizing criticism. Then the spoken words convince the speaker and it can begin a vicious circle of destruction of a relationship that did not need to be destroyed.

As James talks about the tongue, he begins with a description of how a bit in a horse's mouth is used to turn the horse in one direction or another, and how a small rudder steers a ship through storms (see vv. 3–4). Then he says:

> Even so the tongue is a little member and boasts great things. See how great a forest a little fire kindles! And the tongue is a fire; a world of iniquity. The tongue is so set among our members that it defiles the whole body, and sets on fire the course of nature; and it is set on fire by hell.
>
> James 3:5–6

Strong words? Yes, God's warnings are strong. I have written at length in my book on the Ten Commandments, *Lifelines*, about the tongue. Throughout His Word God explains what being a false witness involves. The important factor that needs to be considered in the midst of every relationship in life is that the tongue, or words formed on the tongue and spoken audibly into the ears of another person, have the potential to accomplish marvelous things in the continuation of a relationship—or horrible things in splitting that relationship into bits and pieces.

The tongue is dangerous. Why?

Because with a few words, we can destroy something we have taken months or even years to build up. We go along building, sometimes destroying bits that have to be rebuilt, but we keep on building. Then, we tear down!

Proverbs has a lot to say in warning and in teaching us to think before we pour out harmful sentences.

> Every wise woman builds her house,
> But the foolish pulls it down with her hands.
>
> Prov. 14:1

> A soft answer turns away wrath,
> But a harsh word stirs up anger.
> The tongue of the wise uses knowledge rightly,
> But the mouth of fools pours forth foolishness.
>
> A wholesome tongue is a tree of life,
> But perverseness in it breaks the spirit.
>
> Prov. 15:1–2,4

Women and men are in danger of pulling the beautiful continuity of a family—generations of togetherness, reunions made up of a flow of generations, the most preciously fulfilling things of human life—down around their ears. In so doing, they cause themselves and others to live among broken pieces of memories, and the ugliness and desolation of living in the midst of broken continuity.

People shudder at pictures of the smashed and smoldering ruins of Beirut, where human beings wander aimlessly. Yet people "bomb" with harsh and dangerous words the treasures of their home, their children, and their personal continuity—that which should be protected with gentle, sensitive words expressing that reality of "Love suffers long and is kind" (1 Cor. 13:4). The ruins of Beirut are no more ugly than the ruins of families divorced from each other and divorced from the realities of what God made human beings to know in the fullness of lives that have some measure of continuity.

Dissecting and analyzing each word destroys freedom of expression, and makes it impossible for some people to say "I love you." It takes them months to come around and say, "Well, I do love you." And if the question "Why?" comes, does the answer have to be a profound analysis of the whole gamut of possibilities that the word *love* covers? There are lots of reasons we love each other, and we can use those words to express very *simple* everyday things. It is the critical analysis of every word, or every feeling that you are expressing that can be destructive to a relaxed and warm natural relationship.

There is also danger of being honest in the negative or opposite direction, or rationalizing harsh criticism by saying, "I have really got to tell him what I think of him" or "I'm going to be honest with her and tell her right down the line what I think about her." As harsh words spill out, exaggeration so easily underlines it all, and adds word after word. There is no way of your seeing from the outside what effect your criticism is having inside another person.

Creativity can be stopped by harsh criticism. A person's freedom for creativity can be a very delicately balanced thing. The creative mental work of a sensitive violinist, a talented composer, a painter, or an architect cannot be "seen" in the traditional sense of the word. Crash in on creativity, and something may die! The birth of creativity may end in miscarriage. An individual piece of creativity means a great deal to an individual.

A child can be planning a play with mother or dad. He may write the script in a crooked handwriting, he can bring in neighbor's children to be the bride and bridegroom or other characters, and he can direct the play. And as this creativity is in the midst of taking place, someone shouts out and begins to criticize, saying harsh, cutting things. Suddenly the sensitive young artist, or cook, or musician, or playwright, or poet, or gardener stops enjoying the creativity and the flushed excitement over the lovely unfolding of beauty, and crushed embarrassment floods him or her. Creativity has been stepped on, squashed.

Just as there are limits to the areas of things that are never to be referred to in anger, so there must be limits to the *timing* of criticism. Creativity should not be crushed through scolding, no matter how legitimate, just because a family member or friend is angry. *Time* can be chosen carefully . . . and that kind of a setting up of limits should be done when we are not angry.

No, we are *not* talking about perfection in relationships. But if we are to fight for reality in the continuity of our relationships while things are falling apart around us, we need to go to the source of wisdom. We must discover the common sense danger signs as well as the trail marks on the paths God has laid out to fulfill the reality of our being human beings, made in His image, to whom continuity is basically important. "It is not good that man should be alone" (Gen. 2:18) coupled with "till death do us part" speak of lasting togetherness, even though imperfect since the Fall. The rules or commands of God are given in the Bible to help human beings be human. Inhumanity of one human being to another fills our newspapers with a variety of horror tales. Human beings need help in the way of finding true patterns for life.

"Set your hearts on all the words which I testify among you today, which you shall command your children to be careful to observe—all the words of this law. For it is not a futile thing for you, because it is your life, and by this word you shall prolong your days in the land which you cross over the Jordan to possess."
Deut. 32:46–47

Common sense Christian living, in the framework God Himself has given, is the path to life *now*, as God means it to be.

Eternal life is for later in the perfection that will be God's future for us. But—at present—God's words to us in His Word are profoundly important and urgent: "[They are] your life" (v. 47).

Another aspect of creativity in relationships with husband, children, relatives, friends, is an honest look over the past (in privacy) to discover your most irritating habit—the one that has most often preceded a tense situation, or an argument. This kind of a check-up can become a creative challenge to yourself. As you plan a skeleton outline of your week, do a very attractive poster or chart, for your own encouragement, using whatever artistic ability you have, and listing what you hope to get accomplished in addition to the essentials. In this reminder to yourself, try to fit in the *timing* of things you have always been too late doing. Put a star, a candle, a flower, or some sparks, beside items like "pack suitcase," "make the pumpkin pie for Thanksgiving," "sew buttons on pajamas," "write the promised letter," "take clothes to the cleaner," "prepare for the committee meeting with refreshments made and frozen, and the outline of business"—whatever things have been often forgotten, or done in great haste too late, and have caused continual outbursts in the past.

This is a creative way of preparing for situations long enough ahead to avoid the old patterns of difficulties in your relationships. The *timing* of what to do first should include not only a rearrangement on your list of things to do, but a rearrangement of your attitudes, a self-discipline consciously concerned with the fact that we have ridiculously ignored the common sense recognition of danger points in our relationships. Perhaps it will be maddening to prepare your suitcase ahead of time, and have it ready by the front door, and to have no one notice with praise that change in timing. But your reward is in improving a situation by avoiding the habitual mistake. Your reward is in seeing the artwork of relationships begin to take a new shape here and there, like a painting the great artist improves with each brush stroke.

The beauty of preparing an artistic colorful list or poster— "TEN SPECIAL DAYS from OCTOBER 24 to NOVEMBER 4" or "WORK TO BE ACCOMPLISHED AND EVENTS TO OCCUR BEFORE CHRISTMAS"—is that you are really being your own helper and inspiration. You encourage yourself with incentive, ideas, and originality and treat yourself as significant enough to receive creative help! It is my own secret weapon. Childish? I really don't think so. It encourages you to improve without nagging. It is never too late to work on your own irritating habits, your own weaknesses in down to earth, practical, and creative ways.

Before finishing a chapter on continuity in life, it is imperative to remind ourselves that as human beings we have a need for continuity in the area of familiar physical surroundings. God's promises to His people in the Old Testament strongly emphasized being brought to a land that would be a good land and would be handed down from generation to generation. Land to build homes on, to plant trees that last from one generation to another, to fertilize and grow crops on, to landscape with artistic care for others in the family to enjoy, is something God has pointed to as good.

> And you shall do what is right and good in the sight of the LORD, that it may be well with you, and that you may go in and possess the good land of which the LORD swore to your fathers.
>
> Deut. 6:18

> Honor your father and your mother, as the LORD your God has commanded you, that your days may be long, and that it may be well with you in the land which the LORD your God is giving you.
>
> Deut. 5:16

The Creator speaks of that which is good for those whom He has made to be finite, yet with needs He understands perfectly as He made them in His image. The created earth was made to be inhabited—to provide families a familiar home, familiar trees and grass, familiar hives of bees or flocks of sheep, familiar looms on which to weave, familiar wood to cut and season and carve into art objects or musical instruments, or build into another dwelling place on the land. God is describing as good and natural for His people, the possession of a piece of land to supply shelter, food, and creativity, as well as fulfill a need of security.

Yes, God makes it clear to His people that the world has been spoiled by the Fall, that history is abnormal, and that He is preparing perfection for us for all eternity in a heavenly land, a home He is getting ready for us. But while we are in the land of the living, we are still human beings who have a need for continuity of some familiar things. Material things do affect us. To have to change geographical location every day, or week, or even year, and to have *nothing* familiar in sight, is something that can have an effect not only on children, but on adults.

But so many of us are unable to have a piece of land with a home which is our familiar dwelling place for our lifetime and which is ours to hand down to the next generation. Perhaps one day the Lord will give you and me a comparatively lasting piece of land or house, tent, or tree house that we can have as home, and prepare for someone to follow us. But if not, we can still be surrounded with familiar things even in unfamiliar geographical locations.

There are many reasons to move about—floods, famines,

wars, earthquakes, volcanos, fires, as well as changing jobs. For those who can move a household of furniture—chairs that belonged to a grandmother, a bed that "daddy slept in as a child," dishes that bring back memories of day-by-day meals as well as a stream of Christmas dinners—it is important to do so. It is a mistake to believe it is possible to buy all new things because of an increase in salary, and to start out without any of the memories that are bound up in things that have lived with the family for years. Other people may not be able to take a large number of things, or anything as big as chairs and beds and barrels of dishes because they have been burned or stolen!

I feel so very strongly that human beings were made for continuity, and that continuity makes a difference to us emotionally, psychologically, intellectually, and spiritually. I believe we all need to work at taking things along with us from one location to another! Memories and a feeling of reality go along with the material things, across mountains, land and sea!

Babies need a "security blanket," the same bed, familiar toys and the favorite dishes in order not to feel uprooted and bewildered. Children's need of the familiar should always be taken into consideration if parents are in diplomatic or military service, or any other kind of work that makes frequent moving the pattern of life. Books are important—not just the same titles, but the actual books themselves with their smudges and markings as well as content. It is important to fill the new home with the music that was always played on Sunday or on Friday night! Candlesticks, the shell collection, tablecloths or mats, pictures, other art objects need to be placed lovingly to turn a bleak, unfamiliar place into a set of familiar surroundings. It isn't just the children who need to see the familiar old things come out of boxes and trunks to make the strange place "home." Adults need this just as much.

One does not need to be apologetic about taking things that are familiar across the world. It is a way of taking along the only part of "the land" that can go with you.

A very creative and wise niece of mine just put together an ingenious and practical piece of continuity to be put into her son's trunk as he went off to college for his first year away from home. She carefully made a quilt with pieces of corduroy from all the past years—from jeans and skirts of brothers' and sisters' clothing as well as from his own. These recognizable parts of years of incidents, celebrations, school life, home life, made a practical bridge, and helped the continuity to be real.

Each of us should use our imagination to prepare things for each other in our families, or to tuck things into suitcases that help to substitute for the continuity a family homestead is really meant to give us. In a torn and broken world, fast becoming unfamiliar in tragic ways, nothing is too trivial to carry out our own and other people's need for help in our feeling at home in strange situations and places. Be sure to record as much as possible in diaries, or in photograph albums, in treasured recipes of grandmother's pumpkin chiffon pie, or Aunt Elsa's sponge cake, or Prisca's rose hip jam. Recipes carry flavors and smells from one generation to another in families who cannot live on the same land!

The smell of Thanksgiving, of pine freshly cut, of a wood fire, of roasting turkey, of currant jelly bubbling on the stove, of fresh bread baking, of leaves burning in the fall . . . these help not only to bring back memories, but to give a security of continuity! It is common sense to live in the light of who we are as human beings . . . made for continuity . . . in life.

CHAPTER FIVE

The Lost Arts of Serving, Privacy, Discovery, Imagination

H OW CAN WE POSSIBLY show God that we love Him? What kind of a formula has He given? Is there an acceptable offering of love pleasing to the Creator?

I would like to read Matthew 25 with you, in searching for a practical way to show God over and over again, time after time, that we love Him and that we take His Word literally and seriously in everyday life.

Jesus is speaking of a future time:

"Then the King will say to those on His right hand, 'Come, you blessed of My Father, inherit the kingdom prepared for you from the foundation of the world: for I was hungry and you gave Me food; I was thirsty and you gave Me drink; I was a stranger and you took Me in; I was naked and you clothed Me; I was sick and you visited Me, I was in prison and you came to Me.'
"Then the righteous will answer Him, saying, 'Lord, when did we see You hungry and feed You, or thirsty and give You drink? When did we see You a stranger and take You in, or naked and clothe You? Or when did we see You sick, or in prison, and come to You?'
"And the King will answer and say to them, 'Assuredly, I say to you, inasmuch as you did it to one of the least of these My brethren, you did it to Me.'"

Matt. 25:34–40

God's economy is fantastic! He allows us to do several things at one time, even though we are finite. As we serve someone, a human being, we can be serving the Lord. We can do several things at one time with the same energy, or love, or money. It is an amazing reality, not made up by human beings, but told us by God.

As we give money or material goods to others, with love of the Lord and desire to give unto Him, we are giving it directly to Him. The widow put her mite into the box and the Lord spoke of it as having been given to God. And as we give to Him, we are at the same time giving to a human being or to a particular project, and that gift is accomplishing something in present history. At the same time a mysterious thing is going on in heaven, for we are told that treasures are being laid up for us in heaven when we honestly give to the Lord. We will discover in the future what these treasures are, but we *do* know that an additional thing is taking place now. Our hearts are being affected in a good way. "For where your treasure is, there your heart will be also" (Matt. 6:21) is a statement of fact that describes what is going on within us as we give in a variety of ways.

We are to be doing things in what I call "a backwards way." A person who wants to find life must lose it. A person who wants life to be productive must bury it as a grain of wheat. What a backwards way to approach the accomplishment of something real and important in life! Is this the avenue to accomplishing something? It doesn't sound exciting, and it doesn't sound very spiritual. What is meant by "losing your life"? Losing your life means you don't say, "me," "me," "me" all the time and insist on "my rights," "my rights" with concentration on what those consist of. Losing your life means you don't insist:

"I did the dishes last night; you jolly well can do them tonight."

"Fifty-fifty; everything has to be fifty-fifty."

"I'm *not* going beyond that! I'll do so much and no more."

"I'm not being imposed upon and that's that."

What am I talking about? Serving. Like *continuity, serving* is a word not very well known today. These two words are not central in most people's living. In the first place, continuity is not a part of the schedule of life to most twentieth-century people; in the second, serving is not a part of the search for human rights! How to serve my own rights might be worth considering . . . but serving someone else? What for?

"He who loses his life for My sake will find it" (Matt. 10:39). Finding life is interesting—but finding by losing seems nonsensical. Yet this is where common sense Christian living starts. You see, God's wisdom sounds like foolishness to people, and fools turn away from God's wisdom.

You may think this a very trivial illustration of the stuff of daily service, but it provides one tiny glimpse of the wide diversity of opportunities each of us has to serve the Lord.

Through the years, especially at Chalet les Melezes, my husband has called, "Edith . . . Edith," without saying what he wanted. I would know. A tray with a pot of tea would be prepared, with a teacup and saucer, some hot muffins, cookies, or cheese and crackers, depending on the time of day. If he was talking to someone, I would add another cup and saucer, a bit of cream and some lemon, a candle (always a candle), and enough food for two.

Back in the early sixties, people who came to L'Abri had been reading *The Feminine Mystique* by Betty Friedan. Many discussions sprang up around the ideas expressed in that book—not the fully formulated feminine movement of today, but seeds of ideas being planted in minds. Someone said to me as I was walking out of the kitchen door with one of those trays for my husband, "Why in the world do you run up the stairs with a tray of tea for him? Can't he do it himself? Why don't you say, 'Just get it yourself'?"

This is what is being said today to most children, as well as to most husbands or wives. Relationships are being built by people saying to each other: "Just get it yourself" or "Do it yourself; do it yourself; do it yourself." It becomes a refrain, without a very pretty tune: "I have my rights." "I'm tired." "I'm reading a book; I don't want to be disturbed." "I'm ironing; I don't want to be disturbed." "I'm sewing; I don't want to be disturbed." "I'm talking on the telephone; I don't want to be disturbed." "I'm watching TV; I don't want to be bothered." "I'm composing some music; leave me alone." "I have my rights—you live your life" (whether it is a five-year-old life or a fifty-five-year-old life). "My rights." "My rights." "My rights." "Don't intrude on my plan for these five minutes or five months."

Serving!

How do I regard my having run upstairs with tea, or having served breakfast in bed, or having continued for years to do this kind of thing for a diversity of people, as well as for husband and children? How do I look at it? Do I feel like a martyr? Let me tell you exactly how I see it.

First, I say silently to the Lord, perhaps not always, but really almost every time: "Thank You that there is a *practical* way to serve *You* tea [or breakfast in bed, or whatever it is I am doing for someone]. There would be *no* other way of bringing You food, or doing some special thing for You. Thank You for making it so clear that as we do things that are truly in the realm of giving of ourselves in service to others, we are really doing it for You. These things can be done so often!"

Second, I go on to remember something of this sort: "Now Fran really needs this. He is talking so seriously to this person, and right now this refreshment will pick up both of them. I'm sure they both need a bit of blood sugar. This wheat muffin and cheese will give good nourishment, too, for whatever is coming next." I walk up the steps, you see, really thinking of the individuals I am serving, whether adults or my children or grandchildren, in one or another circumstance of life. A flair of imagination gives me the idea of putting a rose on the tray, or adding some hot nuts toasted in the oven, as I imagine the pleasure the sight and fragrance will bring to ears and nostrils! This is the fun of serving. If you never have surprised anyone in the midst of ordinary daily life, you've missed a lot of the satisfaction that can be spread through days.

Third, I then walk up the stairs with another thought flying in and out of my mind. I think this is very real and valid, and that it does not diminish the reality of the other two things that are taking place simultaneously. I think: "Who is keeping their waistline? Here I am doing my aerobic up-and-down-the-stairs exercise. Now breathe in . . . one, two, three, four, five, six . . . and breathe out through the lips . . . one, two, three, four, five, six."

I have had periods of doing XBX exercises very faithfully every morning for months, and have then started a different set. I enjoy doing exercises, I enjoy swimming laps, but often the exercise time slips away. I have had good resolutions time after time. "I'll do it every day *this* time." I've resolved to get a book and record in order to exercise to music. However, one thing I can continually do is to run up and down stairs for fifty million reasons. It is something to be said to oneself, and to be remembered: When you are serving someone else, in any tiny physical way, and in many, many other ways, *you* are the one benefiting. You are benefiting physically, emotionally, intellectually, psychologically, and you are benefiting spiritually. Serving with a growing recognition of what it consists of is an exercise of spiritual growth.

Why?

Because it happens to be God's way of doing things.

Freedom is much stressed and needed by human beings. Freedom from tyranny is to be treasured and sought after and fought for. The freedom for which Christ died is the freedom from the tyranny of sin. It is made clear to us that we do not need to be slaves to sin, but that we now have a gorgeous freedom. However,

Paul spoke in the power of God to the Galatians, and to us, with a strong warning: "For you, brethren, have been called to liberty; only do not use your liberty as an opportunity for the flesh, but through love serve one another. For all the law is fulfilled in one word, even in this: 'You shall love your neighbor as yourself'"(Gal. 5:13–14). The plea, "Let us not grow weary while doing good" (Gal. 6:9), does not simply refer to missionary work, or to great exploits to save lives in a flood. It is that which applies, moment by moment, to our not becoming weary or tired of doing the little things that give us reality in *serving* other people. We are not to tire of giving a glass of cold water to a thirsty child or of taking a bowl of soup to an old grandmother, or roses to a person in the retirement home, or a fresh ivy plant to the tired scrubwoman who cleans the office. To not use freedom to indulge the sinful nature is not simply referring to blatant sexual sins but to the self-indulgence that ignores the needs of other people living in the same house, or on the same street. Every day we should search for someone to really serve in love, remembering that only in that way can practical kindnesses be given directly to the Lord.

We are to imitate the Lord Jesus. He has shown us the way to show love to God the Father. In Ephesians 5:2 we are told that "Christ also has loved us and given Himself for us, an offering and a sacrifice to God for a sweet-smelling aroma." That double gift is amazing! His sacrifice was a fragrant offering to God the Father, even as He was dying for us because of love for us. "I was thirsty and you gave Me drink . . . I was sick and you visited Me" (Matt. 25:35–36). Amazing! Why are people not more eager to serve one another in love and with imagination?

God the Father is personal to us. We may come to Him privately, alone, communicating directly to Him, talking to Him in prayer with expressed love, adoration, worship, praise, as well as with requests. Because of His infiniteness He can receive each of us as if we were the only one praying at that time. This is such a comfort when we realize no human being has time for us at every moment of need. Other human beings have to wait for a free moment, taking time for only one at a time. Jesus, the Lamb of God, died for each one of us individually, for the sins each of us has committed as if each one were the only one. It is correct to sing, "Jesus loves *me*, this I know, For the Bible tells me so." The "me" is correct. It is correct to tell someone, "Jesus died for you," and to comfort oneself with the realization that we can truly say to the Savior, "Thank You for dying for *me*," knowing that is a true statement, not a nonsense statement.

Then, as finite human beings we can do for God our Father, and for Jesus our Savior, that which is truly personal, by doing something for one individual human being in a most personal way. What a beautiful understanding of our finiteness God demonstrates to us in this:

> I was hungry and you gave Me food;
> I was thirsty and you gave Me drink;
> I was a stranger and you took Me in;
> I was naked and you clothed Me;
> I was sick and you visited Me;
> I was in prison and you came to Me.
>
> Matt. 25:35–36

God understands us. Although He is infinite, He understands our finiteness. Although He is unlimited, He understands our limitedness. He has given us a reality in the area of serving Him which fits in with finite, limited minutes and hours of the day at any time of history and at any place geographically. There are always *individuals* who are hungry, thirsty, or are strangers to us. There are always individual people who need clothing, or who are sick, or who are in prison. These people are one, and one, and one. We show our love to God by showing love to this one, and this one, and this one, and this one! Within the family? Yes. To those among our Christian brothers and sisters close to us? Yes. To those far away? Yes. To strangers? Yes. The possibilities are limitless, although we are limited, and God puts the daily practice of love, or the daily practice of serving, within the reach of each one. Even a sick patient can encourage a nurse by being appreciative, by smiling, by showing thoughtfulness, rather than total concentration on self.

God's way of doing things is the measuring stick given to us to measure ourselves by. We are not to use it to judge each other, but to stand directly alone before God and to check up, time after time, on whether or not we are sincerely and practically serving and with the right motives.

We'll read this passage later in another context, but it fits in as a searchlight to me, and to you, right here:

> Let love be without hypocrisy. Abhor what is evil. Cling to what is good. Be kindly affectionate to one another with brotherly love, in

honor giving preference to one another; not lagging in diligence, fervent in spirit, *serving* the Lord; rejoicing in hope, patient in tribulation, continuing steadfastly in prayer; distributing to the needs of the saints, given to hospitality."

Rom. 12:9–13, italics added

Today not only the patterns of serving have been lost, but patterns that are meant to be passed down from generation to generation have been either deliberately thrown in the garbage, put on a dusty shelf, or discarded in the desire to have something more up-to-date or new. When God gave the commandments as a base for living in the framework that would make living possible for human beings whom He had made, He commanded that the understanding of this framework should be passed down by discussion, verbalization, words said in answer to children's questions. "Talk of them when you sit in your house, when you walk by the way . . ." (Deut. 6:7) gives a vivid picture of family discussion times around a fire, in the garden, at the kitchen table, as well as during family walks along a road, among rocks, in the woods, or by a lake or sea. It is impossible to talk unless you are in *some* way together (with the exception of the modern convenience of a telephone, of course!). Communication is made up of talking or of letter-writing.

Families are meant to hand down patterns *accurately.* Anyone who sews knows how important an accurate pattern is, and the same principle is true for many other forms of creative work— recipes for family favorites, formulas for medicine, or scripts for plays, or notes for music.

Patterns are meant to be passed down, then, by word of mouth and by example. There has been a terrible neglect or wicked and deliberate throwing away of the patterns during the last number of years that has brought us to the place of lost patterns in which we find ourselves now, not only in the United States and the United Kingdom, but in many other countries.

There has been a loss of the patterns for family. Many children have no idea of what a family is meant to be. There has been a loss of the pattern of "oneness" in a sexual relationship—the richness of human beings having a possibility of being one physically, spiritually, and intellectually . . . not with perfection, but with a measure of reality. This concept is foreign to many people because no one ever unfolded such a pattern of possibility to them. The sex education of today's children is through films, books, and programs that are being put in the schools or on television. Such "sex education" makes it clear that the sexual act exists, and even demonstrates how it is performed! There is teaching about homosexual acts and lesbian relationships. Even sex with animals is illustrated in certain pictures and charts. It is suggested to children that these are interesting portions of life. They are told these are alternative lifestyles, choices to be made with no real absolute alternative to the ideas being presented. With moral absolutes left out, beauty and humanness and artistic sensitivity of relationships are left out too.

Ignorant and twisted ideas may have been given to some people in the past, rather than a healthy understanding of one's body and the honest answers that should be given when any question is asked. But the blast of so-called "education" today—as if human beings were machines to be oiled, repaired, and used for a variety of purposes, differing only in whether they are Rolls Royces or Fords, as if no sensitivities, differences, and varying personalities made people individual and unique—can be damaging, to say the least. There is such a difference between machine-made, production-line objects and no-two-alike creations of God. Humanness is that which needs emphasizing so that people may appreciate the *wonder* of individual human beings and their unique relationships.

Forgetting the matter of standards, morals, or right and wrong for a moment, I'd like to speak of something else that is being lost in our day, and that is the breathless beauty of discovery. Few children are allowed to discover anything for themselves, whether morally and at the "right time" through the counsel of loving, wise family members, or whether immorally at the "wrong time" with another child in curiosity and stumbling upon something never heard about before. Even the immoral discovery of one person by another person is very different from being given a deluge of illustrated instruction by films or charts, including all kinds of sex acts—whether a variety of positions, or partners, or homosexual acts—as valid alternatives, like choosing between downhill skiing and cross-country skiing, or going on a vegetarian diet or eating roast beef. The shattering effect on artistic, sensitive personalities can be drastic. The need for true sex education has been ignored by those who prepare the secular humanistic materials that treat human beings with a polluted view.

Children need to be told that there is far, far more to human sexual relationships than what they have been taught. They need to be told that the ingredient of beauty and awe has been left out altogether. There is a great difference between seeing a deer shot and broken by a hunter and seeing that same deer leaping through the silent woods, fulfilling the wonder of all that God intended it to enjoy. There is a great difference between seeing a bare skeleton and seeing that same skeleton with all its warm flesh covering the sinews, tendons, and muscles, performing in a gymnastic event or diving from a high board. If x-ray pictures were all you were given to explain who human beings were, and you saw *only* those x-rays, what a warped view you would have of that one whom some day you might meet as "Jane, whose x-rays you have seen."

There are two dangers constantly present in explaining any portion of human life. One is that it is possible to be too romantic, failing to point out that perfection does not exist because there are no perfect human beings, therefore there are no perfect relationships—physically, intellectually, or spiritually. The other danger is that it is also possible to rob human beings of any expectation or hope of *beauty*. To disregard the existence of romantic love—the possibility of two people finding the wonder of being drawn to each other physically for the first time, giving a gift that has been wrapped and waiting for that one person—and to fill young imaginations instead with how-to directions at ten, eleven, and twelve years of age, is to rob someone, *many* someones, of something very precious.

Television programs and magazine and newspaper articles constantly speak of the "sexually active" age. "Just when should girls be given the Pill by social workers?" "Should it be twelve or is it needed by the age of eight?" "Does the parent have to be told when a young girl, say eleven or thirteen, is pregnant and is being sent to an abortion clinic?" Such questions are asked as if it were a foregone conclusion that sexual activity were a normal, necessary part of the lives of young school children—a part that has nothing to do with the home, let alone morals. The word *active* sounds as if it refers to something quite good, like being "bright." The whole atmosphere takes for granted that this "activity" *is* taking place.

Not only are people being robbed of discovery, but of being allowed to consider chastity as a commendable and attractive period of life. Being chaste carries with it some dignity and privacy! And privacy is being lost on a *very* large scale.

A child should learn early that the body is beautiful, and that

God designed it to be good. The body is so important and so wonderful that Jesus Christ died so that the *body* of each believer can be raised from the dead, changed in a twinkling of an eye when He comes again, to be with the soul forever and ever! It is because the body is so *precious* that we are told that promiscuous sex is not for Christian lives. Paul told the Corinthians, who were puzzled about this aspect of life, that common sense Christian living does not include promiscuous sex. Christ died that our bodies may be raised one day; therefore, it matters what I do with my body. This is clear in 1 Corinthians 6:12-20, but in the seventh chapter Paul goes on to say that one gives one's body as a gift—the husband to the wife and the wife to the husband. The beauty and pleasure and wonder of that physical relationship is not to be diminished by a twisted view taught at an early time in life. The privacy of saving a gift for a loved person is a rare and lovely thing to experience. Wrapping that gift and saving it until the right moment is a lesson that can be learned in the giving of a variety of things, so that the specialness of preparing and saving surprises becomes an important part of all of life.

Privacy is being intruded upon in a variety of ways in life, and we need to resist spoiling the privacy of our relationships with the constant barrage of how-to manuals, or urgings to go to a counselor with every aspect of our relationships. Privacy is being wiped out as a treasured part of life, and we need to be careful we don't fall into that trap! We need to help each other to understand how special it is to urge young human beings to be diverse and human and to make discoveries.

We need to encourage imagination and creativity, not only in looking forward to unwrapping the gift of a fresh, saved body as a gift to the person they will marry, but also unwrapping special talents such as writing a bit of love poetry for one person, not to be read by anyone else. It should be realized that it is not a waste to make a creative original arrangement of bark, moss, and fern for one person, never to be copied exactly again. A song written for a wife or husband, for a child or a mother or a friend does not have to be published to be worth a great deal. The joy of a secret offering, the entrance into the privacy of a sheltered experience, is lost to people who are brought up to think that every step of life has to be shared with the psychologist, the counselor, or another professional.

The freshness of a new morning, with dew on the grass and daisies opening to the light with a look of being the original daisies, and ferns unfolding their perfectly untouched, unbroken tendrils, is exciting to view alone with the Lord in the privacy of being the first one up on a spring day at sunrise! The privacy of greeting a fresh day and new green leaves after a cold winter is something everyone ought to have in memory! The words *innocence, purity, glowing* are words that belong to childhood and should be connected in people's minds with beauty we remember as unspoiled, fresh, untrampled . . . as lovely as a virgin forest filled with breathtaking flowers and fern. It is a horrible thing to be an adult who has thrown all his or her broken trash and garbage over eager new plants just putting out their first buds and leaves. Vandalizing a beautiful garden is an ugly activity, but vandalizing beautiful young human beings is a million times worse! Such vandalization comes in many forms as it invades the whole realm of privacy.

Children love secrets, and the sharing of an occasion or an original creation of some sort should be anticipated by children as enduring parts of lasting relationships. Privacy is part of purity and is something to be enhanced, not spoken of as "lower" and "less fun" than living by someone else's ideas. If every word spoken by wife to husband, and husband to wife, by children to parents and parents to children, by friend to friends, or employer to employee has been suggested and advised by some sort of a counselor or psychologist, and if the *results* of the time of communication are to be reported at the next counseling session, the whole atmosphere of privacy and originality, as well as having the beauty of one's own imagination appreciated is spoiled. People are then in danger of living on a kind of stage constantly. Perhaps the tender moments of life or the big disagreements of life are not actually being viewed by a big audience, but the artificial element of living for the next report to the counselor makes it close to the same thing!

So often the things being said to the husband or wife or children have already been said to the psychiatrist or counselor ahead of time, so that there is a lack of spontaneous communication. I'm talking about a sad loss of humanness, of the beauty of growing and discovering together new facets of another personality and of one's own personality that nobody else has ever found out. Freshness of communication needs the excitement of feeling that "this has never been said before," even if the words *have* been used by other human beings.

Have you ever watched a young couple as they look adoringly

at their first baby in the hospital, and say, "This is a miracle! Look at those perfect fingers and toes"? They haven't had a baby before, and this one might as well be the first baby ever born. The baby is a discovery, unwrapped from the mother's body and placed into the father's arms during a climax moment in the natural childbirth process. This is still, in many good places, a private moment of discovery. Nobody has unwrapped this human being before, and this person has never been born before. Although modern obstetrics can partially unwrap the mystery and discovery ahead of time, no one really has met this human being before or is able to predict what is ahead of him or her. This moment can still retain freshness and privacy, at least among those who will not, and firmly declare they will not, tamper with a new life.

In any discussion of common sense Christian living, it cannot be remembered too often that God has given us understandable comparisons between our human relationships and His relationship with us, and ours with Him. Anyone who feels she or he has already been so spoiled by the deluge of garbage dumped upon her or him by twentieth-century education or attitudes from early childhood on, and to whom the freshness of daisies and dew on the grass is a freshness only to be seen through a crack in the door into a secret garden into which he can only wistfully look and never enter, then she or he should read this carefully—twice at least—before going on.

It was not by accident that Jesus spoke of the new birth to Nicodemus: "Unless one is born again, he cannot see the kingdom of God" (John 3:3). This is a concept that makes clear the possibility of a fresh beginning! Nothing is so new as a newborn baby. No one has met this human being before. The moment of spiritual birth is one of discovery in a special way, with a personal acceptance on the part of the Heavenly Father and the Elder Brother, the Lord Jesus Christ. A new life is being accepted into the Family in a *very* private moment. Tender care is promised. People who have had good parents are able to understand this more readily than those who have had broken and neglected childhoods.

God not only tells us that our sins are washed away in the blood of Christ when we accept His death on the cross as His having taken our punishment, and that we may realize that although our sins were as scarlet they now have been washed white as snow, but He also impresses us with the possibility of a new beginning—a fresh life, the reality of being a new creature in Christ Jesus—by allowing us to read over and over again that which Jesus said to Nicodemus. Don't let the misuse of the phrase *born again* spoil anything for you. Being born again means something historic and *real* in one person's life after another through history. That moment of birth is the unwrapping of a new person who is put into the arms of the heavenly Father as a child in His family.

Yes, we still live with scars, and we will still live in the devastated, abnormal world with temptations surrounding us until Jesus comes back. But the door to the secret garden has been opened to us, and we can walk into it. There is a freshness of morning in the daisy field that belongs to us.

The comparison, the relationship, the mélange, the sandwiching of Christ and the church—Christ the Bridegroom, the church the bride—and the human relationship of a husband and wife is another marvelous thing to contemplate. This God-given pattern of how a man and woman are to care for each other has been lost by many Christians. It is only common sense to read over and over again that which God has given—not just as a suggestion, not simply as advice, but as a command. How foolish can we be? If "The fool has said in his heart, 'There is no God'" (Ps. 14:1), certainly a Christian who makes his *own* rules about how a man is to behave as a husband and how a woman is to behave as a wife, rather than acting upon God's Word in these things, rather than showing his or her faith in God by attempting to *really* live by His directions, is a fool indeed! If we talk about *common sense* as the opposite of *foolishness*, it is very plain to be seen that to believe in an all-powerful Creator God who will be judge of us all, and to hold His Word the Bible in one's hand, reading day by day and in church in a pious act of worship . . . and then to totally disregard what it says, is utterly stupid.

Harshness of a man to his wife, beating her down as an inferior creature, relegating her to second place, thinking of her as an inferior citizen, has nothing to do with the framework God has given in the Bible for the relationship of a husband and wife, a male and female, in the oneness of marriage and family throughout a lifetime.

As you look at John 14 you quickly see the example Jesus gave husbands as He spent time with the early church, His disciples. As we will see in Ephesians, this is a parallel and model as to the relationship of husband with wife. At the beginning of John 14 Jesus promises that He is going to prepare a place for His bride, a home that will be forever. This perfect, everlasting home will have no flaws, but the example is there in the loving preparation of a place in which to dwell, a home. He goes on to speak of the openness of communication that is the reality of the relationship of Christ with His bride. Can it be perfect? No, because the bride (all of us) is not perfect now . . . but it will be someday. Two imperfect people in the earthly relationship of husband and wife are to strive day by day for open freedom to ask as well as to express love, and to talk over needs and worries.

In John 13, what is the Bridegroom Jesus doing? How is He treating the early church? He knelt and with His own hands washed their dirty feet! " 'You call me Teacher and Lord and you say well, for so I am. If I then, your Lord and Teacher, have washed your feet, you also ought to wash one another's feet. For I have given you an example, that you should do as I have done to you' " (John 13:13–15).

This is an example for anyone who would minister to others in the church, but it is also an example on the part of Christ the Bridegroom to any husband who would live according to God's pattern for life in the *now.* If any husband can possibly come anywhere near Christ's gentleness with His disciples, with those who loved Him, that husband is going a long way! Of course, no man and no woman are perfect, but this is the pattern, the example.

How very grotesque is the picture given by some Christian (or professing Christian) husbands as to how God intends for a man to treat his wife. How very wrong has been the idea that the Bible teaches tyranny of man over woman. This is not the relationship God unfolded in His Word, but it is what women have rebelled against in wanting to do away with men. The beauty of oneness— "so then, they are no longer two but one flesh" (Matt. 19:6)—is a beauty that has been marred so often. And the beauty of a day-by-day diversity of serving and a continuity of serving has been demolished by many horrible examples.

Jesus is God. Jesus did not have to worry about His "image," to use the modern, overused word, as He knelt down and felt the ground under His knees, dirtying His hands and arms as water trickled over them, washing the disciples' feet. The Son of God did not lose His place as truly Lord by serving His disciples. He made it clear that only by serving one another could the disciples serve Him. However, He also made clear that the beauty of human relationships would emerge in marriages where the husband realized the seriousness of His place as head of the home, representing Christ who is Head of the church. Is the husband to be a proud and arrogant tyrant as he makes pronouncements?

How far, far, *far* from the Word of God people have gone when they think that harshness and loud commands—"You have got to do this because I say so, and no discussion"—is the way that Christ demonstrated how the bride is to be treated by the bridegroom.

When Jesus spoke to His disciples (His bride—of which we are part) just before He ascended, He gave the Great Commission—the tremendous responsibility of making the truth known. He did not say, "You are not capable of doing anything so important as to tell the world about Me, and about eternal life." He simply gave a titanic job to be done, with trust that His bride would carry out that work. Yes, He promised His presence with us throughout life as the work is carried on, but the fact that we are given the precious truth to give from generation to generation is astounding!

The example Christ gave to husbands is one of tenderness to the bride in menial serving, and of entrusting to her the *most* important work of all history.

"You gotta serve somebody," sings Bob Dylan, and it is so true. There is a lost art in the area of serving. Nevertheless, whether people are artistic and skilled in serving or not, whether they have rebelled against serving or not, they still *do* serve somebody. As Dylan sings, "It may be the devil, or it may be the Lord." So it is true . . . it may be a twisted serving of someone in the midst of running away from serving someone else, but "you gotta serve somebody." Why? Really it is human beings acting on the basis of what human beings are. As people turn from the true God, they serve false gods. As people turn from proper, true, beautiful service, they serve in ugliness that which is abnormal.

Whether wives serve husbands without recognizing any balance in the reciprocity, or husbands serve wives without the proper appreciation; whether employers serve their employees without the right recognition of what they are doing, or employees serve their employers without fair reward; whether we visit prisoners who do not say thank you, or care for cranky sick people daily . . . our art in serving is meant to be improving daily as we serve the Lord and each other. A diversity of restored patterns should be emerging out of the junk heap of the twentieth century to give some true pictures of what has been *lost*!

CHAPTER SIX

Choice and Time

ANY CHOICE INVOLVES the use of time in a way that cannot be used over again.

I met a brilliant career woman a day or two ago. She has had two marriages, a diversity of experiences in many parts of the world, and several involvements in Eastern religions and what the Bible calls the worship of false gods. The wistful longing in this woman's eyes needed no interpretation as she watched my nine-year-old grandchild jump off the bus, kiss me, accept a glass of apple juice at our sunny outdoor cafe table, and then breathlessly say "Goodbye, Mommy might be worrying." The woman expressed her longing eagerness as she said, "I *wish* I had a child . . . I would like a child more than anything else in the world." She could easily have had a child of that age by now, had her choices been different.

Among other misconceptions about "choice" is the one that no one points out—a piece of time, a section of time, a certain length of time is the price of choice! Time cannot be used over again. Time cannot be taken to the cleaner and brought back as good as new, to be used in another way. The use of time is a very permanent thing, whether one wants permanency or not! Time moves from the present tense into the past tense very relentlessly . . . a minute, an hour, a day, a week, a year, nine years! There it is. Childhood cannot be used over again for another set of preparations nor a different set of memories. The teen-age years cannot be lived over again, but neither can the twenties, nor the thirties.

I am not saying that a career is wrong for a woman. Some women are able to do amazing things because of an abundance of energy, efficiency, and talent and can have both a successful career and be an imaginative homemaker.

101

It is important to say, however, that the first home of every human being that has ever been born throughout history has been the body of a woman. It is an incredible wonder that needs recognition—that only a woman can *be* a human being's home for nine months, as well as using artistic skill and creative imagination to *make* a home for that and other human beings! The word *home-maker* may be applied to a father after the new person is born, but the nine months a human being is growing from conception to birth are spent in the only perfect home.

The wistfulness of wanting a nine-year-old to be eager to run home to *you* is based on an accompanying wistfulness of wanting to *be* a home for nine months of private, personal living on the part of a new human being. What a potential to be given! However, that possibility exists only for a certain period of time—shorter or longer, depending on the individual woman. This possibility needs protection. Disease and injury can render the body incapable of being a home. Also, conditions such as sterility that are no fault at all of the individual woman, may make it impossible for a woman ever to *be* the home of a new human being.

Never to realize that the first home of peasant or prince, of rich or poor, of handicapped or athlete, of artist or farmer, of doctor or college president, has been a woman's body is to be cheated of the need to stop and think of the variety of possibilities in the use of time. The use of those nine months is a very precious use of time. No career can compare with bringing forth Beethoven or Bach, or Leonardo da Vinci or Michelangelo, of Shakespeare or John Bunyan, of Thomas Edison or David Livingstone, of Ethel Waters or Mother Teresa, of Amy Carmichael or Madame Curie. What could be more fantastic than being the home of another human being you have not yet met? That person may be a great football player, or a girl who will excel in ice skating, or a president of your country, or a scientist who will find a cure for lung cancer. Or that person may be someone who will need your special care because something has gone wrong during those nine months of living in the home that is you. Perhaps your excellence in caring in such an imaginative and special way for your handicapped child will blaze the way for other mothers, teachers, and therapists with ideas and successes that will help others. There is an unknown result of the use of those nine months, but there is also an unknown result of the use of that same period of time in a career.

After that nine months, there is another period of time that can be used in one way or another, but never used over again. The mother may become the first person in her baby's life (and later in her growing child's life) from whom help is sought, to whom is spilled out all the first precious bits of communication, and to whom the first questions will come—or she will turn that priceless and irretrievable piece of time over to someone else.

It is true that some children are filled with dismay when asked in school, "What does your mother do?" and their answer, "She makes a wonderful home for Dad and all of us," is laughed at with scorn. "What a crazy thing to say! *That* isn't a career. Doesn't your mother have a career? *My* mother is president of General Motors" (or it could be "My mother is an actress," or "My mother is a doctor," or "My mother is a teacher," or "My mother is an astronaut," or "My mother is a lawyer").

The child whose mother is right there when he or she runs home in dismay can have his or her questions answered. That mother can tell something of the wonderful career and artwork involved in making a real home for a growing family. She can talk about the museum of memories she is helping to build for them all, and about the education she is involved in as she adds concerts, reads a good variety of books aloud, cuts out articles to discuss, plans restful vacations that also encourage new skills such as hiking, swimming, playing tennis, bicycling, or visiting art museums. She can explain to the child that she feels home is meant to be a place where human relationships are to be understood for all the situations in later life, and where a shelter is to be found for all sorts of hurts, physical and emotional.

In other words, it is at such a time as during a barrage of questions—"Why aren't you out working like other mothers?" or "Why don't I have a key around my neck?"—that I feel my book *What is A Family?* would be useful to explain, bit by bit, to the child whose friends either have broken homes or homes empty of anyone when they come back from school, what is missing in the lives of most of those children they know.

The imaginative homemaker will find that her home is often filled with other children, enjoying the dough she has prepared for rolls; finding out what it feels like to twist "snails" or "rosebuds" or to make "mice" with raisin eyes from wonderful oatmeal and honey dough; watching it rise twice its original size; and sampling the finished product with a glass of milk.

A new desire for the future may be planted in the mind of some child who has never had a mother at home, or whose parents have been divorced two or three times—a desire to also have such a home to share, a place where a treasure-hunt supper can be a part of the children's friends' life as well as a weekly event for the family. Planting the seeds of future homes by really spending a few years' living this way can accomplish more of lasting importance than giving clever lectures at women's clubs on the psychological needs of children.

A child who is ashamed of having a mother at home, waiting with a pleasant surprise or with a job to be shared in the house or garden, confuses the normal use of a lifetime of time periods. It is impossible, when a mother wakes up and finds that a twenty-year-old child is not going to be at home any more, suddenly to try to grab a year and try to squash into it all the lost years!

When we live in an alien atmosphere we need to be careful to explain just why our way of life is different, and what we consider to be the most important use of precious time. This is important for mother and father and children who are in the midst of using time as a family. "Daddy doesn't answer the phone when we are having our evening reading. You see, either Mother or Daddy reads aloud, and we pull our quilts around us in front of the fireplace in the winter, or we sit in a cool spot in the summer and watch the sunset while we all enjoy the book. Our reading time is the most important time of the day." It may sound crazy to the person who had called in vain during that reading hour—or it may put a question mark in that person's thoughts and give them pause to consider whether their own use of time is as wise.

Common sense Christian living? Common sense should tell each of us that the use of our time is an hourly, daily, weekly, monthly consideration. It is foolish to use time talking or writing about family life, or as a preacher or evangelist preaching about family life, without *living* it. The only way to live anything is to have courage to make *choices* in this use of time. Choices in the use of time—choosing to use an hour in one way always means choosing *not* to use that hour in some other way. Any choice involves a sacrifice of the use of that time in another way. It is not just that a person turns away from a career for a few years while children are growing up, or turns away from the use of time and money for a personal vacation in order to be together at a family reunion, or saying "no" to some seemingly advantageous appointment because of promising the children to go to a concert and a special dinner afterwards; it is a mentality or a basic determination to *put first things first*.

"Ah . . . but aren't you talking about 'common sense *Christian* living'? Doesn't that mean that a church service, or an evangelistic meeting or some religious lecture, or even folding bandages for a hospital *always* should come before a family evening or special times with the children?"

I say, *"No . . . No . . . No!"* Someone has confused you altogether about what is "spiritual." The frantic use of time to "do good works," which then leaves no time to care for the needs of a husband or wife, children or grandparents, sisters or brothers, aunts or uncles, or wider family is part of what is responsible for the terrible breakup of families.

God knew what He was commanding, and why, when he made it clear that husbands and wives were to fulfill each other's sexual needs day by day. You can't read 1 Corinthians 7:1–7 without realizing that men and women are meant to spend *time* together. Forgetting all the details of that passage, concentrate on verse 5: "Do not deprive one another except with consent for a time, that you may give yourselves to fasting and prayer."

This is written in the context of the physical needs of both husband and wife sexually. This is to provide fulfillment, even as food fulfills the needs of the body. At times it is good to fast and pray for a day or two in order to concentrate on an unbroken time with the Lord. The putting aside of the physical relationship is placed in that same category. There must be mutual agreement, and the reason for putting the time used normally for lovemaking aside is for nothing other than for prayer. The picture here is that this is the *only* way for Christians to live "because of sexual immorality" (v. 2). This verse makes it clear that in an immoral atmosphere such as that in which the Corinthians lived, it was important that each Christian man have his own wife, and the woman her own husband, in order to fight the temptation that surrounded them.

This is the basic command for use of time in marriage as a safeguard against immorality. With the statistics of an enormous proportion of divorce among Christians, one knows that this command and teaching has been ignored. Some people seem to have felt they could be more spiritual than the commands of God!

Our children should grow up loving both the Lord and the family, and with a desire to have a continuity through the generations. *Time* is meant to be given to talk *together*, to answer questions, to eat together, to *be* together at bedtime, to have special work *together* as families. *Choice* of the use of *time* is an everpresent reality. It can't be put off. Friendship and closeness among family members grows through years, and lost time is hard to make up.

A grandmother took care of her grandchildren during her daughter's brilliant career. This grandmother lovingly gave her time and energy to do her very best, but in spite of this her daughter has now turned against her with a rather ugly bitterness. Why? Because the love of the children has turned to the grandmother. Their secrets and longings are shared with her. They ask for their grandmother at moments of fear or special need. The mother is suddenly waking up to the fact that she has not simply lost love and relationship, but *time*.

You cannot go back to having a two-year-old. That precious year between two and three is like no other year. Who is going to hear the first awed discoveries of your three-year-old expressed in his beautiful or funny little remarks? Who is going to write down the priceless observations of a four-year-old? These need to be recorded in the mind, accompanied by the memory of the sparkling eyes and smile, or to be written in a notebook.

Who is going to have the treasure of watching and listening to the unfolding of this mind and personality—different from that of any child who has ever lived before? *The person who is with the child.* That person who is taking care of him, or her, may be sensitive and full of delight in appreciating the wonder of this special personality, or may be dull and unappreciative and ready to squash all the beauty of delight and discovery.

There is a choice to be faced by many career women today. Remember, I am not saying a career is wrong. I am saying there is a choice that must be honestly considered, with one's eyes really open. "Experiencing pregnancy and birth" is something even unmarried career women babble about today as they decide just how they are going to include that "experience" in the potpourri of their lives' "experiences." "I don't want to miss out on the experience of childbirth. It's one of the important things of life." This is the sophisticated non-Christian speaking—someone who really feels the universe is a chance universe anyway, and there is no God, so why not? "Yes," I would say. "On your base, why not indeed?"

But there are two things to be said next.

First, you who are reading this in a serious search for the ingredients of common sense Christian living need to recognize that you have a different base for life than the sophisticated non-Christian. "Well," you may say, "I am married and am a Christian and therefore can't be compared with that woman you have just quoted." True, but realize that when this woman puts the child she has "experienced bearing" into the hands of someone else to care for, she is depriving that child of the kind of a home he needs.

The comparison comes here: What kind of growing-up time is *your* child having, and what about your own fractioned life? In what are your choices resulting? You also may be giving your child a deprived childhood if he or she is not experiencing a home with a mother's attention. In addition, you are depriving yourself of this precious irretrievable section of your and your child's life history.

Life is not a frozen thing. The time of having a tiny baby is extremely short. Preschool years pass quickly by, and soon the three-year-old is towering over you as he searches for his football gear or his tennis racquet. Who has been answering this child's questions, or winning his love? When is there going to be time to catch up? The biblical picture of an ideal mother and wife indicates a great diversity of the use of time, but not a diversity that would be the same every day through the years. Life has its different periods of time, and while the loss of one period cannot be made up, often the freedom to do very different things comes with a rush as children leave the nest!

Second, even the non-Christian woman, though attempting to live on the basis of a chance universe without God's existence, cannot escape the reality that her needs are based on who she *really* is, a human being made in the image of God. She has been made to have the desire to be a mother, and she has discovered this and has given in to the strong longing to go through pregnancy and childbirth in order to have "all that is coming to her as a woman." However, if she walks away from all that God planned for male and female, she is still going to be frustrated and empty, perhaps without knowing why. The family life of mother, father, and growing children, and the delightful relationships among personalities at various ages in life—the awe of seeing children discover the wonders of music, or nature's mysteries, or the feel of water flowing by a canoe, or the warmth of a campfire as the family has a cook-out on a cool evening—is something human beings often miss out on altogether. The one who does not have a philosophical base for family life or for continuity in relationships, nevertheless is continually searching for something that is always missing!

Unhappily, there are Christian families who break up and give an ugly picture to the world, while there are agnostic families who live as human beings were made to live and therefore have really beautiful family lives. I do not say "unhappily" because I am sorry the agnostics have found the fulfillment of living on the basis of what God made them to have together. I rejoice in the beauty and example of marriages and families that have had generations of continuity and beauty in the midst of diversity and creativity. But I do say "unhappily" for the twisted, blurred demonstration of "truth" that many Christians give when they do *not* live as God made human beings to live, as they throw away continuity and the place of family life.

At times, a false view of spirituality turns people away from the basic guidelines God has given in His Word concerning the contrast between wisdom and foolishness in everyday life. People who fail to understand that the whole of life is under the lordship of Christ also fail to treat with respect and tender care the parts of life that are under attack by the enemy, who wants the Lord's people to fail in living for the Lord moment by moment.

Choice of the use of time is so often a devastating thing because when the choice is made, there is no possibility of going back. The words "too late" are crushing!

I feel that the woman described in Proverbs 31 points out the fact that life is not meant to be regarded as a frozen or static situation. The matter of being a wife and mother who makes a career of the art work of family and home with its great variety of facets is not a thing that would be the same from one year to another, or from one month to another. Certainly all the admirable things written about this woman did not take place in one year. It seems to me it is a summary of the great diversity of accomplishments and the results of her work and imagination and talents over a long period of time.

Her husband's full confidence in her has been built up over a long enough period of time for that confidence to grow and deepen, as her life has emphasized that she is a trustworthy person. When the statement is made, "She does him good and not evil all the days of her life" (v. 12), you know immediately that there have been many years involved in order for such a sweeping statement to make *sense*. It would be nonsense to speak of "all the days of her life" concerning a young wife who has been helpful to her husband for two months. Day by day, month by month, year by year, there is something being *lived* that can then be pointed to as worth observing because of continuity.

The description of this woman getting up while it is dark to prepare interesting food for her family, and working with eager hands to spin and weave flax, is a picture of something that has had a continuity, something that has taken place over a long period of time. Flax has had time to grow, to be harvested, to be spun, to be woven into cloth, to be made into an amazing array of things. We are not being told about a short spurt of energy and imagination which soon turns to another man, or to another career after a minimal trial!

This description of the "wife of noble character" describes someone who certainly cares for her family with all the diversity of her talents, and in her discussion with her children and husband . . . "She opens her mouth with wisdom, and on her tongue is the law of kindness" (v. 26). Her opinions and ideas and advice are described as being "wisdom" . . . not folly. Through years that are long enough to develop the relationships with her husband and children, years that are long enough to have them grow in their appreciation of her ideas as well as of her, she has influenced her husband and children. This is not the picture of a drudge who is kept at a sink, cowering in a kind of dumb submission. This woman, we are told, has earned her reward in a great variety of work, creative work, as well as just plain diligent, industrious work. However, her praise is not pictured as praise only for a fruitful production of material results, but as we are told, "Her children rise up and call her blessed; her husband also, and he praises her" (v. 28). That praise shows forth the reality of warm friendship and relationships that recognizes the intellectual, spiritual, and emotional help his mother and wife has given, as well as an understanding love.

However, there is a wider thing than a family being pictured through a lifetime of living, as this woman considers a field and buys it out of her own earnings, and in that field plants vineyards. She is pointed out as someone who has the intelligence *and* the freedom to look over real estate, make a judgment, and choose a field that will be good for growing grapes. She knows something about soil, and something about grapes. She could develop her knowledge into a full career, but she obviously limits it to only a portion of her time. She also grasps the spindle with her fingers. She holds the distaff in her hands. She makes coverings for the beds of the household, and clothing for herself of scarlet and purple, as well as fine linen. A creative person is being described with many talents, much energy, and full use of her time . . . but a use of time that covers years, not simply a few months!

You may say, "I don't have that many talents." But you do

have *some* talents. Talents are meant to be used as a creative diversity fulfilling who you are, as well as in the context of providing something for other people. This is not a picture of endless, unchanging drudgery, but a creative diversity . . . doing all kinds of basic things with surprising variety.

A lot is covered concerning this woman's use of time and her choice to extend what she does beyond her family's needs in verse 20: "She extends her hand to the poor, yes, she reaches out her hands to the needy."

The emphasis, I feel, is on her hospitality, as she brings in the poor for a picnic, for lunch, or for dinner! We are told in the New Testament that we are to invite "the poor and the maimed and the lame and the blind" (Luke 14:21), not simply people we want to impress or whom we want to invite us back for dinner. Is this woman doing social work? Is she extending her provisions of food and clothing to the poor around her? Yes, I am sure this verse is given to us as an example of the use of time on the part of a busy mother and creative person. *Time*, as well as material goods, is to be shared with the poor and needy. But taken in the context of the whole Bible, care for people is to be personal—and there is nothing so personal as a visit to a person's dwelling place with a surprise gift, or an invitation to come share a meal in your home.

A widening of the picture in Proverbs 31 would unfold all sorts of common sense Christian living—from George Mueller's opening orphanages for needy children in England; to Amy Carmichael's making a home in South India for children who were being put into temples to be trained as temple prostitutes, and giving her life to bring them up in a Christian atmosphere; to the thoughtful opening of the farms of Christian families to poor children in neglected city slums for summer periods of discovery of nature, good food, and healthy activities. The myriad possibilities of opening one's hands to the poor and extending one's hands to the needy are limited only by time and money, by energy and willingness.

Think for a moment. If every married woman has a career outside her home, or has a timeclock to punch for daily work, plus whatever she can hurriedly do at home, *who* is going to have compassion translated into action to do lovely, imaginative things for the poor? It seems to me that there is very often less diversity and fulfillment offered to women's talents in their being under the burden of a contract, rather than having freedom to arrange their time from week to week and month to month.

While I was writing this chapter, a family came in for tea. The couple had been L'Abri workers years ago, had been married in our chapel, and had had their wedding dinner in Chalet les Melezes, and a reception for all the L'Abri family outdoors on that terrace. An account of what had been going on during the intervening years did not speak nearly so loudly as the beauty of four little girls—ages four and a half, seven, nine, and eleven. These were four totally different faces and personalities, four very delightful little people, with eagerness to read, to quietly play a game in a corner while their parents were talking, four bright happy human beings whose vividness and response gave evidence of having a mother and father, a home, a family life that pointed out a fulfillment of another generation following in the line of that one described as being "clothed with strength and dignity" (v. 25 NIV). She has "the reward she has earned" (v. 31 NIV)!

Choice? True choice requires the careful study of alternatives. Although the same piece of time can never be used again, never forget that time is not frozen. Time is never static. One day follows another. Time flows. Springtime planting precedes autumn harvest. Autumn's freezing of vegetables and making of jellies and jam precedes eating that food in front of a roaring fire as the snow blows against windows in the winter's storms.

These obvious statements are often lost in the modern world. To forget that if the seeds are not planted and weeded and watered, there will be nothing but wilderness at harvest time is the same as forgetting that the richness of growing relationships that continue in togetherness and love right up through old age may be experienced only through *time* and *choice*. There is no possibility of picking corn and roasting it to eat outdoors if the corn has not been planted and cared for. There is no possibility of having loving grandchildren to keep one alive and young if the choice has not been made to use life earlier for continuity of planting, weeding, watering, and caring for the *relationships*. There is a moment when "too late" is an agonizing realization! Life's time has been spent in that which has provided nothing at all for the winter blast!

What is a father? What is a mother? What is a family? What is a grandmother and a grandfather? What is a home? These are all questions that may well be asked with curiosity in true ignorance. The answers must be seen rather than heard. Observation of reality in the continuity of the relationships people have been made to be able to have, needs to be seen in the harvest of results from such life. All forms of life have a harvest.

In the August 2, 1982, *Time* magazine, an article titled, "The New Scarlet Letter" recounted an amazing collection of facts concerning a harvest. The article begins:

> After chastity slouched off into exile in the '60s, the sexual revolution encountered little resistance. . . . The revolution looked so sturdily permanent that sex seemed to subside into a simple consumer item. Now, suddenly, the old fears and doubts are edging back. . . .
>
> "The truth about life in the United States in the 1980s," says Dr. Kevin Murphy of Dallas, one of the nation's leading herpes researchers, "is that if you are going to have sex, you are going to have to take the risk of getting herpes." An estimated 20 million Americans now have genital herpes, with as many as half a million new cases expected this year, according to the Centers for Disease Control in Atlanta.

Promiscuous sex has a harvest! People are reaping herpes, a disease that at the present time has no cure and is spreading rapidly. Blisters appear within fifteen days after infection! A swift result, and the only continuity is a continuity of the disease . . . uncomfortable, downright painful, and possibly harmful to future babies. Forgetting morals altogether for a moment, even forgetting the commands of God concerning the way human beings are meant to live to fulfill the reality of who they are, the choice to use time to indulge in promiscuous sex is a choice which takes a piece of time, or many pieces of time, and in which a momentary feeling reaps a continual harvest of feeling. The *Time* article describes some of the results in various people:

> Part of the pain for herpes patients is the conviction of being damaged goods. George Washington University's Elisabeth Herz reports "intense guilt feelings" among women who get the disease, and hears again and again the feeling that they are unclean, dirty. . . . Many people who contract herpes go through stages similar to those of mourning for the death of a loved one: shock, emotional numbing, isolation and loneliness, sometimes serious depression and impotence. . . . Some people act out their fantasies of revenge. A Midwestern woman says she has infected 75 men in three years.

This is the description of the harvest that is being reaped by millions because of choice. God has always given freedom of choice, but He has made very clear what the results of choice would be. Choice to turn against His carefully explained laws as to how human beings are to live in communication with Him and with each other have always resulted in devastating disaster . . . a continuity of devastating disasters.

Time is meant to be used for the sexual relationship only within the framework of marriage. Jesus made this very clear when He said in answer to a question from the Pharisees about divorce:

> "Have you not read that He who made them at the beginning 'made them male and female,' and said, 'For this reason a man shall leave his father and mother and be joined to his wife, and the two shall become one flesh'? So then, they are no longer two but one flesh. Therefore what God has joined together, let not man separate". (Matt. 19:4–6)

People have separated physical oneness from the oneness of the whole person with another person, which is meant to have continuity. People who do not believe God exists, and who base their lives on a chance universe, have no reason to feel guilty about how they live! Amazingly, however, *Time* magazine's article concludes with a very new note in the consideration of what human beings are gaining or not gaining from their new freedoms.

> For now, herpes cannot be defeated, only cozened into an uneasy, lifelong truce. It is a melancholy fact that it has rekindled old fears. But perhaps not so unhappily, it may be a prime mover in helping to bring to a close an era of mindless promiscuity. The monogamous now have more reason to remain so. For all the distress it has brought, the troublesome little bug may inadvertently be ushering in a period in which sex is linked more firmly to commitment and trust.

This final paragraph ought to cause some very serious re-examining as to the truth of the universe. Might there be a mistake about the base . . . if there is such a disappointing result of life lived on that base? Might there be a wrong seed sown, a mistaken lifestyle accepted if there is such a frighteningly bleak harvest, with nothing to keep out the freezing winds and wild storms, and no fire in the hearth for the winter ahead? Relentless march of time: youth, middle age, old age!

God speaks of those who chose to worship false gods, to bow to their own idols, who ignored His communications, and who chose to use the time of their lives to follow their own paths away from Him.

"Just as they have chosen their own ways,
And their soul delights in their abominations,
So will I choose their delusions,
And bring their fears on them;
Because, when I called, no one answered,
When I spoke they did not hear
But they did evil before My eyes,
And chose that in which I do not delight."

Is. 66:3–4

It sounds like a description of the plight of the many millions of people just described, but it is a vastly more serious thing than that. People have chosen to kill their own babies before they can be born, to kill handicapped babies, to let old or unwanted people die—not only during Hitler's regime, not only in Soviet Russia, not only in Red China, not only in heathen domains in various parts of the world, but in the western world with its supposedly compassionate rules and regulations.

Evil? What a variety of evil is chosen by people sitting in committees, in councils, piously making choices as they cast their votes. Choice of the use of time? What a serious thing it is! An account is to be made of our choices, and of our time.

Common sense Christian living calls upon us to use some time to consider the daily choices we make concerning our use of time. It is not just in the area of the breakdown of the standards all around us that we need to be wary of being influenced to put the wrong things first in our use of time, but in our positive response to the Word of God.

In the area of money, Paul makes it clear that the choice of using money generously brings amazing results to the giver. Read this passage in the light of giving *time* as well as money. God points out that giving time in the relationships of life is so important—husband-wife, parents-children, brothers-sisters, grandparents-grandchildren, and the whole family, as well as adopted family members and relationships with other members of the church family, and neighbors. Time has to be given as a result of choice.

But this I say: He who sows sparingly will also reap sparingly, and he who sows bountifully will also reap bountifully. So let each one give as he purposes in his heart, not grudgingly or of necessity; for God loves a cheerful giver. And God is able to make all grace abound toward you, that you, always having all sufficiency in all things, have an abundance for every good work. As it is written:

"He has dispersed abroad, He has given to the poor;
His righteousness remains forever."

2 Cor. 9:6–9

As the banners flutter around us . . . "choice–choice–choice" . . . may we be pricked to consider our own choice as to the use of our time in this particular moment of history—for things we can never do again, for our friends, for our families, for our churches, but also for the lost and stumbling people around us. This moment of history will never return.

"The harvest is past,
the summer is ended,
and we are not saved!"

Jer. 8:20

It is the sad cry of the virgins who did not have oil for their lamps! There is a time; then that time is ended.

However, those of us who really are a part of the Lord's family also have a warning. We have been given time—however long our lives last before we die or before Christ comes back. That time is measured; it can not be lived again. The *now* is the period when I need to look around and see what I can do that is precious, even priceless. It is not to be exchanged for a senseless, mindless choice.

Joshua sets forth to the Israelites that which is very much the appropriate word to the Christian people of this moment of history, that which is needed as we face honestly the reality of choice:

"And if it seems evil to you to serve the LORD, choose for yourselves this day whom you will serve, whether the gods which your fathers served that were on the other side of the River, or the gods of the Amorites, in whose land you dwell. But as for me and my house, we will serve the LORD."

Josh. 24:15

Only God knows how many church members are serving "the gods of the Amorites" today, "in whose land [they] dwell."

Your choice and mine make a difference in history. When Ruth chose to follow Naomi and declared, "Your people shall be my people, and your God, my God" (Ruth 1:16), her choice placed her as an important woman in the line that led to the birth of Christ: Boaz, Obed, Jesse, David. Choice makes a difference, not only at the time of the choice to the person choosing, but to the future.

CHAPTER SEVEN

Questions and Answers

THE FILM SERIES *Common Sense Christian Living* consists of questions and answers as well as lectures. As you know, it was filmed in Rochester, Minnesota, in a private library, and very real people asked their very honest questions. This book includes more material than was possible to put in the films, but the questions you will find here actually *were* asked.

Perhaps these are your questions too . . . or the questions you hear from troubled or confused people in your church, neighborhood, family, or community. My answers are far from perfect, far from complete, but they have been born out of a constant search for God's help in understanding the needs of a great diversity of people. We have met these people as they have come to us for years in L'Abri, and by following the lives of individuals who have been with us in seminary or in our church work as long as half a century ago.

The answers are not to be thought of as pat, or as push-button responses. Individuals differ and individual situations differ tremendously. Thank God He is available to help individuals, and that they may come directly to Him. Thank God also for His wonderful provision of forgiveness—on the basis of the shed blood of Jesus Christ—for each of us for past sins and mistakes, and for His giving us the strength to go on to make needed changes in humility.

QUESTION:

Sometimes a couple goes through a crisis so severe as to leave them emotionally drained or exhausted. They question their love for one another, yet they feel committed to the continuity of their relationship.

117

What practical suggestions would you offer such a couple during the reconstruction period?

ANSWER:

I would say first of all that the attitude of permanency is a very important thing. If a couple has an attitude of lastingness, of continuance, of durability in marriage, their practical actions following a crisis will be very different from those of a couple who do not have this attitude. In this day in which we live, when the general attitude is one of temporary relationships, the emotional pressures can be far too great for two people who accept the norm of this changed attitude as their framework for marriage.

Rather than having the attitude that the life of the relationship is meant to continue for the length of the life of the two people ("till death do us part") the attitude is that it may die before the people do. After a fight, a flare of tempers, a complete disagreement, a spilling out of exaggerated accusations, a threat to leave, a breaking of some valuable material object or of a beautiful plan for an evening's dinner and concert together—whatever it is that has brought about a heated set of feelings that are far from love—a search is so often *not* for the right thing to do to nurse the relationship back to life, but the search is for an answer to the new question: "Shall we do anything at all, or shall we just let the relationship die?"

Dr. C. Everett Koop has said that a similar attitude has been revealed in recent years in the questions asked by young doctors who have recently graduated from medical school. When a very needy baby is admitted to the hospital, the question of today's young doctors often is: "Shall we do anything for this child?" In the past, the question of any fine young pediatrician as he approached the wisdom of an older specialist would always have been: "What shall we do for this child?"

There is a direct parallel between these two situations: letting a child die and letting a relationship die.

"Shall we let this child die, or shall we try to do anything?"

"Oh, we can't let this child live, because its quality of life will not be what we think the quality of life ought to be."

And so a sign is placed on the crib: "No antibiotics, no food, no water."

"Oh, we can *not* let this relationship go on because the *quality* of this relationship is not what it ought to be." (Or . . . the quality is not what someone else judges that it ought to be!)

And so a sign might as well be placed on the marriage, "No attempt to reevaluate what love is all about. No use of imagination or sacrifice of any kind. Let it die without water or nourishment on any level!"

A very long time ago, a couple in one of our churches was on the verge of a breakup, and the husband had planned to go away with a young girl with whom he worked. My husband visited that home and stuck his foot in the door, although he wasn't at all welcome. He literally kept his foot in the door so that it couldn't be closed and said, "Here I stay, and I'm going to talk to you tonight."

I stayed at home and prayed while I did other things that night. He didn't come back until five o'clock in the morning. My night was well used in getting the week's ironing finished and doing some dressmaking.

I'd like to say something about our own relationship here. Everyone does *not* have the same amount of energy, nor can we all do things the same way. We are not carbon copies of each other. That cannot be said too often. Please do not think I am saying this is the way other people should find time to be together. However, I never went to bed without my husband. Whether it was five o'clock in the morning after an important time of conversation like that, or one o'clock after a session meeting, or eleven o'clock after a committee meeting, I was always up. This was when I got my sewing done, posters painted, ironing finished, curtains made, or letters written. Then when he arrived, we had our "evening" together! It was the coming-home-from-work welcome that I felt was important. Whether a short time or longer, we stopped for something to eat and a talk of some length. I realize now that had I not done that, we would have gone for days without really being properly together because of the busy schedule of a pastor!

Well, in this case he came back saying it had been tough going. "But I helped him to see that the problems he had run into were going to be run into again. Rather than going off with a new person, there were things that needed to be done differently from his standpoint, and from his wife's." Because his wife did not have an understanding of the importance and beauty of the physical relationship, my husband said to her: "Have a talk with Edith tomorrow!"

To the husband, Fran had advised a very drastic thing. "Change your place of work; just quit your job. [These were not people with enough money to do that with ease.] Quit your job and go away together on a honeymoon. Your marriage and the family life for your children is more important than any financial consideration right now. Tomorrow Edith will tell your wife some things."

The next day I had a long talk with the wife. Among other practical things, I advised her about getting her hair redone and buying new and different clothes, including a black lace nightgown. But in addition to revamping her looks for a fresh start, we talked and prayed about an entirely new attitude. Obviously there had been a neglect and misunderstanding of what Paul made clear in 1 Corinthians 7:1–6.

The wonderful thing was that these two people did actually go off on their first airplane ride to a very different part of the country. They blew their money, but not their marriage! They had a vacation that was the most different time together that they had ever had, and discovered two different people—each other. When he met my husband after their return he said, "Hey, I didn't know who I had for a wife. I almost lost a rare treasure."

The problems that bring forth a crisis are not always in the physical area, of course. Naturally, there are as many varieties of irritating and frustrating difficulties that could spoil relationships as there are people. There are blind spots that do not change, and must be recognized as part of that character to be taken into account and forgiven, even before the next irritation or blowup takes place. But, I could repeat this kind of story with other elements in other combinations of people—where people have made drastic new beginnings by reevaluating each other and recognizing the need for *both* to make changes.

There are other cases where people realize in time how precious are the memories of their past mistakes, as well as of their past joys. They begin to see that the complications of a breakup, trying to adjust to two new people, along with the heavy burdens of trying to make up to the children what they are losing, will *not* produce a perfect situation.

The temporary attitude toward the possibility of two people having a growing relationship is similar to continual transplanting of all the garden plants to other gardens before roots can take hold. It is no help to growth!

A crisis such as you have described in your question means a really drastic change is needed. There needs to be a willingness to go out on a limb financially and in many other ways, with the attitude that the precious relationship of two people that is supposed to last "until death do us part," is more valuable than all the other elements involved. One's desire for one's rights must be put aside, with a recognition that the tearing apart of one's own house with one's bare hands is a ridiculous price to pay to win an argument! There is a cost to be faced—cost of time, energy, thought, "death to self," attention, money—plus the turning of a deaf ear to the deluge of opposite attitudes shouted at you from the media, and even from many Christians.

QUESTION:
You spoke of relationships needing to be warmed up. I have struggled for years with a problem regarding one of my three children, for whom I do not have the feeling of love. But, I still try to show her through my actions that I love her. Is my goal to be that I will one day receive and have this feeling of love, or are my actions adequate?

ANSWER:
First of all, I would like to say to anybody with children that it is not possible to have exactly the same kind of feelings toward each child. There are differences of personality between mother and children. Each child is an individual personality, a human being, and no two are alike. Your children are not carbon copies of the genes that you and your husband have put together. People do not have six children who are carbon copies of each other. We don't each have a stock of chromosomes that come together to produce the same kind of temperament in each child.

I have heard a mother saying after her first child was a few years old, "I really *do* know how to bring up a child. I know because of the results. This is the way to do it." After a second and third child came along, that same mother confessed she had spoken too soon. Their reactions were so different, and her problems changed her assurance that she had hit upon exactly the right formula! Sometimes the third child or the fourth is the easiest one, but for others it is the first who is the easiest one to understand and enjoy. Then comes the unexpected shock of stubbornness or lack of response from the second child to the same series of things that brought pleasure to the first.

By "easiest" I don't mean not throwing ink at a white wall or not crayoning the new wallpaper. But there are a variety of things one human being can do to irritate another one! Children are not the only ones who can irritate a mother or father; it can be a neighbor, a friend, a grandmother, or an uncle. A boss can be irritating or a secretary can be irritating, or the conductor on a bus!

You alone know what irritates you; perhaps you just feel "fussy" without analyzing the cause. A too loud person, or a too silent one, a too perfectionistic person, or a too careless one, a too energetic person, or a too lazy person, a person who bursts out laughing all the time or a person who never smiles . . . there are a variety of things that irritate one person but do not irritate another. These are not destructive or naughty traits I'm talking about; they are simply traits of personality, or "tics," or habits that "get under your skin." We all know some human beings who make us feel as if suddenly a porcupine had gotten inside our tummies! We feel prickly!

Now, children are human beings. These human beings have been born to you; they are on your family tree! Each child has some talents, or gifts, or traits that have come from your family line somewhere, quite different from the talents, gifts, or traits of his brother or sister. As you meet your baby for the first time, you look at someone who is different from anyone else who has ever lived, but who might resemble a number of other people in face or form, in intelligence or in talents, in traits or in personality.

This baby has been a human being—with a life of his own— from the time of conception. Even his time in the womb was different from others. As soon as this child was born, he met the only mother he or she has, and the only father! Children are not pets! They are not the property of the parents; they are not something to be owned. We must think of babies and children as human beings with lives that need to be respected. They are under your protection as parents, and under your care to educate, to learn to know, and to love. As far as coming to know what the relationship of a mother and child can be, you are the only mother each one of your three children has.

Now this little girl has only you as her mother. If she is going to know the love of a mother, it's only going to be your love she will know, not that of another. First of all, then, it is something to be praying about as you try to find the cause of what is troubling you.

I am *not* suggesting professional analysis and a lot of introspection, but simply common sense consideration of your present situation. Try to discover what the irritating things are, and when they take place. What are the things that make you feel the "I-could-shake-her-until-she-is-jelly" kind of feelings or bring the tense "I-can't-stand-this-anymore" kind of pressure? Find out when this happens (keep the information private) and how often.

Is there a time when it does not happen? Contrast in your memory the incidents when you have been totally unfair because of your overreaction, and when you have been able to be reasonable and calm.

Now review something else entirely. What is her greatest interest, her greatest talent? What is the thing that needs encouraging and enhancing in her personality? What work does she do well, even reasonably well? Separate yourself now from your feeling of love, or lack of such feeling. Forget your struggle to have an emotion you could label "love." Give your attention to thinking about this growing human being you are influencing. (Never forget that a mother influences children, and a wife influences her husband. . . . A woman may be influencing Congress or the decisions of the agricultural department, or some business, but it is ridiculously foolish to forget that as a mother, she is influencing someone of the next generation. Common sense underlines the need of remembering that the influence of each one of us may be changing history!)

Does this little girl have an ability in music? . . . or drawing? . . . or making up fanciful stories or poetry? Does she love animals or have an interest in gardening? Would she like some seeds to plant and care for in a window box or garden of her own? Would it be good to take her to another city—Minneapolis, New York, Boston, San Francisco, London, Paris, or whatever place is possible for you—and go to a natural history museum, or an art museum, where you could purchase books to study together at home? "Remember we saw this one?" "That was in the exhibit near the fountain . . . remember?"

Could you go out alone for lunch or a picnic together? Forget that she is a child you are *supposed* to love, and for whom you are trying to conjure up a proper feeling, and think of her as a friend—perhaps an irritating one, but one you want to get to *know* better.

Try to find out where there is a beginning spot, something you can *do* together. The talking will open up later. Real communication can't be forced. If possible, find something creative that will continue to grow, or something in the area of education in the humanities . . . certain kinds of movies, certain concerts, a children's play, the circus. Would she love a ballet? Find a classical ballet, if such exists near you, and surround it with a good time of enjoying each other's reactions. In due course you will find you have enjoyed her as a person.

And then the next stage of things will flow from these beginnings. You will have your own recognition of what should come second and third. Naturally, being finite is a problem each one of us has. It is impossible to divide time with perfect balance, having time for husband and each child, as well as for togetherness of the whole family. None of us is wise enough to map out such a course for ourselves. Perfection does not exist!

However, the really important second stage can be put in one sentence. You ask the God of love, who is her God as well as yours, not to allow that child to be deprived of the richness she could have in having your love. *Pray* hour by hour for a measure of love for her for that hour, just as you ask for strength and ideas hour by hour in your work in the house—ways to make things more beautiful for all the rest of the family. You know you cannot perfectly arrange the days for that diversity of people that make up your family, but you ask for the Lord's help—not for a block of time, but moment by moment. Then you also ask specifically for the reality of love to come to you as a surprise in the midst of doing what God has outlined as the things love *does do*.

What do I mean by the verb *do* as connected with love? What is love's definition? "Love suffers long and is kind" (1 Cor. 13:4). Two things to *do*. You can be patient with that child. You can bite your tongue and stop the words of criticism or sharp retort because something annoys you, and you can be patient in the midst of the things you can't stand. This is an active thing God has said is to be done, which is definitely love. "Lord, help me to be patient." How long? "Well, long enough to count, Lord." Patience is not an exciting emotion. It consists of a period of time during which you are putting up with something because you do not want to hurt that other person! It is an act of selflessness.

Secondly, "Love is kind." That is an outward thing you can do. You can do something kind for her. As you help her with her arithmetic, or you put her pajamas on the bed the fancy way they do in an Italian hotel . . . "Look, Dear, see? You can pretend you are in Italy! The waist of your pajamas is pinched in, and the pants laid out, as if it were in a store window." Or you can think up your own kind of surprise. As you do an outwardly kind thing, you are expressing to her what God says love *is* even if you don't have the wave of warm feeling inside that you think love is made up of.

Read 1 Corinthians 13 over and over. Point by point, use your imagination to figure out ways to practically practice love as defined by God. "Tomorrow I will specifically ask that I show love by not being easily angered when I normally would. The next day I'll show my trust of her in some specific way." Point by point, you can try to be realistic in *doing* that which love is meant to do, rather than simply struggling with feelings. Day by day, we each can show patience in our relationships with children, parents, husband, or wife . . . as well as all the other relationships of life. With this little girl, try watching for opportunities to show love simply by being patient.

Since patience is the opposite of impatience, patience can only be shown when impatience comes naturally! The minute you feel impatient with her, pray inwardly without shutting your eyes, "God, help me to know how to show love with some patience right now." Patience is made up of tolerance, sympathy, understanding, generosity. Patience has an expectancy of the other person's gradually going on to the next stage of whatever he or she is doing, or of life! Patience is not made up of a great rush of feeling welling up inside of you—an "Oh, how I love you" kind of feeling. The feeling will come with time. Patience is made up of saying to yourself, *I know this music is noise to me, but she is listening with a kind of eagerness. I must try to understand what it is she likes about it.* Patience is thinking, *It's supper time but that puppet show doesn't have to be spoiled. I'll try to be really generous and sympathetic to her creativity and turn down the oven for a few minutes to watch her little "show."* Patience reads one more story, or lets the child look for her pencil for one more minute.

In the midst of trying to get to know your child as a person, and also of trying to follow the reality of what God says love consists of, it seems to me that slowly and surely the feelings of love will come. Memories will help that, but distance will also help. It is important in all relationships to have some short periods of time alone, away and quiet . . . to put a bit of distance between yourself and the next demand upon you. This is true in the most intense of relationships, in old relationships of long marriage, in short relationships with someone you have just met. It is therefore especially true for anyone having a problem with the personality of their own child. Whether it is an hour, a day, or a week away at camp, the distance itself helps your perspective and brings you back together ready to recognize new interests to be talked about and shared.

The word *love* has often been depicted as a bolt of lightning that strikes where it will with an overwhelming romantic emotion. This kind of emotion does exist for children, husbands, wives, and for grandparents too. But what God gives us in the context of the word *love* is a list of things to continue *doing* over a long, long period of time. This list takes the word out of a romantic, unreachable fulfillment and puts it into the place of possibility, right where we can reach out and touch it!

QUESTION:
   How can we keep from placing unfair pressure and unrealistic expectations on our children as we try to raise a Christian family?

ANSWER:
   I think that many children have gone berserk, if I could put it that way, from being given too-high standards and by being treated as if they would have to be perfect to please you . . . no matter how imperfect you parents are as people! You live out your imperfections in daily life. We all do. To be fair to children, your (our) imperfections must be a subject of conversation. You must say without hesitation that no one is perfect, and that, of course, you are *really* imperfect.

   "Look at little John Lewis. He's being imperfect right now. He has been told not to touch the sound system, and he's touching it while he is saying, 'Don' touch! Don' touch!' All right—that is imperfect!"

   We have an overwhelming appreciation of imperfection at times, as it is so interesting in a brand new little person. Then all of a sudden it hits us the wrong way, and we reach out and *Whack!*

   Is there to be no discipline, then? Yes, of course there is to be discipline—but fair, even discipline, recognizing that no one is going to achieve perfection until Jesus comes back again and we are all changed to be really perfect. Discipline is to teach a child acceptable behavior or to protect against terrible dangers of being burned or hit by a truck. But to expect perfection is not only unrealistic, but totally unfair in really teaching the truth of what the abnormal world is like, and what human beings are.

   I would rather put aside discipline than have the child think I thought that I was always perfect. Bitterness has come among the children of Christians when they have received what they felt was totally unfair treatment. They were punished for things they observed their parents doing, or for behaving in ways they had observed their parents behaving.

   It is important to say to children when it is true: "Look, I did something that was really wrong. I'm awfully sorry; I lost my cool.

I lost my temper; I got mad; I was angry. I shouted about something I should not have shouted about. I realize you were just being creative over there, playing your recorder, while I was trying to concentrate on something I was composing. *Your* music clashed with my notes. I'm sorry I screamed." You need to say enough to put it into the context of reality and life. Their lives are not going to be easier than yours, and your help is needed.

There must be no pressure for perfection when perfection is not possible. We all put pressure somewhere, and we need to be careful to evaluate the fairness of the pressure our demands are causing. (Of course, we can't be perfect in our fairness, either!)

As we try to be balanced, our basic attitude must be: "Here are imperfect children, and here are two imperfect parents. We are going to spend a certain portion of our lives together living in the same home. After that comes the 'whatever'—the career, the wedding day, the study and travel—and never again is it going to be the same. Never again are we going to live in the same way under the same roof, with each other's clashing ideas, or clashing music, or clashing schedules. How can we be *real* in our influence, and teach more by the reality and honesty of our lives than by our rules and regulations and very unrealistic expectations?"

Paul is speaking to the children when he says, "Children, obey your parents" (Eph. 6:1). But in that same chapter, he strongly cautions parents: "Fathers, do not provoke your children to wrath, but bring them up in the training and admonition of the Lord" (v. 4). There needs to be time for careful examination day by day as to what you might be doing to exasperate your children and turn them away from both you and the Lord, rather than giving them excitement and interest in pursuing truth.

One way of having the right kind of influence on our children is by making it clear that we are all together in the same boat of being imperfect, but that we may have help. Nobody is perfect but the triune God. Nobody else is. However, as a family living with the desire to be what God wants us to be, we don't expect to follow the lead of the unbelieving people around us any more than the Israelites were expected to follow the standards, customs, and lifestyle of the Baal worshipers living around them. We expect our family life to be different, and we expect each other to be different . . . even if not perfect!

One other thing needs to be said in answer to this question. Don't forget to give praise and appreciation to your children. People have told me that their parents never praised them: "No matter what marks I got in school, my report was always met with 'You could have done better.' " People of all ages need encouragement. Pianists and orchestras need applause to feel the appreciation of the audience; they don't need someone to stand up and say, "In such and such a bar I heard a mistake." It is bad enough to read critics' disparaging remarks later, but in the flush of performance people need applause, appreciation, and acceptance.

Children need praise and acclaim from their parents for tiny performances as well as great ones!

"Darling, how wonderful! You carried that glass of water as well as any big person!" (to a three-year-old lovingly bringing you water, with his mouth all screwed up in concentration).

"I'm so proud of you for making your bed alone; that was such a help" (to a six-year-old who has a bit crookedly made her own bed).

"The table is set so well, and daddy will love your flower arrangement" (to a ten-year-old who has not only set the table but picked daisies to put in the center).

"Don't worry about failing the math test. I know you tried hard this month, and we'll try to see together what your problem is. I am so proud of that poem you wrote [or of the collection of shells or grasses from the nature walk, or the map made for geography class . . . or some other accomplishment during the same period of time when the failure took place]."

My children joke today about my always thinking they were the best, no matter what their studies were, or what the results were. I really always felt that way! I thought my children were great, and still do! I don't think my letting them know that hurt them any. I felt they could do anything they put their minds to— building a tree house or a raft; making a puppet show; learning French as they dropped into French-speaking Switzerland; studying at the University of Lausanne; painting; or whatever! Of course each person's talents are different, but that doesn't make any one person less special and worthy of praise for what he or she has done or is doing.

Yes, please don't forget praise! The word *worthy* can be applied to imperfect people. Praise does not wait for perfection, God tells us He will say, " 'Well done, good and faithful servant; . . . Enter into the joy of your lord' " (Matt. 25:21). No one will have been a perfect servant, but God our Father is not going to withhold praise from His children because of our mistakes and imperfections. We don't have to be afraid of "running the good race," becoming exhausted, and never reaching the finish line. Don't discourage your children by withholding praise.

As a final thought in answer to your question, it comes to me that unfair pressure often comes through trying to reach the expectations of others, rather than dealing directly before the Lord with plain good common sense as to what is important for the child at that particular time in his or her life.

Let me illustrate. The first of August is the Swiss national independence day, a day of old-fashioned bonfires, patriotic parades and speeches, and fireworks. At that time, when Franky was a small boy, each village family had their own fireworks. Franky had always asked if he could collect money for the fireworks. Now L'Abri had a principle of praying for financial needs, rather than asking for money. But this was *not* money for L'Abri; it was a little boy's desire to put on a great production! He was asking for contributions from people who would be enjoying the production. Our answer each year was "yes." Our conviction was that this was an important occasion to Franky, and that all the people certainly got their money's worth. When he had collected the freewill contributions for the celebration, he went off happily to the store in Villars and made his careful selection.

Then came the day itself. Franky made great preparations year after year as he nailed pinwheels to the plum tree and put up elaborate wooden frames for various kinds of fountains and so forth to be fastened at different heights. There were rockets laid out in a neat row as the time approached, and various other interesting-looking affairs. Franky had also marked places for the wheelchairs of the children in Bellevue, the cerebral palsy home next door, and benches for all the L'Abri people and the workers, therapists, and nurses, in Bellevue. My part was to make enough cakes and ice cream for everyone.

The audience was satisfied and excited as they listened to the master of ceremonies, Franky himself, announce each event and as they watched the display, knowing there would be homemade ice cream and a selection of cake after the grand finale. Any of you who were in L'Abri or Bellevue at that time will remember the specialness of those first-of-August occasions with as many as 135 people enjoying that widened family time, talking of the climbers who were lighting flares on the tops of the mountains, and thanking Franky for his earnest hard work as the "producer" of this evening's memory. Unforgettable.

Now it was approaching the first of August one year when

Franky was about seven or eight years old. His usual box with the hole in the top had been taken from person to person throughout the day, and he was listening to the jingle with obvious satisfaction.

I was in the Chalet les Melezes kitchen doing dishes with a young man who was bitter and superior about Christianity. He had come from a Christian home, and had gone to a Christian college, but had turned away from it all. Suddenly he whirled around from the spot where he stood drying dishes and spoke to me: "It seems to me that *you* [and the "you" was spoken with a sarcastic sneer] . . . *you* ought to stop *your* boy from collecting money for fireworks. *You* ought to send that money to the *heathen* . . . to preach the *gospel*." I can't express the kind of sneering malice that came forth in his voice.

I whirled around from the sink and spoke with just as much emphasis in my voice, I hope not a sneer, but I am afraid I was strong and not sweet, as I said, "If your parents had let you collect money for fireworks . . . and had let you put on the kind of production Franky does, perhaps you wouldn't be against Christianity as you are."

Money has a variety of special uses to provide memories and beauty and the fulfillment of creativity on the part of children. The "heathen" and "the preaching of the gospel" will be helped more by giving your children a rich and full childhood than by sternly sitting them on a chair and giving them lectures about the starving or the heathen. Please remember that I really believe in sharing the gospel with the lost, food with the hungry, and clothing with the poor, and in teaching children to have compassion, but it all has its proper place in the balance. Anyway, the fireworks were being shared!

All this is a part of *not* having an unrealistic expectation.

QUESTION:
Would you consider continuity to be a practical priority in today's society for a single career person who has made frequent moves, has a scattered family and broken family ties? Is it a practical consideration?

ANSWER:
A single person does have a family, and this is where I would bring in the importance of the family reunion. If at all possible, over a period of time, families should try to pick up the threads by

face-to-face togetherness in some kind of a reunion. This has to be planned and prepared for, with some sacrifices and inconvenience involved as far as time, finances, travel, and interruption of work or vacation or other plans are concerned.

Here is a lifetime—a block of years. How many years in a lifetime? Sixty-seven? Seventy? Eighty? Less, or more? Some time during that block of years there should be breaks in the business-as-usual or life-as-usual or success-as-usual or too-busy-as-usual kind of life, to come back together with those who comprise what is left of your family. There needs to be a face-to-face kind of continuity in being a family—for each member's need, if indeed there is anyone else at all who is living, and whose address you know.

There needs to be a person-to-person communication that continues over a lifetime . . . keeping alive a friendship, a sharing of ideas and convictions with those who are closer than acquaintances of your same generation. This is something everyone ought to do for their own stability in life as well as for continuity of whatever family relationships there are.

I don't know you personally, and so I don't know your position in life as far as having any living relatives. But for others (perhaps this is you, too) who are single, with their parents gone, and with only one or two distant relatives anywhere in the world, or no known relative alive, there is a second important thing to do. There is an adoption process that is important. I think people should adopt as an aunt, an uncle, a grandparent, or a cousin, some lonely person or a number of persons who also have no caring family. I am not talking about financial support of such people, but of really communicating with them as you would with your own family. This means some planned time of being together and consideration of what to do for birthday, Thanksgiving, or Christmas surprises. It means listening as well as telling your hopes and fears, joys and sorrows, to someone you feel you can really adopt. It means listening to that person's interests, ideas, and accounts of what has been going on.

The feeling of responsibility for a family member is a good thing in this world of inhumanity. Your own being human to another human being, with kindnesses and thoughtfulnesses, is a healing balance to your own feeling of being suspended as you "live in a suitcase."

Whether you decide to contact relatives with whom you have lost touch or whether you adopt a family, not only should you plan for a reunion once every two years at least, but letter-writing is very important.

You say your job causes frequent moves and travel. Some lonely person who never can travel and has no opportunity for a new job in a new location would love to know what Australia is like from your postcards and letters . . . as you describe the heat in January when they are having summer in Australia, and the cold, wet weather in August. Your adopted aunt, or grandmother, or grandfather would love to see Hong Kong through your letters, with perhaps a Chinese bowl for rice, and a pair of chopsticks arriving as a surprise one day!

You can adopt a person or several people some distance from you to write to, as well as adopting someone close to you geographically. The compassion for another person, expressed through communication and providing surprises, is one aspect of what the Bible calls losing your life in order to find it (see Matt. 10:39). That is to say, it is one way you can lose time, money, energy, and imaginative ideas without foreseeable return! The "finding" will be recognized when you discover that as you wander through a market place you have had a small thrill in seeing just the right thing, a scarf or a trinket of some sort, for "dear Mama Jones" or "my adopted aunt in the nursing home."

The disconnected feeling, the "separated-from-roots" kind of feeling, can really be helped by taking on this kind of family responsibility, rather than living, traveling, working, entertaining yourself as a single person with no ties, from whom no one is waiting to hear. It is good for each of us to be conscious that someone is waiting for a phone call, a letter, or a visit, and that we should not neglect that someone! This is a practical, common sense outworking of: "Be kind to one another, tenderhearted, forgiving one another, just as God in Christ also forgave you" (Eph. 4:32). It is doing that which is within our reach to do in fulfilling the law of love.

QUESTION:
You said that continuity in our relationships requires verbalizing, yet our society pushes us off in a hundred different directions. How can we cultivate better communication in our homes?

ANSWER:
Finding time for communication in the midst of a very heavy schedule is difficult. I would say that the only time I have found

for valuable communication with each of the members of my family has been when it has been inconvenient!

If you are not willing to stop and take the inconvenient moment, you are not going to have any real communication. A phone call comes when you are just ready to turn out the light and go to sleep, or when you are halfway out the front door. The person on the other end of the line is your child, your grandchild, your sister, or your parent, who will take your time, but whose conversation is a special continuation of your close friendship.

You realize that at least a few minutes are essential. To cut this time off would be to lose something precious, not just for the moment, but for the reassurance your attention is giving that other family member that you really care. Naturally, if you are a surgeon running to do an emergency operation, you say so, and your son or daughter will understand as you say, "I'll get back to you as soon as I can." It is the pattern that is important, and the exceptions are then easily accepted. If, however, everything else *always* comes first, your children will feel they are always last in being considered important.

You are just in the midst of writing a chapter of a book, and one of your children comes in and sits on a chair and says, "I have something I need to talk to you about." My feeling is that there is no use writing about life, in any area of living, unless you are willing to stop writing and *live.* Being available at an inconvenient time is part of really living as a mother, a father, a family member.

Your child begins to talk to you after you've read a story and you are tucking him into bed. Your mind is outlining what you will do next: *I'll do the dishes now . . . then I'll do this and that and the other, and so on. . . .* But your child is opening up with a question important to him or her or is about to confide some special thing to you. *This* moment is not going to come at another time. If you slam the door on this particular use of the next half hour, you are finished with whatever this close moment was going to consist of. That specific time is never to be repeated.

Learn to stop your brain and actions to ask yourself a question: *What's more important: my relationship with this child or getting the child in bed at the right time?* You answer the question by telling yourself: *Stay. Do the dishes later.*

Naturally, there are myriad examples of inconvenient times for shared confidences or precious discussion of ideas or accounts of projects that have been completed. Inconvenience is the shared ingredient of a variety of pieces of time.

QUESTION:

At what point does self-sacrifice stop, and self-preservation become right?

ANSWER:

It would be impossible to give a hard and fast rule in reply to that question. There are different personalities and characters, and different combinations of people. There are people who would be so selfless that they would never sleep and never eat, keeping on working for the rest of the family and serving others until they really fell apart!

Each person needs to know something about his own physical energy, amount of sleep needed, psychological makeup, point of emotional fatigue, and tension levels. You can't say, "Well, Edith Schaeffer stayed up until her husband came home every night, so I've got to do that too." I would *not* say that at all. That was *my* life, and it was my kind of energy at that stage of my life. It worked out well for me, and for us.

You can't say, "I'll do it the way Mrs. Jones does it." You are not a copy of somebody else. You have to know what and where your own limitations are. You need to recognize when you need to have your feet up and read a book, sip some juice, get away from everything, and say, "This is my rest, and I am going to sleep a little while, or read a little while, *because* I can't talk to my children later today if I get into a falling-apart state." You have to face yourself in the mirror and say, "OK, I have limits" . . . and remind yourself what your danger signals are.

Our oldest daughter, Prisca, is a person who becomes very nervous and tense at times. She has come to know herself well enough to recognize the signs. She is a birdwatcher. So off she goes with her binoculars, up to the woods to do some birdwatching for a time. Then when she calms down, she gets back into her L'Abri work with her students and so on—listening to other people's troubles and talking to them, as well as cooking, cleaning, and caring for her own home and family.

Susan, our second daughter, has her own manner of living so that pressures don't carry over from one moment to another, or from one part of the house to another! The Manor House at Greatham contains a very big kitchen, a dining room where students and L'Abri guests are served, the Farel House study room with desks and tape recorders, the library with its books and cassette tapes, the big entrance hall, the office, the living room where lectures are given and high tea is served, and the new lecture room with its provision for showing films. Upstairs are student dorm rooms with eight in some rooms, and an apartment for a worker couple. Then there is a portion for Sue and Ran and their four children, with bedrooms and family room.

Susan has her own way of coping, which no one may be able to copy. When she goes downstairs she becomes totally absorbed in L'Abri, in the menu for lunch, cooking, running out to the garden, telling people what their jobs are for the day, having a cup of tea for some minutes with someone who needs help with a personal problem, talking about some current issue like the war in Beirut or abortion in China or whatever with all those who are peeling carrots and potatoes. She says she is completely involved with the people and their needs and in what she is doing down there in her L'Abri work.

But, when the children come home from school, or when it is time to teach Ranald John, who is studying under her teaching, she can go up to their family room and just as totally shut out L'Abri. Now, she is a mother and a teacher for her own children, a wife and a homemaker in that part of the house, which is the only home her family will ever remember. In the same way, she finds she can sympathize with someone in a tragic situation without going to bed to weep or dream bad dreams about that person's problems.

"I really can turn it over to the Lord practically," she says. "I can honestly feel the reality of the fact that Jesus died in order to bear burdens of this sort *for* us, and since in my finiteness I cannot, I tell Him so openly, and I can be free of that person's burden, except when I am with that one. I don't feel this is false, but the only way that human beings can help other human beings. Only God is infinite."

Udo Middelmann, our youngest daughter Debby's husband, for some years now has taken the Thursday evening meal as his time to cook for the L'Abri students and guests who are eating in their chalet. That is Debby's time to prepare and enjoy a meal upstairs alone with their children, while Udo uses his chef's abilities to try out various new recipes! Then, of course, he also sits at the head of the table and leads discussion. This gives a change to Debby, and gives the children some time to be away from the people for their own conversation. A switch, a variety, a change in the schedule or kind of pressures needs to be tried out.

Debby and Udo keep track of when there are organ concerts

in the Cathedral of Lausanne, or in some other church, as well as of other events. Their day-off excursions with the children include a variety of diversions, with perhaps a picnic, a walk, a swim in the lake, and a concert. The important thing to remember is that we each differ in our basic needs, as well as our amount of energy, so for some the need for "serving self properly," if I could put it that way, is to read a book late into the night (as Debby often does) while for others (or for the same person) jogging or skiing or exercising with a specific program is the more complete preparation for the next portion of the day.

In every area of life, balance is needed, and not one of us finds a perfect solution. In this as in all else, we need to pray for help in finding what will fulfill the true need of the moment. When there is a string of emergencies following each other, we call out for the strength that God has promised us He will give . . . His strength for our weakness—a beautiful, exchange—and practical, time after time!

People have to know what relaxes *them,* and not feel guilty about using a piece of time when it is necessary for them, or when they do not use it exactly as somebody else would. Each person has a very different measure of energy, of original ideas, of creative talents, of determination to finish a job, or opportunities to do various kinds of things, and of obligations assumed. The president of the United States has a very different set of obligations from the real estate man or woman. When we take on an obligation, at the same time we make a commitment to fulfill our promises. I am not talking about shirking obligations and being lazy or careless about responsibilities.

But if you and I drive ourselves to copy some other person's achievements or energy output, we could easily fall apart and, in the end, accomplish less. If we try to live outside the circle of who we really are, there is a danger that some kind of disaster could affect us, as well as other people. By suggesting that you know your limitations, I am not talking about being analyzed or analyzing yourself, but of gradually coming to a practical, common sense understanding of your limitations. There is a need to recognize that when certain signs come along, you should rest in some way, or change what you are doing for another kind of job for a while, so that you won't fall apart in some way!

This is one of the most common sense rules of living. When a man becomes tense and nervous in his office work, he should be able to go home and chop wood or charge around his piece of land cutting scrub brush, planting trees, weeding his corn and tomatoes, or don a chef's apron to make a charcoal fire and cook supper for his family. When a woman gets tense in whatever she is doing, there are many things she can do. If she has a loom, she can weave for a while; or she can make bread dough and punch all her frustration in the kneading of that dough.

She can turn from a typewriter to a sewing machine, or from ironing clothing to painting a picture, or from telling her two-year-old a story to drawing pictures and writing the story to be retold over and over again, perhaps eventually to become a book. Just as I thoroughly believe that God meant us to have continuity to fulfill the way He made us as human beings, so I feel God meant us to have diversity—which brings its own kind of rest and needed change. People are not machines that work well if simply oiled and turned on for hours and hours of unchanging work.

I know your question dealt with how much serving is necessary in relationship to the fact that each person has his or her own needs, but the matter of diversity fits into this. No matter for whom things are done, variety, diversity, change of occupation are forms of meeting one's own needs.

In today's world of "city dwellers," some form of getting out among grass, trees, rocks, sand, hills, lakesides, seasides, into a rowboat or running shoes is extremely important. Such balance is needed by a human being made to dwell in the midst of nature . . . or the "real world" . . . as it was created as a proper environment for the human beings who were to dwell in it.

QUESTION:
Where do you draw the line between educating your children to make responsible choices and destroying their joy of discovery?

ANSWER:
Of course, there needs to be careful instruction. You are not going to allow a one-year-old to discover what feeling a hot stove is like, and then have him in pain from the blisters for days. You are not going to let your three-year-old discover what it is like to walk off a landing where the stairs have been torn out to build a new staircase in the house so that he can discover what such a fall is like. You grab him back! You may give him a spanking to emphasize that the landing or the stove are forbidden. However, you try to explain as carefully as possible, according to the age of the child, just what it is that your love is trying to prevent. The need to be

careful before taking a step in a house that is being built or remodeled must be learned by adults too! A Swiss builder of whom we were very fond, and who had built hundreds of chalets, one day in careless thoughtlessness stepped right off a stair landing and fell on his head. Impressing a child early in life that we all have to warn each other at times to "be careful" or "watch out" because we love each other is an important lesson.

There is a need of instruction. Human beings are not meant to be dropped into the world to learn everything without instruction. This is why in Proverbs, when fathers and mothers are being spoken to, the emphasis is that children are expected to have a male and female parent with slightly different kinds of instruction to contribute.

> My son, hear the instruction of your father,
> And do not forsake the law of your mother;
> For they will be graceful ornaments on your head,
> And chains about your neck.
>
> Prov. 1:8–9

This command is preceded by a very important verse, a statement of fact, spoken to parents as well as children in verse 7 of the same chapter.

> The fear of the LORD is the beginning of knowledge,
> But fools despise wisdom and instruction.

It is of vital importance in trying to be common sense Christian parents to remember that we need the Lord's discipline throughout life. We never arrive at being "finished products" as human beings. We have a lot yet to learn, daily. We need to gain continually more knowledge and wisdom, and our awe of the Lord is the constant beginning place. Foolish parents are not very capable of giving a balanced variety of good instruction to their children. In today's world of broken homes, however, it is necessary to constantly remember that children are to be in relationship with their mother and father. The father is meant to be around to give instructions, and the mother is meant to be present to impart her wisdom. Note, please, that this is far from sounding like putting the woman in an inferior place. Wisdom is hardly an inferior quality, and the mother is meant to have real wisdom!

There should be sensitivity on the part of the mother and father as to where there is a need for discovery. As seeds are planted in the garden, there is a need for the child to experience the delightful discovery of that plant's bursting through the soil with tiny shoots or dividing leaves. Not even a five-year-old child would, of course, know enough to take the seed and plant it unless you have instructed him. "These little brown seeds [or white ones or whatever] are going to turn into lettuce plants [or pea vines, or tomato plants]. Come on, let's put them in the ground here, and pat them down, like this." You are not spoiling discovery; you are introducing your child to its reality. One day you can say, "Oh, come, look. They are breaking the ground." (Or perhaps your child will call you, if he goes out every day.) Then this is the time to explain what has happened.

This instruction is in contrast to showing the children a movie or a set of pictures to illustrate how a plant comes up. The first experience of seeing a seed grow should be as real as possible— growing in a garden, or a window box, or at least in a flower pot if you live on the twentieth floor and have no outside space on the balcony. They are able to see how a seed bursts, how tiny shoots come out of it (and how the root turns down if they are watching sprouts in a bottle). As days go by, you discuss the progress and add other information about plant life—maturity of corn or beans or tomatoes, how to tell when it is time to pick them, and so on.

If you use your ingenuity, you can recognize opportunities in many things in life for introducing your children to discovery they will never forget. Let them discover rather than doing it all for them, feeding them with a spoon, which cuts out discovery.

Debby and Udo have chickens in a chicken house built at the back of Chalet Gentiana (a part of Swiss L'Abri). These chickens are fed daily with both chicken feed and with peelings and scraps that are boiled together for a tasty hot mash each day. They are good layers and the eggs are delicious—fresher than anyone could buy. Recently a Farel House student asked Mike as he placed a bowl of eggs on the kitchen table, "Do those eggs come from Udo's chickens out back?"

"Yes, they do," replied Mike proudly.

"Oh," said the fellow, with both surprise and a bit of condescension in his voice. "They look almost as good as if you bought them in a store."

And, of course, we will never forget dear Claire from California when, years ago, she was asked to go out into the Melezes garden and get some carrots. "There aren't any," she said. "I looked everywhere." She had been looking for bunches to be hanging on bushes, the way they looked in the supermarkets in Los Angeles!

Discovery needs some guidance and instruction, and preparation by wise and imaginative parents, so that many things are learned in various areas of everyday life.

You introduce your child to discovery when you expose him to finger paints, or tempera paints and a brush, or modeling clay or a dish of play dough. As you get out the mixing bowl and ingredients, you grit your teeth and say to yourself, *this is going to be a mess, but I want him to do it himself.* Then you say aloud, "Go ahead and break the egg in that bowl. That's right. Oops! Never mind, we'll get another one. Here." You point out what comes next in the simple recipe for muffins or sugar cookies. "Go ahead, measure it in this cup. Now put this in, and then that. Now stir it up with this big spoon. Take this margarine and grease these muffin tins like this . . . see?" Let him discover what it is like to make muffins for the first time. When he is older he will be able to follow a recipe. Boys need to learn to cook as much as girls. Tell them that most of the chefs in the famous restaurants of the world are men!

Let them discover what it is like to put peaches in boiling water to loosen the skins, to carefully lift out one at a time with a slotted spoon, and when cooled a bit to see the skin peel off like magic! Let them cut up the peaches (two or three cupfuls for the first time) and add an equal amount of sugar, a couple of handfuls of raisins, a teaspoon of cinnamon, and stir it as it boils to a proper thickness. It will be their first peach conserve, and can be enjoyed later in the week . . . a discovery that canning and jelly and jam making last longer than the making of one meal.

I actually made this peach conserve when I was nine years old—the first jam I had ever made alone. My mother let me melt paraffin in a tin can to carefully pour over the conserve to preserve it. I had the fun (which I still remember) of watching the paraffin gradually cool and harden into a white seal, not to be broken until we wanted to eat the peach conserve on fresh hot biscuits which I had then learned to make by myself. I still remember my satisfaction.

It is a being-allowed-to-discover-what-it-is-like affair in a variety of areas—without your mother's saying, "You are too young to make a dress. Here, hem this handkerchief." Again, I remember that same year, when I was nine, I made my first dress. Admittedly, it was extremely simple—like a doll dress, a front and a back, with raglan sleeves, all cut together. I laboriously put bias binding around the neck and sleeves by hand. The stitches were crooked, but I wore the dress proudly!

Opening discovery is introducing children to one step when the next step can be totally original—trying something out for the first time; not having everything done for them so that all they learn to do is push buttons in an electronic game.

Naturally there are areas that are for later in life, that are to be kept wrapped for the proper moment of opening. There is a difference between your careful sensitive sex instruction, with emphasis on the marvels of the human body and childbirth, and the ugly presentation that reduces it all to mechanics.

Can you protect your child from everything, from all the threats around you in your particular "neck of the woods"? Can you foresee every temptation and prepare him or her for that? Were our parents or grandparents in different moments of history able to achieve the unfolding of a perfect childhood as they cared for us or for our parents, giving them a measure of wisdom, understanding, and instruction?

No, there is not, and never has been, a golden age for children. As we live in *this* moment of history, we need to use our own common sense, we need to pray for the wisdom of the Lord beyond our own, we need to help each other all that we can possibly do within the "circle of possibilities" not to allow childhood to become "extinct" because of the pollution of the media, supermarkets, and schools with the great variety of poison that is designed to do away with any possibility of a hopscotch, rope-jumping, hide-and-seek, tree-climbing, walking-on-stilts, fishing, rowboating, campfire cooking, imaginative, discovering, childhood.

One of our most important goals in common sense Christian living should be to do something for our own children and for other children in preserving this thing called *childhood*, which is rapidly growing extinct and in some circles is a meaningless word.

There *is* discovery that is ghastly—discovery of drugs at the age of eight or nine, discovery of alcoholism at ten or eleven, discovery of sex and pregnancy at eleven or twelve. These discoveries are ones by which human beings are actually making money, polluting and wiping out the childhood of little human beings.

Yes, of course discovery needs mothers and fathers in the background—with the kind of wisdom and instruction God is talking about in Proverbs!

CHAPTER EIGHT

---◁▷---

Spiritual Issues of Life

I N THINKING OF WHAT is meant in the Word of God by the life-style of a Christian, it is important to recognize that there is not meant to be a division in life. Life is not meant to be sorted out like clothes for the washer—white, colored, delicate, and so on! We are not to sort some things out as "very spiritual," and other sorts of things as "medium" and other things that we think of as having nothing at all to do with being a Christian as "kind of neutral." When we speak of what it means to be a Christian in the whole of life, it includes everything that any one of us does. The new you and I, as we live according to the teaching God gives us in His Word, are meant to be affected moment by moment in our work, as we face the new day morning by morning, in everything we do.

The kind of spirituality the Bible talks about affects how we treat other people in the family, in the wider circle of people we work with, in the community, and in the even wider circle of the world. We are to be interested in people thousands of miles away. But we are to be interested in people across the street too, and those who live under the same roof with us!

There is a definition of the Christian life in Romans 12:9-13:

> Let love be without hypocrisy.
> Abhor what is evil. Cling to what is good.
> Be kindly affectionate to one another with brotherly love,
> in honor giving preference to one another;
> not lagging in diligence, fervent in spirit,
> serving the Lord;
> rejoicing in hope,
> patient in tribulation,
> continuing steadfastly in prayer;

distributing to the needs of the saints,
given to hospitality.

We need to read *all* the Epistles, and study longer together, but we can begin with this much to clarify a few things. At the beginning of chapter 12 of Romans, we are told, "Do not conform any longer to the pattern of this world" (v. 2 NIV). Our need is to read and reread God's very different "patterns."

Love must be without hypocrisy. We are to hate evil. What an antithesis these two statements present to us. Love and hate are opposites. What a sharp negative after the positive statement about love being real and sincere. Hating evil is to be a part of our true spiritual life. We are not just to love each other and love what is good, and do compassionate things for people, but we are to hate evil and whatever is evil. That hating must also take some kind of action. Therefore, as we consider the spiritual things of life we must include a great many things. And part of it is to be hating what is evil—actively!—as well as clinging to what is good—actively—in order to be devoted to one another in brotherly love, and to be honoring one another above our own selves.

We are never to be lacking in zeal. Zeal for what? Zeal for the issues of our period of history. There were actions taking place as people worshiped Moloch and burned their children in that worship. Jeremiah spoke into the midst of the issues of that day. Today there are actions taken by those who do not believe in God's existence and have a humanistic base. Actions come from that base as naturally as one plus one equals two. There are actions Christians ought to be taking that are also natural, commanded actions, upon the Christian base.

Before going on, I would like to look into a few of the things we are told God hates, or detests, or abhors. This should help us to have a bit more spine or backbone in hating what God hates, and in taking action when He would have us take action.

Proverbs 17:15:

He who justifies the wicked, and he who condemns the just,
Both of them alike are an abomination to the LORD.

God is interested in justice, and we His children are in danger of trying to be more "spiritual" than the living God if we say that the things that happen in the justice department of the country we live in is of no interest to us. Justice should matter to us. God has said so.

Proverbs 20:23:

> Diverse weights are an abomination to the LORD,
> And a false balance is not good.

Business affairs of the people of God—whether they run enormous companies or are grocery-store owners or sell apples by the road—matter to the Lord. He expects His children to be honest in their dealings and this is a part of spiritual action.

Isaiah 1:13–17:

> Bring no more futile sacrifices;
> Incense is an abomination to Me.
> The New Moons, the Sabbaths and the calling of assemblies—
> I cannot endure iniquity and the sacred meeting.
> Your New Moons and your appointed feasts My soul hates.
> They are a trouble to Me;
> I am weary of bearing them.
> When you spread out your hands,
> I will hide My eyes from you;
> Even though you make many prayers,
> I will not hear.
> Your hands are full of blood.
> Wash yourselves, make yourselves clean;
> Put away the evil of your doings from before My eyes.
> Cease to do evil,
> Learn to do good;
> Seek justice,
> Reprove the oppressor;
> Defend the fatherless,
> Plead for the widow.

God hates false religions, and a *mixture* of false worship combined with worship directed to Him is detestable to Him. Many false religions have been involved with killing babies as a part of their worship, and literally their hands "are full of blood." The mockery of using God's name and addressing Him in prayer in false worship, God calls "evil."

Proverbs 1:7 speaks of the fear of the Lord as the beginning of knowledge, and says that fools despise wisdom and discipline. In other words, the honoring of God, the adoration and awe of God, should bring forth understanding and knowledge. Such awe and adoration would honor God's Word sufficiently so that one would seek truth in the Bible itself. Fools, as described in the Bible, are those who have disregarded the truth of what God has said.

I would like to consider together with you Isaiah 58, which

gives us practical conditions for acceptable prayer and true spiritual living. At Swiss L'Abri we often read this passage on our days of fasting and prayer. Isaiah has been told by God to make clear to the Israelites why He has not been hearing their prayer. He tells Isaiah, "Shout it aloud, do not hold back. Raise your voice like a trumpet." God wants to be sure His people understand. He is not just scolding; He is unfolding a definite pattern for them to follow if they want Him to listen to them.

> " 'Why have we fasted,' they say,
>   'and you have not seen it?
> Why have we humbled ourselves,
>   and you have not noticed?' "

God replies:

> "Yet on the day of your fasting, you do as you please
>   and exploit all your workers
> Your fasting ends in quarreling and strife,
>   and in striking each other with wicked fists.
> You cannot fast as you do today
>   and expect your voice to be heard on high.
> Is this the kind of fast I have chosen,
>   only a day for a man to humble himself?
> Is it only for bowing one's head like a reed
>   and for lying on sackcloth and ashes?
> Is that what you call a fast,
>   a day acceptable to the LORD?
> Is not this the kind of fasting I have chosen:
>   to loose the chains of injustice
>   and untie the cords of the yoke,
> to set the oppressed free
>   and break every yoke?
> Is it not to share your food with the hungry
>   and to provide the poor wanderer with shelter—
> when you see the naked, to clothe him,
>   and not to turn away from your own flesh and blood?"

I have quoted the New International Version, verses 3 through 7, here. Do read the rest of chapter 58. The passage goes on to say that if these things are done, then your light (and my light) will break forth like the morning, and many wonderful results will follow in our communication and relationship with the Lord.

But stop a moment . . . and reread the last line of the quotation: "and not to turn away from your own flesh and blood." In *that* context I would like to discuss some very clear issues of this present day. I believe God is speaking to us concerning what we are doing or neglecting to do. "If anyone turns a deaf ear to the law, even his prayers are detestable" (Prov. 28:9 NIV). Does He want to observe our spiritual activity, or hear our prayer, if we are allowing destestable things to take place in our community, our country, in our moment of history without raising a voice, or without taking *action* in some way?

"Your own flesh and blood." How could you turn away from your own flesh and blood? In no way more throughly than in the issue of abortion. A mother turns away from her own flesh and blood as she refuses to give birth to her child. This is the flesh and blood of the grandparents also, and of the aunts and uncles and others of the family line. The family line of 1,500,000 babies involves an awful lot of people. And there is a father as well as a mother. Proverbs 23:22 speaks of the father as the one "who begot you," and later of the mother "who bore you." An interesting distinction!

Who is responsible for so many turning away from their own flesh and blood? First of all, there are those who urge others to make a choice for abortion. If this takes place without our protesting in any way, then our silence is giving consent in a very real way. In Jeremiah 5:28–29 God calls "doing nothing" in this context an "evil deed."

> "They surpass the deeds of the wicked;
> They do *not* plead the cause,
> The cause of the fatherless;
> Yet they prosper,
> And the right of the needy they do *not* defend.
> Shall I not punish them for these things?"
> says the LORD (italics added).

God is saying that the fact that these things had been neglected amounted to an "evil deed." In various areas of our lives neglect is an evil action. God's Word is very searching, and we can't get away from it by simply shrugging our shoulders and saying, "I didn't do anything." That's just it; that's what was wrong—you or I didn't do anything when we should have done something.

A poster reproduced on page 148 that I found in Washington, D.C., in Senator Jepsen's office, had been sent to all the senators with a note asking them "not to play God by trying to change the abortion law"! The poster reads:

If they succeed [in outlawing abortion] you will be forced to accept, as law, one narrow religious and moral belief. Even if it is not your own. Your church's. Or your synagogue's.

The Religious Coalition for Abortion Rights of New York State represents most of the country's major religions. We are organizations like the American Baptist Churches, N.Y.S., The N.Y. Federation of Reform Synagogues; The Episcopal Church; The United Presbyterian Church, Synod of the Northeast; The United Church of Christ and The United Methodist Church, whose positions on abortion you might not be aware of.

Note how God's name is signed to this poster! The statement indicates that God approves of the choice of a mother to kill her own child, a person of the next generation.

I quote from the poster again:

We believe abortion is an individual decision. And therefore your God-given right. While we support a woman's choice to become a mother, we also support her choice not to.

This is influencing, urging, putting pressure upon people to consider the killing of a person (who already is an individual at the moment when the chromosomes come together) as a choice quite equal to letting that person live. Life and death have been put into the hands of any woman as within her rights to dictate. The freely given liberty, or "right," to choose to destroy this individual who is growing in one's own body, and the placing of that choice under the heading of a "God-given right" is one of the most vivid examples one could have of replacing "bitter for sweet," and "sweet for bitter" that has ever occurred in history.

What an idea with which to impregnate the minds of the people in our country as they go to their church or synagogue looking for help in the area of how to live. If they have gone to a church or synagogue, there must have been some sort of desire to find out what God's teaching is in the midst of this century. *Choice* is the word being emphasized. *Choice* is the central word. Coupled with that word is the word *freedom*. Both are wonderful words, but they are being misused in this context.

We need to think through a few other areas where choice is being considered a fine thing, whether in the negative or positive use of that choice. Infanticide is the topic of a great deal of discussion these days. A *Newsweek* article (Sept. 6, 1982) entitled "Nature's Baby Killers" traced animals through history—animals that kill their own young or their siblings. This article, because of its

acceptance of the evolutionary theory, does not see any real difference between animals and human beings. Therefore it concludes that infanticide is "hardly a comforting thought, yet it can no longer be called 'abnormal.' It is, instead, as 'normal' as parenting instincts, sex drives and self-defense . . ." says the writer of this article. This is such an illustration of what the Marquis de Sade contended—"that what *is*, is *right*," or what Franky put so well to the tune of "Anything Goes" in the beginning of the fourth episode of his film *Whatever Happened to the Human Race?*

There is a deluge of feeling, emotions, and cold intellectual certainty that it is *right* to let your baby die of starvation or of medical neglect if it does not come up to the standards that some doctor has dictated are the "right standards" for life, or come up to standards that demonstrate an "acceptable quality of life." Acceptable to whom? It seems the criteria is that the person must be acceptable to society or to the parents.

In the August issue of *Science 82*, there is an article on premature babies—"Before Their Time." This tells of the wonderful strides being taken in pediatric medicine that give smaller and smaller babies a chance to survive.

> Many of these very premature babies weigh less than fetuses that can be legally aborted. And the task of saving one is no easy matter. Though 98 percent of Stanford's premature babies survive, 32 percent of those between 750 and 1,000 grams and 76 percent of those below 750 don't. . . .
>
> Still, neonatal intensive care units report not only increased survival rates but decreases in the severity of handicap of those babies that suffer handicaps. At the Children's Hospital of Los Angeles, for example, the survival rate for babies under 2,500 grams who suffer not only from prematurity but from respiratory and congenital diseases as well, has increased from 40 percent in 1960 to 85 percent in 1980. Of the survivors only 15 percent suffer any sort of handicap, and only one percent are stricken with severe handicaps.

What a twisted situation we live in! Doctors are discovering new ways of helping people to live, whose lives have been threatened by prematurity . . . while other people who have every hope of life are being burned and cut up by abortion methods. Amazing. But you say, "I've heard all that before. What's new?" According to this article in the science magazine, what is new is that human beings are being influenced to think that infanticide is perfectly normal, that it is not at all abnormal behavior for parents to decide, "He [or she] *may* not turn out to be without a handicap, so don't try to save life in this case, doctor." The "education" is taking effect in a way that is new.

The article gives two insights into what is going on. Some parents are thrilled with their "miracle baby" who has been helped by operations and special help to live, in spite of some difficulty. Who is to say that a high IQ presents a family with their greatest joy? There is more to personality and character, more to a human being than the mark received on an intelligence test or the achievements in sports! Some very special parent attitudes came through this article, but one very frightening kind of reaction seems to be growing among parents. One parent questioned who should make decisions. This parent felt that doctors only want to save lives, and don't consider the consequences of what they are doing. In other words, the parent began to talk about grounds for a lawsuit! For what? For saving a life that *might* be handicapped!

We are in the midst of arrows flying from several sides at once! Doctors . . . wanting to be true to what they feel is their calling as doctors . . . are being screamed at, or hindered, or influenced, or pressured by certain parents who feel they have a "right to choice" as they choose to have a child with a "normal life" . . . however they define that. And parents . . . wanting to be true to what they feel is their calling as parents . . . are being screamed at, or hindered, or influenced, or pressured by certain doctors who feel *they* have a "right to choice" in the area of declaring that a baby is not going to have the quality of life necessary to be allowed to live! It is a confusing situation, and Christians have a responsibility to *not* just shrug their shoulders and be isolationist and uninvolved. We need to know what is happening.

A very beautiful woman came up to me in the Dallas-Fort Worth airport a short time ago, and said, "I wanted to tell you how much Franky's film and the books have meant to us. We have two lovely children, but each time I was told to abort. Each time the doctor insisted on an amniocentesis test and said, each time, that *that* baby could not possibly be normal." Her eyes shone as she thanked me for the *Whatever Happened to The Human Race?* film and book. She then went on to say, "We had them both, and they are beautiful, bright, lovely children today!"

Another couple came to me who had been told that they should destroy their baby, "Don't feed it; let it starve because it isn't going to come up to a normal standard." In that case the prediction was wrong. Not all cases have these kinds of results, but this particular child grew up to be perfectly normal.

However, God did not say, "Don't turn away from your own flesh and blood *unless* your children are handicapped." People who have to wait until the Resurrection to ever enjoy walking normally, or talking without effort, or seeing anything at all, or tasting anything, or doing anything with their hands because of one or another sort of handicap, need *more* parental love and loving, imaginative unselfish help from brothers and sisters than do the ones for whom everything goes more easily. What a warped view to think otherwise! The "perfect race" of the Greek States or of Hitler's dream would certainly have been a race built on the bones of other human beings. The living would be heartless and totally selfish.

When you think carefully as a Christian, your common sense tells you that the drive toward abortion, infanticide, and euthanasia of the aged is a drive to get rid of any people who might need to be given unselfish care! True unselfish compassion is being exchanged for a very selfish idea of "freedom from care."

No utopia will ever work because there is no way of sifting through human genes so that the only ones left will produce brilliant, kind, good people. It is a vain and hopeless search for happiness without difficulties to mar that happiness. It is doing evil that someone's idea of good may come, in the worst sort of way.

There will be the sound of a trumpet some day, which really will announce the arrival of joy as it announces the arrival of the Prince of Peace Himself. That trumpet will spell disaster to those who have turned away from the true and living God. How often God has made clear to His people what the dangers are, and how clearly He has called human beings to Himself in compassion: "Return to me." People who do not return are called "silly."

> "For My people are foolish,
> They have not known Me.
> They are silly children,
> And they have no understanding.
> They are wise to do evil,
> But to do good they have no knowledge."
>
> Jer. 4:22

Choice is involved in "doing." Choice sounds like a special thing we should all be interested in. Why can't everyone have choice? The answer is that God *has* given choice, has given choice all through the history that Scriptures reveal to us. He gave Adam and Eve the choice between life and death. The choice was theirs. Results followed.

We need to read again Isaiah 66:3–4 concerning choice to see that God continues to point out that *results follow choice.* Right and wrong exist; therefore right and wrong choices exist . . . and the results differ.

> Just as they have chosen their own ways,

Who? Among the many, the people who have chosen to make that poster promoting abortion in the name of God and to hang it that others may be influenced.

> And their soul delights in their abominations,

God would surely call the killing of babies an abomination. He makes clear that He detested false religions, as the Israelites were often tempted to do what was being done around them, and were caught up in the worship of Moloch, which involved the destruction of babies. Over and over again in the Book of Jeremiah God speaks of the detestable idols, and the infanticide connected with the false worship. He hates the killing of the innocent, and so God says next:

> So I will choose their delusions,

For whom? For the people who make these choices in their own foolishness against Him and against His Word.

> And bring their fears on them;
> Because, when I called, no one answered,

This is God speaking. Often people say they have called upon God and He hasn't answered them. God is saying in Isaiah 66:

> . . . when I called, no one answered,
> When I spoke they did not hear;

God *has* spoken through Scripture. People *have* the Scriptures. People who make such posters have Bibles in their houses, as well as in their churches. This is the Old Testament. People may read

Isaiah and Jeremiah freely. At least these words are on their shelves!

> But they did evil before My eyes,
> And chose that in which I do not delight.

We who do read our Bibles and claim to believe God's Word to be truly from Him should be doing something practical in these areas. To speak against what is wrong? Yes. That is something practical, but we all need to do something more practical in the area of abortion, infanticide, and euthanasia.

I am very excited about what some people are doing in various parts of the United States in starting crisis pregnancy centers to help people in their moments of need.

Please don't be lulled to sleep, or fooled, as you see posters about choice, perhaps in your churches or other places where you go with friends—for a Parent-Teachers meeting or some other event. Don't just shrug your shoulders and say to yourself, "Oh well, you know, people *ought* to have choice, I guess. After all, they are living on a wrong base anyway . . . so why shouldn't they have choice?"

I feel very strongly that the answer to that is that women are *not* being given a choice, because they are not being given a careful presentation of *two* sides of the matter. Nobody who walks into an abortion clinic, or into the office of a doctor known for practicing abortion on demand, ought to do so without first being shown *both* sides. If you are talking about choice, there have to be things spread out from which to choose!

They ought to see the whole film *Whatever Happened to The Human Race?* first, and then make a choice. That would be a choice. You can't choose "between" one thing! "Here is a cup of coffee—there is your choice." Choice is not being properly given in the areas of infanticide or abortion; all that is given is pressure to do one thing. It is one sided. Public TV told Franky they could not show his film because it did not present two sides, but they then showed films that presented only the so-called pro-choice side. That is extremely narrow, to say the least.

The woman who told me about her baby said that the doctor argued flat out: "You two people don't have very much money. Your baby is going to be a hopeless human being and this operation will cost seven thousand dollars. I advise you to let this child quietly die."

With tears in her heart but stars in her eyes, she replied firmly, "Thank you just the same, but no thank you. We'll raise the seven thousand dollars—and we *will* have the operation." She went on to say that this child is walking today, and beginning to talk, and is a much-loved and delightful three-year-old person.

The doctor was wrong in his one-sided advice for several reasons. One reason is that his prediction was quite wrong. Human beings are not God, and so they don't always *know*. The element of possibly making a mistake is always there. But the big mistake is the treating of life as a dispensable thing. These parents feel chills when they look back and realize that without a second thought that doctor would have thrown away the life of this child . . . now a person so precious to them.

Choice is not properly given in the area of abortion, infanticide, and euthanasia, either by many doctors or by the media. People have not heard two sides, nor have people been given equal voice in discussing the issues. For me to live my little period of life of sixty, seventy, or eighty years, for you to live your little period of however long . . . and for us to think we are living a common sense Christian life without speaking to the issues of the day in *some* way is to be blind indeed. We need to speak in every way we can think of so that another voice is heard, to make sure, in whatever comes to your mind to do, that something is done in a positive way, too.

The spiritual things of life are the things that God has given us—the diverse talents, the variety of gifts, the preparation we have been given and are being given to do well for Him—during our time of life as His representatives. In the midst of our doing good to others, in the midst of our making truth known, our hating evil is a part of that spirituality as is our appreciation of beauty.

If you are a publisher or a pastor, a ditch-digger or a pilot, a fisherman or a fruit grower, a garage mechanic or a furniture maker, a writer or a homemaker, an office worker or a congressman . . . there are unique things involved in your moment-by-moment work since you are a child of the Creator of the universe. Your work should be different; your conversations with others at break time should be different. But when we are at home, the reality of our living a common sense Christian life will show up as either solid oak all the way through or simply a thin veneer on top. Perfection? No, but there is a difference between being real or fake both in our careers and in our lives at home.

True spirituality at home is caring about the things of the home—the relationships, the atmosphere, the serving, and the longsuffering—in action! Then there is to be the historic reality of opening the home in hospitality to others. It can't be always "someday"!

You are to do well, whatever you are doing, to the glory of God (see 1 Peter 4:11). Just as flowers that grow on the Alpine peaks, beauty in the cracks of rocks with perhaps no one ever passing that way, are not growing in vain because God sees them, so it is true of the human being. A person may live alone, walk alone, and feel that no one is recognizing that he or she is being patient in the tribulation of loneliness . . . but God does know, and is aware of the whisper, "I love you, God. Please accept my praise as I walk alone today." This is true of people in prisons, in concentration camps, in hospital beds, or in wheelchairs. What can be done in such places to the glory of God is really a spiritual work. "Work" to the glory of God can be done in every part of life . . . which is what makes it all so fair. No one gets a bigger opportunity than another. And no one is "out of work"!

But, as we do what we do unto the Lord, it is to be in the negative as well as the positive. The Bible does not indicate that we must beat ourselves (as certain religions demand of people), nor do we need to try to do some sort of penance to please God. It is quite the opposite. Yes, God hates evil, and so it is a spiritual act to go out and fight the idea that killing a small handicapped baby is acceptable, or that killing a perfectly normal unborn baby is a fine thing. A spiritual act *is* to fight twisted wrong ideas.

But—a spiritual act is also to enjoy a flower as it comes up in the spring, to go out into the woods to look for the first snowdrops as they come after the snow melts away a bit, to watch the river go down with a rush as the spring snow melts into the mountain streams, to watch the sunset over the mountains or the lake or the fields of corn, or to get up early to see the beauty of morning at the seaside or on the desert. Planning to go out to see the new moon and first stars at twilight is important. It is spiritual; it is good in the eyes of the Lord for us to enjoy the beauty that God made and to acknowledge in the midst of it that we appreciate His creation. We should be spending some time communicating to God and expressing to each other something about the wonders of what He has created for us to enjoy. In 1 Timothy 6:17 we are told:

Command those who are rich in this present age not to be haughty, nor to trust in uncertain riches but in the living God, who gives us richly all things to enjoy.

This is a wonderful and strong word to each of us, no matter what our financial status! Hospitality, sharing, serving, kindness, putting others before one's self, loving, fighting evil, standing for truth, laying up treasures in heaven, fighting the good fight for the faith, enduring all things, having gentleness, being generous and willing to share . . . all these admonitions are to rich and poor alike! This is very clear in 1 Timothy. We are to be concerned with what each one of us is doing, as to whether or not we are pleasing God, loving Him, serving Him, and following His clear commands in His Word. We can't push it off because we are "too poor" or "too rich" or "too medium" or "too old" or "too young" or "too anything"!

Enjoying what God has given us to enjoy does not depend on how much money we have in the bank, or how much success we have had in our work, or what we do or do not have in material possessions. Affluence does not give us more or less enjoyment. We are given so much that we can richly enjoy just by standing out in a field, or on a balcony, and looking up to the sky and watching the first star come out or the first snow softly fall down. We can richly enjoy making music, or if we cannot make music we can richly enjoy the music of other people. We can't all make music. I can't. I can richly enjoy the great violinist's music, or the cellist's, or the flutist's, or the great pianist's. It isn't wrong to enjoy richly the music of some human being who is not a Christian. Do we have to enjoy the music only of a composer or musician who is a Christian? Do we have to sing hymns to have it be Christian music?

At this point some people seem to be confused, because they are apt to forget that God made human beings in the first place. The music that pours forth could never do so had He not made such amazing creatures as human beings with their diversity of talents.

I know that my husband's books have gone into the following statements much more fully, as have Hans Rookmaaker's and Franky Schaeffer's books. But I do feel a few sentences need to be said right here in the area of the arts, because a true picture of common sense Christian living could *not* be given without saying at least this much.

In the area of all the arts, the same thing must be said as in the area of painting. A Lutheran pastor told me that Franky's book *Addicted to Mediocrity* gave him a feeling of release as he read it. It gave him a great sense of freedom, because for years this painter, Jerry Raedeke had painted nature—geese in flight and a variety of midwestern wildlife. And during all those years people had come up to him and asked, "You are a pastor; why don't you paint Christian paintings?"

"Since I have read Franky's book," he said to me, "I simply reply, 'I do—all that I paint are Christian paintings.' "

Paintings do not have to be of religious subjects to be Christian. Films do not have to be religious to be Christian. Interior decorating does not have to be religious to be Christian. A piece of music does not have to be in the form of a hymn to be Christian. Great music can be listened to with hearts full of praise to God.

Praise and thank Him that we have ears to hear! Praise Him and be full of awe that such a great diversity of musical instruments have been made by human beings through the years . . . instruments of fine wood, wonderful brass, silver flutes and gold harps, gleaming violins, great pianos, and wonderful organs of all sizes with the amazing hidden pipes as well as the ones to be seen. God created human beings in His image to be creative. Part of that creativity is shown in the instruments, as well as in the compositions that can be played, and by the performers who are so skillful as to be among the great of history in performing music. *How* can it be? Only because God created human beings in the first place to be capable of being so fantastic.

We are not meant to have a narrow, limited view of our God, nor are we to have a narrow, limited view of what He richly provides for us to enjoy. ("[He] gives us richly all things to enjoy" 1 Tim. 6:17.)

I love what James 1:17–18 says concerning what God gives:

Every good and perfect gift is from above, coming down from the Father of the heavenly lights, who does not change like shifting shadows. He chose to give us birth through the word of truth, that we might be a kind of firstfruits of all he created (NIV).

He chose to give us birth!
Am I mixing things up? I don't think so.
Our dear and wonderful God has given fabulous gifts to His people. The turning away from what *He* has given, polluting of the

beauty of life by death, spoiled all history, and so we can see only bits and pieces of the wonder of it all. He has given us "the word of truth" so that we may have everything someday, with none of the pollution, none of the twisting ugliness spoiling the view. The perfection is ahead, but in the time of our own lives we are to be "firstfruits" in our being freed to enjoy, more than ever before, what He has created, as well as in our being well assured that the hope of future perfection is *not* a shifting shadow, but certain.

He chose to give us birth!

God created us in His image to be creative. We are made in the image of the Creator. So part of being spiritual, part of the spiritual life, is fulfilling what He made us to *be*. We are to enjoy the flowers He made. We also are to plant gardens even though we cannot create the plants. We also are to enjoy the beauty of creativity that comes forth from other people who have talents we don't have . . . because they couldn't be creative had He not made them.

Use your common sense! This makes sense, doesn't it?

Jesus gently welcomes children to Himself. And He also says that unless we become like little children we won't see the kingdom of heaven. He says, " 'whoever receives one little child like this in My name receives Me' " (Matt. 18:5). This is another strong word directly from the Lord as to what we can do for Him. It is another of those amazing couplets in reality . . . we are to be received by the Lord into His family when we come to Him believing, but we also are to receive little children—not push them away in *any* sense—and when we receive them in His name we are receiving Him!

Jesus says, " 'But whoever causes one of these little ones who believe in Me to sin [that is the negative coming in immediately], it would be better for him if a millstone were hung around his neck, and he were drowned in the depth of the sea' " (Matt. 18:6). Read the next verses there . . . the words are strong to those people who influence others to do the wrong things! Think not only of child pornography and all that includes, but also of drugs being pushed on small children in order to make money. God is not unaware of what is going on. But think also of parents exasperating their children and turning them away.

As Jesus points to small children we usually think of the fact that they believe more easily, and accept Him as Messiah and Lord more quickly. This is part of it. However, I think we have often overlooked another aspect of small children's reactions. They are more appreciative of the miracle of what they see in God's creation, whether it be a butterfly coming out of a cocoon, a tiny new leaf on a plant, or tumbling new puppies. I believe that the phrase "become as little children" (Matt. 18:3), alludes to something of this ability to see the wonders of God, and to their freedom to react with joy and appreciation.

As I read George Will's column in an international copy of *Newsweek* (July 19, 1982), I was struck with his last paragraph as he compared his not-yet-two-year-old daughter's reaction and appreciation with a scientist's. In the context of what I have just been saying, I believe this illustrates the difference Jesus points out between adults and children.

> The epigram that credulity is an adult's weakness but a child's strength is true. Victoria Will (21 months) croons ecstatically at the sight of a squirrel; she sees, without thinking about it, that a squirrel is a marvelous piece of work—which come to think about it, it is. For big people, science teaches the truth that a scientist put this way: the universe is not only queerer than we suppose, it is queerer than we can suppose.

"By faith we understand that the worlds were framed by the word of God, so that the things which are seen were not made of things which were visible" (Heb. 11:3). What an exciting "crack in the wall" God gave us in Hebrews to give us eagerness and expectancy as we look forward to finding out much more when we have eternity in which to make discoveries and ask questions, with no hindrances like false experiments or lies of any kind being given as answers! I want to say "wow," but I suppose it isn't dignified. Anyway, "Wow!"

Now let me quote George Will again:

> But modern science teaches that things are not what they seem: matter is energy; light is subject to gravity; the evidence of gravity waves suggests that gravitic energy is a form of radiation; to increase the speed of an object is to decrease the passage of its time.

There are so many mysteries that we are waiting to discover in that "someday," that no one needs to worry about it being boring. When Franky was about five years old he said once, "Mommy, I'm afraid that when I grow up there won't be anything left to discover, because there are so many things being discovered right now." Knowledge is endless; if you were going to read everything written about one portion of one field in order to become "expert," it would take you ten years. And by the time you had finished, you would be ten years behind!

Common sense Christian living consists of a measure of expectancy, of eagerness in looking ahead, as well as recognizing the marvel of what God has given us so richly to enjoy now.

Ahead of us there is a time of creativity, a time of enjoying God's creativity without hindrances and without the need to be fighting ugliness. There won't be ugliness of death, of abortion, or of any kind of violence or sorrow. There will be joy forever. However, at present our time needs to be divided between the enjoyment and the fighting, or standing against what is wrong. God has made crystal clear to us the knowledge of right and wrong.

I recently made a study through the Bible of the Ten Commandments and all the nuances of God's careful guidelines for us in today's history. This is in a book called *Lifelines,* and all of that book should fit right here between these two paragraphs.

The Bible does not leave us floundering as to what is right and what is wrong in the basic areas of life. We do have an absolute base for choosing. The choices are not so vague that we need to be frightened that we are choosing the wrong thing. We also have a God who says He will be our God and our Guide to the end—not just halfway through, not for the first months of being a Christian—but to the end. He even mentions gray hair.

> For this is God,
> Our God for ever and ever;
> He will be our guide
> Even to death.
>
> Ps. 48:14

> "[You, Israel,] have been upheld by Me from birth,
> Who have been carried from the womb.
> Even to your old age, I am He,
> And even to gray hairs I will carry you!
> I have made, and I will bear;
> Even I will carry, and will deliver you."
>
> Is. 46:3–4

Right to the end of our lives, God will be our God. But He warns us in this thing of choice. He tells us to choose Him, to choose whom we will serve. Through Joshua God challenged the Israelites to choose among "the gods . . . on the other side of the River, or the gods of the Amorites," or the Lord. Elijah presented the choice on Mount Carmel, and made the difference very vivid. Choice continues to be important time after time for each of us, but there are crisis moments in each of our lives when we are tempted to make a tremendously wrong choice. Joshua said to the people, "Choose for yourselves this day whom you will serve. . . . But as for me and my house, we will serve the LORD" (Josh. 24:15).

My husband made a choice when he was nineteen to do what he believed God was leading him to do, in opposition to his parents' wishes. As our daughter Susan read about that portion of history in *The Tapestry* (my book about the story of our lives), she wrote him a letter: "Dear Dad, I do want to thank you for your choice when you were nineteen, because you didn't know who your 'house' was going to be." He was one child with two unbelieving parents. They told him not to go to college. They did not want him to be a pastor. Years later they became Christians, and he feels they never would have become Christians if his choice had been the opposite one.

Fran had chosen with tears that day, "As for me and my house, we will serve the LORD." Who on earth was he talking about? Susan caught it when she wrote, "Dad, you were choosing for the four of us. And for the fourteen grandchildren. This is who you were choosing for." Many years before any of them were going to be born, a year before Fran was going to meet me, he made a choice that would affect all of us.

What are your choices? Whom are your choices for? *Not* just for yourself. Choose now whom you will serve, and that choice is going to affect the next generation, and the next generation, and the next. Choice never affects one single person alone. It goes on and on and the effect goes out into geography and history. You are a part of history and your choices become a part of history.

This song is in the film *Whatever Happened to the Human Race*? It was written and sung by Dallas Graham. It haunts me as the tune and words keep going through my brain. Get the film and watch, and listen, get the record also, but please finish this chapter by reading the words in the context of *choice, choice, choice*. Please learn the music and sing this song whenever you see banners or posters telling people they have a "God-given choice" to do anything they want to for their own happiness. Sing it inside your own thoughts.

> When I was in my mother's womb,
>   you nearly put me in the tomb,
>   Yes you did.

When I was in my mother's womb,
    you nearly put me in the tomb,
        Yes you did.
I know you don't think it's a sin,
    but you sure tried to sucker me in.
When I was in my mother's womb,
    you nearly put me in the tomb,
        Yes you did.

By the time that I was seven,
    you told me there's no heaven,
        Yes you did.
By the time that I was seven
    you told me there's no heaven,
        Yes you did.
You said we just got here by chance,
    but doncha worry boy, we're going to advance.
By the time that I was seven,
    you told me there's no heaven,
        Yes you did.

When I got into my teens,
    you said we were machines,
        Yes you did.
When I got into blue jeans,
    you said we were machines,
        Yes you did.
You said all we are is just a brain,
Then you wonder why we're goin' insane.
When I got into my teens
    you said we were machines,
        Yes you did.

When I got to twenty-five,
    you taught me to survive,
        Yes you did.
When I got to twenty-five,
    you taught me to survive,
        Yes you did.
You showed me how to play your clever game,
    and how to make myself a big name,
When I got to twenty-five,
    you taught me to survive,
        Yes you did.

When I got to seven-O,
    you said I had to go,
        Yes you did.
When I got to seven-O,
    you said I had to go,

Yes you did.
So you wheel-ed me off down the hall . . .
You said, "This is better for us all . . ."
When I got to seven-O,
you said I had to go,
Yes you did.[1]

It is so true that false ideas and a wrong base are being handed down from one generation to another, and that people all around us are living on that wrong base, and making choices on that wrong base . . . the base that there is no God, and that we live in a chance universe with no possibility of saying anything is right or wrong!

God describes this very well for us in Isaiah 32:6:

For the foolish person will speak foolishness,
And his heart will work iniquity:
To practice ungodliness,
To utter error against the LORD.

Common sense Christian living is to be a life full of speaking wisdom rather than foolishness. Go through the verses of the song, and aloud to yourself speak wisdom concerning the opposite of each verse! Our minds are to be full, busy with good things, with what we can do to refute, change, reform the evil. We are to think of lovely things to replace the evil, not selfishly drawing up the drawbridge to be alone in our castle or ghetto, but reaching out. We are to practice godliness so that our lives are a contrast to the practice of ungodliness that is taking place all around us. And we are to spread truth concerning the Lord. This last is intensely important.

Recently a Jewish girl from the heart of New York, a successful girl in her place in the media, came to L'Abri. As she listened to Debby and Udo, Prisca and John, and others in discussions and at meals, as she sat at our table one Sunday, and lived at Gentiana . . . she was amazed. Why? Because she had accepted the opinions of her peers and associates in her various circles, which were based on what they had gathered from the Christians they had heard speak. Their opinion is rather total: "Christians are a bunch of goons."

Fair? Maybe not, but we all need to be careful of what kind of truth we are spreading concerning the Lord. Are we really repre-

---

[1]© 1978 by Franky Schaeffer V Productions and used by permission.

senting Him fairly? Again, of course, we cannot be perfect. And again, people in Jesus' time spoke terrible lies about Him and about His disciples. Of course, the unbelieving world will not all come to think well of us.

With that said, as we seek help from the Lord, as we ask for His strength in our weakness and for His words as we attempt to answer questions fairly and give truth understandably, we need also to ask that we will be constantly spreading truth about the Lord, and not error. We need to be careful we are not speaking words or giving impressions that turn out to be spreading error concerning the Lord.

Oh, that people would catch a glimpse of the wonder of who He is, and recognize that His truth has all the answers they have searched for and found missing in the false philosophies and religions, and that it also gives fullness of life.

If we are called "goons," may we be careful that it is not an accurate description. Being called a "goon" falsely for the gospel's sake is all right, but being a "goon" as a representative of the Lord is all wrong!

> May those who hope in you
> not be disgraced because of me,
> O Lord, the LORD Almighty;
> May those who seek you
> not be put to shame because of me,
> O God of Israel.
>
> Ps. 69:6 NIV

CHAPTER NINE

Are We Ashamed of God?
Is God Ashamed of Us?

W HAT ABOUT THE DELUGE of shocks, accidents, illnesses, doubts, depressions, family quarrels, marital
difficulties, wars, prisons, concentration camps, persecutions, disappointments, unjust treatment, misunderstand-
ings, loneliness, weaknesses, temptations, attacks from friends as
well as foes, sudden lack of energy, lack of money, fires, burgla-
ries, muggings, and plane crashes? If God is our Father, if Jesus is
our Elder Brother and Bridegroom, and if the Holy Spirit dwells
within us to comfort us and to instruct us—then what about the
constant barrage of difficulties that come day after day? What does
it prove? Is there a kind of measuring stick to find out what is
happening? When difficulties arrive, does this prove that you are
not living a Christian life at all, and that your spiritual development has either stopped or gone backwards?

Many people question the reality of their salvation just when
they need the comfort of running to the shelter God provides for
His children. Why are they troubled as to whether they are true
children of the living God at times of difficulty? Their doubts often
come because someone has come to them as they sat in a wheelchair or a hospital ward after an accident, or were in a time of
terrible illness or a time of sudden unfair attack, or were sitting
dismayed outside the black ruins of their burned-down house, or
looking at the shambles after a robbery, and has asked, *"What is
wrong with your faith?"* What a cruel question to throw at anyone
who is already struggling with the emotions accompanying severe
shock!

I know of individuals who have been a long time in a wheelchair (I don't mean months, or a year, or two years—but very
many years) and who have been shattered by the "Job's com-

forters" who come and say, "Why are you in this wheelchair? You could get up and walk if you only had enough faith." Not only is the handicapped person shattered, but members of his or her family are shattered because they are the ones who know of the person's faith and patience, and of the growing fruits of the spirit evidenced in that one.

The pointing of the finger and saying, "because of this I think you may not be a Christian" can bring shadows of doubts that loom up in fearful shapes as a midnight kind of horror to people. We have no idea how sensitive people are and how often they have moments of wondering whether really, after all, the commitments they have made, the bowing before God, the saying "yes" were *real*. People differ very much in their inner quietness and assurance, and it is a terrible thing to upset a person's trust and assurance when they are in the midst of a difficulty.

God has made assurance very clear in various places in His Word. We are definitely told that our salvation depends upon what Jesus did for us as He died to take our place on the cross, and that we can add nothing to what He did for our salvation. In 2 Corinthians 4:7–18 (NIV) we are told that we have this treasure in jars of clay, to show that the power is from God and not from us. Listen carefully:

> But we have this treasure in jars of clay to show that this all-surpassing power is from God and not from us. We are hard pressed on every side, but not crushed; perplexed, but not in despair; persecuted, but not abandoned; struck down, but not destroyed. We always carry around in our body the death of Jesus, so that the life of Jesus may also be revealed in our body. For we who are alive are always being given over to death for Jesus' sake, so that his life may be revealed in our mortal body. So then, death is at work in us, but life is at work in you.
>
> It is written: "I believed; therefore I have spoken." With that same spirit of faith we also believe and therefore speak, because we know that the one who raised the Lord Jesus from the dead will also raise us with Jesus and present us with you in his presence. All this is for your benefit, so that the grace that is reaching more and more people may cause thanksgiving to overflow to the glory of God.
>
> Therefore we do not lose heart. Though outwardly we are wasting away, yet inwardly we are being renewed day by day. For our light and momentary troubles are achieving for us an eternal glory that far outweighs them all. So we fix our eyes not on what is seen, but on what is unseen. For what is seen is temporary, but what is unseen is eternal.

Jars of clay! You and I are jars of clay, and all Christians are jars of clay. It seems that some people think that the moment you accept Christ as Savior, the moment you come into God's family, you ought to have that glorious body that Christ speaks of and become immediately something like the "bionic woman" or "bionic man." You should be able to do all things with an amazing separation between you and all other people, as a physical specimen of perfect health and strength.

Contrary to that, it is clear we are still in our frail bodies, and we are still waiting for the moment when our bodies will be changed to be like His glorious body. That which we have now we have in jars of clay. Right now we do not have indestructible bodies for a variety of reasons. But one reason that fits in here is that affliction, trouble, suffering make clear that as we go on our power is of God. "My strength is made perfect in weakness" (2 Cor. 12:9) is not only a nice phrase that is supposed to be repeated in Sunday school or as part of a prayer—it is *practical.* A part of living the Christian life with common sense is living moment by moment in the reality of the availability of God's strength being given us for tasks we could not possibly do on our own.

The weakness is real, or asking for God's strength in our weakness would be a farce.

That promise is meant to be a practical, available help to us when we face performing a difficult operation as a surgeon, or when we are the patient being wheeled down the hall toward the operating room. This promise is meant to be in our minds and hearts, and the request should be breathed fervently when we face a hard piece of work as a lawyer facing a trial, or a factory worker facing a strenuous speed-up of work, as a farmer looking at crops devastated by a hail storm, or as a Christian on a TV spot facing antagonists with hard questions.

The news has come . . . "it is cancer," "it is a stroke" . . . and the wife, husband, children—whoever makes up the family receiving the shock—need to ask for God's strength in their weakness to *be* a demonstration to angels and demons that they love God and trust Him, and seek His strength to do whatever needs to be done. A Christian is meant to call out for God's strength in all kinds of sudden needs and a diversity of weaknesses, in all the difficult things that confront or hurt him or her.

This is true in relationships, too. What is more weak or apt to be broken than clay pots banging against each other? We put cracks in each other as we bang out our relationships, and we simply are not gentle enough or smooth enough in all that we do to avoid endangering each other's fragility. We simply don't behave as we should toward each other all the time. So the difficulty of relationships becomes one of the "afflictions" of life.

It isn't that you consider your children "afflictions." ("Look at all these afflictions sitting around my table!") That isn't the idea; God gives us a very different picture. Children are like olive branches, He says. They are growing things of beauty in which exciting personalities unfold and develop like plants that grow and change.

Nevertheless, just as plants are hurt by disease, by too much water or too little water, by too much light or not enough, children also have times of "drooping leaves," of problems in school work or in what seems to be a plateau of some sort, indicating that something is definitely wrong. Parents can suffer the "affliction" of not knowing what to do and feeling totally inadequate. Our children are individuals with different personalities and we are individuals; therefore, in our limitedness, finiteness, and inability to understand each other perfectly, we bring affliction into each other's lives!

Strangely enough, it is often in the time of deepest affliction that a family grows closer together. The comfort we ourselves have had is that with which we can comfort someone else. This is true with mother and child and with father and child. As a child has some disaster come to him or her, whether it is failing a subject in school, or whether it is an accident or some physical ailment, the mother or father can say: "Look, I had this happen to me when I was a child. I know how you feel. But I also know God helped me through that." It is the vivid memory of the comfort that God has given, or is giving now, with which we can comfort other people.

Frequently my husband says to me, "Although I would rather not have cancer, yet it is true that when I walk into a hospital or people come to me with their troubles, I am really much better prepared to relate to them . . . because of my cancer. I have trouble, too. I'm one of 'the gang' now."

When Paul said, "Don't lose heart!" he was not speaking from an ivory tower somewhere. He knew what it was to experience the feeling and reality of his body "wasting away outwardly"; he understood the contrast of being renewed inwardly day after day. If you and I are living through whatever difficulties we are having right now by asking for God's strength moment by moment and drawing upon the wisdom of His Word, we too are discovering the reality of inward renewal day by day, that is *more* of a victory than physical healing could be. The troubles are momentary; we're to fix our eyes on what is ahead. Our present situation, we are told, is temporary; what is ahead is eternal.

In a sense, we need to experience some measure of the kinds of difficulties other people live through so that we can relate to them with a measure of real understanding.

No, we don't need to be ashamed of our various difficulties as if hardships and difficulties proved that our prayer life were ineffectual or that there were something wrong with our spiritual growth. Look at Philippians 1:12–14,20:

> But I want you to know, brethren, that the things which happened to me have actually turned out for the furtherance of the gospel, so that it has become evident to the whole palace guard, and to all the rest, that my chains are in Christ; and most of the brethren in the Lord, having become confident by my chains, are much more bold to speak the word without fear. . . . [It is] my earnest expectation and hope that in nothing I shall be ashamed, but that with all boldness, as always, so now also Christ will be magnified in my body, whether by life or by death.

Paul asks for and expects prayer on the part of the other Christians not only for deliverance, but for courage to continue in the midst of this extremely painful time. This poor body of Paul's had been beaten, stoned, was cold and hungry many times, and confined to prison in painful chains. I believe he asks for help not only that he might preach the truth of the gospel without any shame, but that he might not be ashamed of his physical condition. He feels that his situation of hardship and affliction has encouraged others to speak fearlessly.

Today, as many of our brothers and sisters in the Lord are in a similar situation in the Soviet Union and in other iron curtain countries, we need to be aware of our responsibilities in living at the same time of history! Had we lived when Paul lived, we would have been involved in praying for him as a part of the network of the early church. The same imperative is upon us today. We are alive right now while people are behind barbed wire, suffering in mental hospitals, working as slave labor, all because they live in a country where it is against the law to proclaim the truth of God's existence, and of salvation through His Son, Jesus Christ. We are not to act as if this were not happening and fail to pray for those who need our prayer right now during our own lifetime.

In 2 Timothy Paul pleads with Timothy not to be ashamed to speak about the Lord, but also not to be ashamed of Paul as a prisoner. It seems to me there is the very strong admonition that can be extended to all the afflictions that come upon the Lord's children. They can come because of direct attack of Satan, or from enemies of God, or as a result of the Fall, but we are not to be ashamed of our heavenly Father, as if we were embarrassed that He could not change things for us or for other Christians.

> I was appointed a preacher, an apostle, and a teacher of the Gentiles. For this reason I also suffer these things; nevertheless I am not ashamed, for I know whom I have believed and am persuaded that He is able to keep what I have committed to Him until that Day.
>
> 2 Tim. 1:11–12

In the midst of all of Paul's suffering—that long list of physical tortures and pain—he is not embarrassed, not ashamed of his heavenly Father, of his Shepherd. His trust is not shaken; his assurance has not slipped away. He is certain that the final solution is ahead, and that all that has been promised will be fulfilled. Paul is proud to proclaim the wonders of the truth; he is not ashamed of the gospel for which he is suffering!

> The Lord grant mercy to the household of Onesiphorus, for he often refreshed me, and was not ashamed of my chain; but when he arrived in Rome, he sought me out very diligently and found me. . . . You know very well how many ways he ministered to me at Ephesus.
>
> 2 Tim. 1:16–18

Paul points with great praise to Onesiphorus, who looked all over for him. Instead of being ashamed to be counted his friend (as Peter was ashamed of Christ when He had been captured), Onesiphorus did refreshing things for Paul. Perhaps with menacing people jeering at him, he ministered to Paul's wounds and gave him food and wine, or washed his feet and face. Whatever he did, he cared for Paul in a miserable Roman prison, not ashamed of Paul as a friend who was a prisoner and "criminal," and not ashamed of Paul's God.

During a family reunion we were visiting a castle where there was a small dungeon with stocks and chains for one person, a stone floor, and only a tiny opening to let light in. The children tried sitting there, tried to feel what it would be like to be chained and left alone. We were not thinking only of Paul, but also thinking of U.S. senator from Alabama Jeremiah Denton who had been in solitary confinement in North Vietnam, and thinking of people in various prisons today. All through history people have been unfairly thrown into literal prisons of mud or stone or cement. Trying to feel what it would be like cannot really be accomplished by taking five minutes in stocks or on a cold floor with some old chains wrapped around one's wrists. We cannot put our finger in a candle flame to see how we would react if we were being burned at the stake as a martyr. We are not asked to "live through," in our imaginations or feelings, all that every child of the living God has gone through in history. We are only to live one life, and that is our own! We are not given the kind of strength that would be needed by someone else in a totally different kind of suffering.

God will hear our individual cry and give what is needed in strength and His sufficient grace for whatever variety of "things" our martyrdom turns out to be—little or big incidents, severe or lighter pain or suffering. We don't get a bowlful of strength or grace to put on a shelf and reach for in time of need. It is given to us on the spot, like a hidden intravenous injection . . . no needle is needed; there is no embarrassment in front of onlookers because no human being can see God giving us the measure of strength we need at the moment.

Although our lives differ a great deal from Paul's, or Timothy's, or Jeremiah's, or Noah's, or those of the people in Uganda, or Zimbabwe, or Russia today, and although we cannot always feel exactly what these oppressed people are going through, yet we are meant to have some understanding, some very real sympathy, a measure of deep appreciation for others of our same "family." The oneness of the entire family of God is meant to be a oneness that causes us to have some measure of pain when others are in pain, as well as joy when others are rejoicing. Perfectly? No, of course we could not be perfect in this, any more than in anything else. Are we to try to be sorrowful and feel suffering because of all the suffering in the world? No, I don't think that is it any more than we are meant to try out a dungeon to see what that would be like.

What is it, then, that hits me as I read the second chapter of Hebrews? The titanic, overwhelming fact that Jesus has declared that He is not ashamed to call us brothers is almost too much to even begin to understand. Can we ever appreciate what Christ has done for us? Read this passage again and again.

> For it was fitting for Him, for whom are all things and by whom are all things [this is speaking of the Creator and Master of the uni-

verse!], in bringing many sons to glory, to make the author of their salvation perfect through sufferings. For both He who sanctifies and those who are being sanctified are all of one, for which reason He is not ashamed to call them brethren, saying,

> "I will declare Your name to My brethren;
> In the midst of the congregation I will sing praise to You."

. . . Therefore in all things He had to be made like his brethren, that He might be a merciful and faithful High Priest in things pertaining to God, to make propitiation for the sins of the people. For in that He Himself has suffered, being tempted, He is able to aid those who are tempted.

Heb. 2:10–12,17–18

Read all of Hebrews 2 again. It makes me feel as if I ought to fall on my face before God in awe and wonder, telling Him I am not worthy of Jesus' astounding choice to become vulnerable to pain and suffering. His pain and suffering did not suddenly come to Him as accident, prison, or pain comes to us. Rather, by clear, definite willingness, He chose to suffer for our sins after His struggle with sin when Satan tempted Him and His agony in the Garden were finished with victory.

"For in that He Himself has suffered, being tempted, He is able to aid those who are tempted." He, the Son of God, the Creator of the universe, He who can say, "Before Abraham was, I am," He did not simply *imagine* what it was like to feel deserted as He hung on the cross alone, did not simply *imagine* what it was like to suffer all the agonies of physical pain, did not simply *imagine* what it was like to suffer the horribleness of actually taking our sin upon Himself; He experienced it all.

Then we are told that which can be put into one sentence . . . yet is earthshaking. It seems almost wrong to write it so easily, black words on white paper, these earthshaking words. "For in that He Himself has suffered, being tempted, He is able to aid those who are tempted" (Heb. 2:18).

This is the One who can truly help each of us in our individual temptations, which are afflictions. The suffering during a temptation is real suffering, and is one of the kinds of affliction we all face. At times we fall, and then we need to be picked up and forgiven by the One who suffered for us! But we are meant to come to Him in time to be given victory over the temptation.

Jesus suffered death. Death is a suffering, too, an enemy Jesus died to one day destroy, but He suffered death in order to give us life. He "tasted death"—a bitter, bitter taste—for us. All this was done that we might be in His family, and that we might be called His brothers, His sisters . . . by Him who has declared to us that He is not ashamed of us.

Jesus is entrusting us to make truth known in spite of opposition and persecution. He is letting us know that whatever we go through in our lives, there will be nothing He cannot understand. As we share in the wonder of being in His family, we need not be ashamed to share some of the battle that rages against God and His people because of the animosity and hatred of the enemy.

Whatever your chains or my chains are today, we are not to be ashamed of them, nor of our dear heavenly Father for not cutting them off, just yet.

> But recall the former days in which, after you were illuminated, you endured a great struggle with sufferings: partly while you were made a spectacle both by reproaches and tribulations, and partly while you became companions of those who were so treated; for you had compassion on me in my chains, and joyfully accepted the plundering of your goods, knowing that you have a better and an enduring possession for yourselves in heaven.
>
> Heb. 10:32–34

We are to ask for strength and grace for our own difficult moments a moment at a time, but our understanding and sympathy is to be growing constantly. We are not to grow cold and hard to others, but rather as we have received help from the Lord in our own difficulties, we are to sympathize with those in various kinds of "prisons." A paralyzed body is a prison indeed, as is blindness or deafness. There are a variety of sufferings we are meant to have some understanding of, enough sympathy to be an encouragement to each other.

> Therefore do not cast away your confidence [don't be embarrassed and don't be ashamed], which has great reward. [You can be proud of your God; He will fulfil His promises. The richness of what is ahead of us is beyond the imagination of any of us.] For you have need of endurance, so that after you have done the will of God, you may receive the promise:
>
> > "For yet a little while,
> > And He who is coming will come and will not tarry.
> > Now the just shall live by faith;
> > But if anyone draws back,
> > My soul has no pleasure in him."

But we are not of those who draw back to perdition, but of those who believe to the saving of the soul.

Heb. 10:35–39

Thank God we don't have to be perfect to be saved, because Jesus has been perfect for us. He did not shrink back. He did it all for us. But as we go on, we need to pray that day by day we may be more patient in tribulation, and with His *help* be asking, "Let me not make You ashamed of me in this five minutes. Help me to bring glory to You."

Another perspective is given us in 1 Corinthians 4. Paul is writing to Christians he knows need a jolt. They evidently are full of pride and boasting that they are doing so well, that things are going better for them than for Paul and the other apostles.

For I think that God has displayed us, the apostles, last, as men condemned to death; for we have been made a spectacle to the world, both to angels and to men. We are fools for Christ's sake but you are wise in Christ! [Note the well-deserved sarcasm to those who think they are wiser than those who are suffering so many things in their lives.] We are weak, but you are strong! You are distinguished, but we are dishonored! Even to the present hour we both hunger and thirst, and we are poorly clothed, and beaten, and homeless. And we labor, working with our own hands. Being reviled, we bless; being persecuted, we endure it; being defamed, we entreat. We have been made as the filth of the world, the offscouring of all things until now.

I do not write these things to shame you, but as my beloved children I warn you.

1 Cor. 4:9–14

This warning is clear and fair. We can think of ourselves as being in a kind of arena, surrounded by those who may be watching—angels, those who have already "finished the course," and also our enemy, Satan, who wants us to fail. The "arena" with spectators, if that picture helps us, must be seen as having a great diversity of "events" going on at any given moment of history. If you or I feel we are such a tiny portion of the whole that we cannot possibly make a difference, then we are wrong. This picture God gives us is not one of statistics in which we are so minuscule a "one" that the "plus" or "minus" doesn't count. No other person in the whole of history has exactly the same part as you have in your succession of "events."

I know a woman in Iowa, on a farm where the snowdrifts pile

high in winter, who has no legs; she lost them at an early age through a series of medical mistakes. But this woman's life is a unique example of common sense Christian living. She is able to do so much in her wheelchair: to cook not only for her mother (who lives with her and does things she cannot do, even though her mother is ninety now), but to make cookies and pies for church events, and to prepare meals for family dinners when others of the family visit on Sundays. Here is a home, a family togetherness, in a time when many people in the country have never seen a home. Here is someone who takes her part in speaking and teaching, living a more full life than many people with two legs to walk about on, who think only of themselves. Her particular "event" in the arena is being won, and courage is being given to other people as they watch from the sidelines.

In the first chapter of 2 Corinthians Paul declares that he doesn't want people to be uninformed about the hardships he and Timothy suffered in the province of Asia. He points out that the hardships made them rely on God, and not on themselves. Whether it is my friend on an Iowa farm, moving about a kitchen in a wheelchair, and peeling potatoes and cooking a batch of pumpkin pies, or whether it is Paul facing what he called "a deadly peril," the really important thing for us to pass down to the next generation, as well as to tell each other, is that ". . . we trust [God] that He will still deliver us" (2 Cor. 1:10). There are many "deliverances" along the way, and the final deliverance is sure.

We come to a very strong word from God in Hebrews 11. The chapter begins with the thought that God our Father formed the universe, and then reviews those in history who have come to God believing that He exists and that He does reward those who diligently seek Him. The list of people includes those who saw lions' mouths shut, who walked across the Red Sea on dry land, and who saw the walls of Jericho fall down. It also includes those who were sawn in half, who were tortured in a variety of ways, who were put in prison in chains, who were stoned, and so on. This is a list that covers all the people who are commended for their faith, and we are included because we are told that God has planned something that not one of them has yet received. It is ahead, and "together with us" they will be made perfect. That future something is what is alluded to when God declares a strong fact to us: "But now they desire a better, that is, a heavenly country. Therefore God is not ashamed to be called their God, for He has prepared a city for them" (Heb. 11:16).

All these people through the centuries have been longing for a better country, a place that will not be abnormal and fallen, but perfect. We too share in this longing. God has declared to them, and to us, that He is not ashamed to be called our God because that longing is going to be fulfilled *perfectly*. Perfection is something we have not yet tasted, smelled, felt, heard, seen. We are going to experience perfection . . . with a perfect set of senses! No wonder God is not ashamed to be our God, even though unbelieving people through the ages have taunted His people, persecuted them, made fun of them, and tried to entice them away from Him to something "better than perfection" (which was Satan's temptation to Eve, and then Adam, in the first place). Many, many people believe the lie that something better than perfection exists!

There is coming a time when not only will we know the wonder of perfection in our bodies, but we will actually come to the moment of future history when the "accuser of our brethren," the one who has made life difficult for each Christian who has ever lived, will be cast down.

> Then I heard a loud voice saying in heaven, "Now salvation, and strength, and the kingdom of our God, and the power of His Christ have come, for the accuser of our brethren, who accused them before our God day and night, has been cast down. And they overcame him by the blood of the Lamb and by the word of their testimony, and they did not love their lives to the death.
>
> Rev. 12:10–11

It will be over.

It is definitely coming to an end—this battle of Satan's against God.

And those who have overcome Satan through all ages have overcome him through the blood of the Lamb. This is our only way now of expecting to overcome him, and of not falling into some trap Satan is setting for our feet. We need to stay in close communication with God our Father, and recognize our need for help.

These few pages are inadequate to discuss all that is included in the Bible about affliction, suffering, and death. I have written many pages of study on that subject in my book *Affliction*, but no study of common sense Christian living would be complete without realizing something of the battle in which we are involved, as well as understanding why the world is *not* as God made it in the first place.

It is imperative right here, however, to make certain that no one is thinking, "Well, God gave Dr. Schaeffer cancer so that a new branch of L'Abri would start in Rochester, Minnesota, and so that he could be more of a comfort to other people who have trouble." Or, "That lady lost her legs as a child because God wanted her to live such an outstandingly special life with that handicap." NO, NO, NO! That is *not* what we conclude at all. That is why it is so important to understand the Fall. Had not sin come into the world at the Fall there would have been no disasters of any kind.

It is also important to understand the Book of Job. It is in Job that we have a curtain pulled back so that we can see *how* "the accuser of our brethren" operates. Satan accuses God of having a servant who does not love Him, but who loves only what God gives him. It is Satan who is trying to make Job curse God, thus proving to God that Job is anxious only to get what God will give him and that he does not love God and trust Him honestly and fully.

Can we understand, then, and have a pat answer to explain each difficulty? Again, *no.* History is very complicated. There are cause-and-effect sequences going on all the time. Human choice is constantly making a difference in history. Satan is attacking God by attacking His people. Yet God is God, and there is no "chance" behind Him on the throne. God is so great that He created angels with choice, and then human beings with choice. Personality and creativity is real; people are not puppets. *All* these things and many more, are involved in the whole matter of history.

We have enough to do to live on the basis of what God has given us to know, without asking for more than finite human beings could understand.

What He *has* given us is so much that if we would contemplate the future with any amount of true expectation, we would be like small children dancing up and down with excitement before the living-room door is thrown open to reveal the wonders of a Christmas tree and piles of gifts, so long awaited and prepared for!

The Bible begins with a family and a home for that family in the perfect garden planned and planted by God Himself. There was a perfect relationship of man and woman in a family oneness, as well as "coupleness." There was then a perfect relationship with God, their heavenly Father, as He walked and talked with them.

The Bible ends with a wedding, and "the family" will be complete with a new beginning!

And I heard, as it were, the voice of a great multitude, as the sound of many waters and as the sound of mighty thunderings, saying, "Alleluia! For the Lord God Omnipotent reigns! Let us be glad and rejoice and give Him glory, for the marriage of the Lamb has come, and His wife has made herself ready." And to her it was granted to be arrayed in fine linen, clean and bright, for the fine linen is the righteous acts of the saints. Then he said to me, "Write: 'Blessed are those who are called to the marriage supper of the Lamb!'" And he said to me, "These are the true sayings of God."

Rev. 19:6–9

What a glorious truth God has given us! How much we have to look forward to! We will all be a part of the bride of Christ. We will all be robed in white linen. We will all partake of that wedding supper. The words "The Spirit and the bride say, 'Come!'" and "let him who thirsts come" (Rev. 22:17) are a true and fabulous invitation at the end of this Book.

In spite of affliction, in spite of all the troubles that come, in spite of the fears, in spite of the fights and discouragements, the hard things as well as the joys and satisfactions, we are meant to work on, to not give up, to endure to the end. We're told it's worth working for, worth waiting for with eagerness. Christ said, "'I am coming quickly'" (Rev. 22:20) and Paul also spoke of the fact that Jesus would come back soon. This is true prophecy of a specific moment in future history, as specific as Christ's first coming when He was born in Bethlehem.

The word that follows the promise of His coming is: "So keep on, work, keep on, keep on." The day is coming when perfection will be there, but there will also be a perfect relationship forever, beginning with the wedding supper of the Lamb.

Heaven is described in a small way, hinting of so much beyond the few paragraphs John gives us. John received some understanding from God concerning what he was to write for us there on the island of Patmos, a geographic spot you could visit today. When Jesus was still with Peter and John, Jesus described the martyr's death Peter was going to experience. Peter then looked over Jesus' shoulder at John, and asked "Lord, what about this man?"

And Jesus answered, "What is that to you? You follow Me" (John 21:22).

We aren't meant to unravel the threads and understand the weaving of history. But as we look back to Peter's death and his entrance into heaven as one of the martyrs for whom we are told there are special crowns, we can also look back in imagination to the old man John. He must have been exhausted on that island that was his concentration camp . . . writing that which was exciting, yet it was very exacting work, too. He was an old man in his nineties, remembering the time when Jesus was there with them all, and no longer having Peter or any of the others to reminisce with. John might have wished he had gone to heaven earlier in life, as Peter had, rather than writing on this lonely island, far away from familiar locations.

How thankful we are that he was faithful to the end, and that he wrote of the gorgeous beauty (as much as we can understand of it) of that which is ahead, making clear that we are going to be part of it all.

How thankful we must be that God gave John sufficient grace, and His strength in John's weakness to write exactly that which God wanted us to have. How thankful also we must be that the final invitation not only comes directly to us today, but to others to whom we can give it.

> And the Spirit and the bride say, "Come!" And let him who hears say, "Come!" And let him who thirsts come. And whoever desires, let him take the water of life freely. . . . He who testifies to these things says, "Surely I am coming quickly."
>
> Rev. 22:17,20

The Bridegroom has promised He'll come to take us to the wedding. He won't fail.

CHAPTER TEN

More Questions and Answers from the Live Audience

QUESTION:

How can we reach those Christians who are convinced that the Bible teaches that true spirituality is just a small part of life, just that part which is religious, not physical, who are suspect of what you are saying, thinking that it sounds so worldly right from the beginning?

ANSWER:

I think it is a matter for education. There needs to be a gentle and slow teaching and demonstration that will hopefully have an impact, and will shake up the cast-in-cement idea that there is a little box in which everything is spiritual. This box contains prayer, reading the Bible, going to meetings, going to church, attending Bible conferences, and so on. I am not saying these things are wrong or that they are not important in our lives at the right times—of course not! I am just saying that some people have been taught all through life from childhood that *"this* is spiritual" and everything else is not spiritual. This teaching says that even if other things are not evil, they are not spiritual; therefore, if you want to grow as a Christian and learn to love God more, you had better go to one more Bible conference.

When this has been our background, it takes time, rereading of the Bible, and conversation to point out things we have not seen before—to be given freedom to recognize that we can serve and love God in the whole of life, bringing Him glory in all that we do.

It is very important to have people in your home informally, sitting around your fireplace, or in the garden, or around the kitchen table having a cup of coffee or tea or a glass of orange juice. Real discussion is a better way to put forth ideas that are new to people among whom you live than simply speaking from a platform publicly. It is very important to show how the other portions of life—the hour-by-hour life of preparing food, serving each other, eating together, working in the garden to produce vegetables or in the field to produce grain, making cloth from the cotton you have grown—are the portions of life concerned with how God made people in the first place.

You are made in God's image to be a communicating creature, to be a creative human being, to do your work faithfully and well, to care for the land you dwell in so that it produces good crops. Much of the Old Testament deals with a man doing a fine job in tilling the field, in taking care of what God has given him, in really having a conscientious attitude toward his work—which is how the Bible says one ought to work!

As you sit around your table discussing things, look up passages in the Bible that deal with the importance of working with one's hands and producing results. You might read my husband's *Art and the Bible* which shows how central the beauty of making art works was in the building of the tabernacle and the temple.[1] Those tapestries and woven hangings, the gold and silver work, were made by skilled people working in obedience to God's commands. They were glorifying Him as they used beautiful wood that had been grown, cared for, cut, and polished. *Work* that was physical work was their work for the Lord.

"Work is connected with spiritual things?" I believe so, but it is because material things are a part of glorifying God. We were created to be able to do such a variety of things in the "art" of living, as He made us to live.

God does not show in His Book that there is some kind of an airy-fairy spiritual realm that isn't connected with daily life. People throughout the Bible were given practical examples of what it meant to be faithful to God.

In Jesus' parable of the pounds, the master says, "Because you have been trustworthy in a very small matter, take charge of ten cities." It seems to me that the Lord is so very fair because the faithfulness required is related to the real possibilities each one has. God clearly sent my parents to be in China for a number of years, and their faithfulness in their work there was important,

---

[1]Also read *Pro-Existence*, by Udo Middelmann (Inter-Varsity, 1974), to help you understand the centrality of work well done.

but no more important than my father's brother Dade Seville in his work as a medical doctor in Pittsburgh. It is doing well and faithfully what is your work at this time, with the very real possibility of doing it unto the Lord, which is commended as "well done."

The virtuous woman described in Proverbs, as you remember, is occupied with many practical things in the material realm. It is clear that she loves and honors God, but she also weaves beautiful materials. What has weaving to do with spirituality? Yet she is praised for being the *kind* of woman God meant her to be. She is praised for fulfilling what women were created to be.

Everybody doesn't know how to weave, or spin, or knit, or sew. Some make their own bread with flour they have ground from grain. This making of bread is a spiritual act. It is a work that is being done in order to feed people with physical food! We are told in the Bible that if someone comes asking for food and we turn them away without food, we are doing a wrong thing!

> If a brother or sister is naked and destitute of daily food, and one of you says to them, "Depart in peace, be warmed and filled," but you do not give them the things which are needed for the body, what does it profit? Thus also faith by itself, if it does not have works, is dead.
>
> James 2:15–17

Is this passage canceling out the doctrine that salvation is by faith not by works? No, but it shows that true faith, a truly growing spiritual life close to the Lord, is demonstrated in a very, very crucial way. The action is to be in the material realm. The food to be given to help the hungry brother or sister has to be prepared; it has to come from something (like grain, or vegetables, or meat) that was grown over a period of time. Clothing to be given was made by someone. The very acts of doing that which is necessary to have some surplus to share is spiritual. To share nothing cancels out evidence that faith is alive and growing, says James. Therefore, the diversity of work that provides food, shelter, clothing for the family and to share with others is obedience to the Lord, and is also fulfilling what a human being was made to be. It is not in a separate compartment from glorifying the Lord, but is part of glorifying the Lord with your whole life.

In Isaiah, when the Millennium is being described, there is a portion that shows that a part of God's blessing in that period of time when there will be no wars will be the freedom to work longer years, because of people having longer lives then.

> They shall build houses and inhabit them;
> They shall plant vineyards and eat their fruit.
> They shall not build houses and another inhabit;
> They shall not plant and another eat;
> For as the days of a tree,
> So shall be the days of My people,
> My elect shall long enjoy the work of their hands.
>
> Is. 65:21–22

This is the righteous reign of Christ being described. Notice that building houses, planting crops, and working with their hands is the Lord's description of people whom He is blessing.

> "They shall not labor in vain . . .
> For they shall be the descendants of the blessed of the LORD. . . .
> Before they call, I will answer;
> And while they are still speaking, I will hear."
>
> vv. 23-24

The Millennium will be a very different period of history, with justice and authority in the hands of the Prince of Peace. But in that period the blend, the melange, the balanced mix pointed to as wonderful is that which points to the wholeness of life. Work with the hands, creativity on a human level, is very naturally blended with calling upon the Lord and having Him answer.

What is held out to us as common sense Christian living is not that which is divided into compartments, but that which is a balance. Do any of us reach a perfect balance? No, because we are not perfect. But our goal individually and our responsibility in discussion with others is to try to find a continually better balance . . . in our creative work, in all kinds of work with our hands and brains, in our care for our homes and our lands, in our hospitality and sharing, in our constant and completely natural communication with the Lord throughout it all.

QUESTION:
How does a Christian cope with the death of a true Christian who chooses suicide?

ANSWER:

As a preface to what I am going to say, let me take your word *choose* and remind us all that to "choose to sin" must always be thought of as the most selfish and unappreciative thing we can do after we have accepted the terrible price Christ paid to forgive us for our sins. We are not to treat sin lightly when it has cost such agony to the Lamb of God.

Suicide is one of the "new freedoms" that is coming out of the same lower view of life that is producing abortion, infanticide, and euthanasia of the aged. People are writing books on "how to commit suicide" in England and France, treating it as a matter of choice. Just as it is wrong to kill the unborn baby, the baby with a handicap, an old person, or anyone who makes life difficult for someone else, so it is sinful and wrong to kill oneself.

We do not affect only ourselves by any choice, and certainly not in such a choice as this! There are many people affected by the decision of a friend or a family member to commit suicide. It is a choice to hurt and influence many, many people, as well as to affect history. It is also a shaking of one's fist at God, saying, "I do not trust Your wisdom and power to provide any solution that will satisfy my need, and so I am indeed going to light my own sparks." It is a defiance of waiting for an answer to prayer, or a refusal to practice patience.

All this needs to be said because of the pressures of the attitudes and discussions putting forth suicide as one of the "rights" and one of the "dignified" ways of ending a bad situation. "Thou shalt not murder" is one of the Ten Commandments, and suicide is a breaking of that commandment.

After acknowledging that suicide is wrong, we need to realize that the whole problem of suicide among Christians must be considered in a wider way. We need to face honestly how often you and I are discouraged to the point that we *think* (hidden in our minds behind the covering of our skull and hair!), *Well, this is too much! I would like to jump off the balcony* or *I'm so upset, I could just jump off a cliff.* We even say aloud at times something like, "I'd really like to just blank out . . . step off the world. I'd like to go down the nearest well!" We have something approaching that kind of sudden feeling. We understand at least in a small measure the desperate extravagance of a desire to escape. We know something of wrong, unbalanced anger or fury.

Jesus has made the Ten Commandments more penetrating in His explanations of our sinfulness. Jesus has said that if you are angry enough to kill somebody, you have committed murder already in your heart. Jesus says to us, as much as to the people to whom He spoke audibly,

> "You have heard that it was said to those of old, 'You shall not commit adultery.' But I say to you that whoever looks at a woman to lust for her has already committed adultery with her in his heart."
>
> Matt. 5:27–28

Jesus is saying that if a human being has adulterous ideas inside his head, hidden from others, they are not hidden from God. And he who looks at a woman (or the woman who looks at a man) with adultery in his or her mind has already committed adultery in the heart.

With penetrating, knifelike, double-edged swordlike penetration, Jesus goes through what sin consists of. We are "hit" or "cut," every one of us, if we are honest before God.

How many of us have thought—for trivial reasons or for reasons that are overwhelming in force, in the midst of psychological depressions, or in the midst of pain and physical illness, in the midst of fatigue with no stopping place in the work at hand, or in the midst of sudden shock—"I'm so discouraged; I don't want to go on."

I believe that Christians have different temptations and different weaknesses. Christians have frailness in one area or another, and we are not all equal in following the instructions God has so carefully given us all. "Call upon Me" is an instruction we are meant to follow when we are hit with unreasonable force in the area of despair. "May those who hope in You not be disgraced because of me." We are meant to plead this with the Lord. "Deliver me out of the mire,/And let me not sink," we should cry in David's words (Ps. 69:14), or in our own. This is the time to silently acknowledge that we are sinful and in need, and not strong enough to stand on our own.

But the frailty and weakness of some Christians cause them to turn away from the Lord at the very time when they should be turning to Him.

Christians who commit suicide (or who are rescued in time from their attempt and live to remember it) already have swallowed the pills, or have pulled the trigger or have jumped out of the window, and this can't be undone! With other sins we commit, we have a time of feeling the overwhelming sorrow and guilt that come before we throw ourselves before the Lord and confess to

Him our sin, asking for forgiveness. We can go to Him, and to a person, if another human being is involved, and say, "I'm so sorry. I ask forgiveness. I was at the end of myself and I am just so sorry for what I said. Please forgive me."

With successful suicide, however, the door is shut to that action. But I don't believe the door is shut to heaven.

Jesus says:

> "My sheep hear My voice, and I know them, and they follow Me. And I give them eternal life, and they shall never perish; neither shall anyone snatch them out of My hand. My Father, who has given them to Me, is greater than all; and no one is able to snatch them out of my Father's hand. I and My Father are one."
>
> John 10:27–30

He is making crystal clear the fact that our salvation does not depend on our own strength in holding on, but on the strength of the Son's hand and the Father's hand holding us fast. Eternity is eternity; it cannot be lived in a week, a month, or a year. Never is never! When we are born into the family of the Lord, when we become one of His sheep, His gift to us is an everlasting gift.

Never let the reality of the statement Jesus made to Nicodemus become so familiar that it loses any of its marvel. God has made a marvelous promise.

> For God so loved the world that He gave His only begotten Son, that whoever believes in Him should not perish but have everlasting life. . . . He who believes in Him is not condemned.
>
> John 3:16,18

Someone reading this who has special need of comfort concerning a loved one who has committed suicide but who has given every evidence of truly believing in Jesus as Savior, may be comforted with the definite assurance of this promise. The promises of God are certain.

Our certainty of being there when the wedding supper of the Lamb takes place, our certainty of being one of the ones Jesus will serve at that time, does not depend on our having time to be given "grace" after committing a sin.

We are secure at the moment of our honest and real acceptance of Christ as Savior, when we enter into the Lord's family, when our name is written in the Lamb's Book of Life. Nobody can be certain of your sincerity except you and the Lord; your becoming a Christian has been (or will be, if it is in the future for you) a private moment with Him. We can't look at another person and say, "I know," because we each have an individual walk with the Lord. We each must depend on His assurances individually, and thank Him individually, and ask for help individually. But it is *not* our individual strength that holds us fast! Our security consists of the two hands locked around our hand—the Father's and the Son's—with the Holy Spirit dwelling in us from the moment of our salvation. We are secure indeed.

This past week, I had a letter from a friend in Texas, a dear woman who has not gotten over the suicide of her son, a very fine man in his thirties. There seemed no sufficient reason to make such a sudden drastic decision. He had experienced keen disappointment and discouragement before that moment, but it was all out of proportion. He knew the heavenly Father and had a well-marked Bible that he read for encouragement.

I had turned away from the book I was writing when the news came to me, and had written her a ten-page letter by hand. She wrote me to say, "Your letter was such an encouragement to me. Thank you so much for taking time to write in so much detail."

Could I know the answer to "why"? Of course not. But this sort of communication is what each of us should be doing for our friends who have that kind of affliction. It is one way of bearing one another's burdens. It is one way of weeping with those who weep. However, we are also to put forth the hope that *is* in the Word of God.

Our human bodies are frail. Some people have bones that break easily in a fall from which others bounce up laughing. Some people have mental breakdowns or small cerebral hemorrhages that may cause irrational actions. We can't know the kind of "accident" there was within a person's mind and emotions that caused a drastic action. Our understanding is incomplete! We can remember that a person had a series of depressions, or we can be mystified as to what caused the terrible decision. We cannot make a judgment of another person.

However, we are each responsible for ourselves. We need to resolve that in our own lives we will *not* allow ourselves to think or say sinful things concerning not being willing to go on "enduring to the end," and we need to resolve that we would never be so unthankful or ungrateful to our heavenly Father, or to our earthly family or friends, as to treat them so cruelly. We have such a short time, anyway, to live and show God how very much we trust Him, as well as to fulfill what He has for us to do as His representatives in history.

Jeremiah and others of God's servants have cried out for death, but that is a different thing. We may ask to be taken "home" as some have done, without sinning. But not to ask for strength to go on if indeed the Lord has something more for us to do and to stop life by killing that life is sin. Thank God for His understanding, and also for His assurance that "the blood of Jesus, his Son, purifies us from all sin."

QUESTION:
How can we respond to people who say that Christians should not have trouble?

ANSWER:
I think we need to inform them that Paul is a very good example of a good Christian, and then show them many passages in Corinthians that stress what Paul has told us, which God wants us to know and understand.

I talked to a man in Texas recently, a well-known person connected with sports, particularly football. He has been hit with a disease that makes motion very, very difficult, so that walking across the floor takes great concentration and talking is an effort. The things that came without thinking all his life are now major achievements. We can all imagine ourselves in the place of this one who was so active all his life, and realize what the struggle would be like.

I walked over to where he was standing and said, "I'm so sorry about what has happened." His words to me were a great help and encouragement, as he replied, "You know what? I was just reading about Paul today in my Bible reading. And boy! Paul didn't have a very good time, did he? He had a pretty hard time. All those stripes when he was beaten . . . all those prison chains . . . the prison . . . the stones thrown at him and all that. Why should I expect more?"

He is a fairly new Christian, but what he said is something every Christian should be realizing and understanding (although many do not seem to understand this after many years of being a Christian). You can't imagine how his response encouraged me. When hard things happen now, I often say to myself, "Think of Paul. Why should I expect more?"

This is exactly what you need to point out to people who tell you that Christians should not have trouble.

Read Acts 7. The first fifty-three verses give you Stephen's lecture. What a strong review of history it is, and how very much it was needed by all the crowd that was listening. But what was the effect? The result? The reaction of the crowd?

The crowd was furious! They gnashed their teeth, covered their ears, yelled at the top of their voices, and all rushed at poor Stephen and dragged him out of the city to stone him. While they were stoning him Stephen prayed, "Lord Jesus, receive my spirit," and then, "Lord, do not charge them with this sin" (vv. 59–60).

The stones rained against Stephen; they must have hit his vital parts because the stoning killed him.

How is it that this was the result when the early church people must all have been praying for Stephen? Were they not full enough of faith? Was Stephen less loved by God? Was he a less valuable preacher than others? Did he not have enough faith to pray for deliverance? How is it that when Paul was stoned later he did not die? Were prayers for Stephen less effectual?

It is important that people think seriously about the fact that God points out to us over and over again that we, His children, do not all have "equal" lives. Each of us is given the grace needed sufficient for the piece of history we are living through, as we pray for help.

In Stephen's case, he saw the glory of God, and Jesus standing at His right hand. What a special thing he was given at that moment! And as he prayed during that stoning, his prayers were answered. The Lord did receive his spirit! Also, as he prayed for the crowd, among those responsible for the stoning was Saul. "Now Saul was consenting to his death" (Acts 8:1). One of the most exciting answers to prayer recorded in the Bible, as far as I am concerned, is God's answer to Stephen's second prayer. Saul was to be marvelously converted, to become Paul, and to be the courageous one facing persecution himself as he made known the truth he became convinced was true!

It seems to me the greatest work in Stephen's life was his having such a tremendous victory in the midst of the terrible affliction of being martyred, during which his face glowed with the wonder of seeing God, and his thoughts were upon other people and their deep need of the Messiah rather than on himself. The fact that he prayed for others in that humanly "impossible" moment was a victory in "the heavenly battle." And *that* prayer was answered.

You can point to that event of history, as people challenge you, and ask: "What do you do with that?"

As Christians we are told that we are in a battle; in Ephesians 6 we are given instructions for preparation and equipment. Trouble? Trouble? A battle is full of trouble!

QUESTION:
I wonder if you could make some comments about discipline in a Christian home on a Christian base?

ANSWER:
I think that the discipline of children in a Christian home needs to be combined with the recognition of the discipline of the parents by the Word of God. In other words, nobody should attempt in a Christian home to discipline their children without remembering (and I am not saying we are perfect and that we do this perfectly) that *we* are under a discipline too—the discipline of the Word of God. We don't make up the rules ourselves.

We need to remember a number of things. For one, a father is not to drive his child crazy. There is to be gentleness and kindness just as our heavenly Father is gentle and kind. We need to remember that God gives us the picture of His being there, ready to catch us when we fall, even as an eagle flies under the young eaglets. God says His wings are under us. In some way we need to demonstrate this aspect of being in the right place at the right time when we as parents are needed! We are to be counted upon, trusted to understand.

When I see a child fall and I hear a parent say, "Oh, you awkward thing, look at your new dress," as he or she jerks the little one up by one arm, I think of the gentleness of God the Father picking us up when we fall into sin, a temptation, a mistake, a foolish choice. We parents need to remember that we are the representation to our children of the word *father* and the reality of what a father is.

Of course I am talking to mothers, too. God speaks in His Word to mothers many times. The love and the wisdom of a mother is an important part of the growing-up days. It is incredible when you consider how much a human being learns in the first two years of life . . . and from that moment until he is plunged into all that our culture surrounds him with. The time is short for teaching the basics on the basis of truth and love. Mothers also need to sit under the Word of God in this, realizing that patience is a part of it. Again, what is love? Love suffers long and is kind. Love has patience.

Discipline?

You have not yet resisted to bloodshed, striving against sin. And you have forgotten the exhortation which speaks to you as to sons:

"My son, do not despise the chastening of the LORD,
Nor be discouraged when you are rebuked by Him;
For whom the LORD loves He chastens,
And scourges every son whom He receives."

If you endure chastening, God deals with you as with sons; for what son is there whom a father does not chasten? But if you are without chastening, of which all have become partakers, then you are illegitimate and not sons.

Heb. 12:7–8

This passage goes on to say that we have all had human fathers who have disciplined us as they thought best, but God disciplines us so that we may share in His holiness. It is specifically for our good. There are no mistakes!

Now no chastening seems to be joyful for the present, but grievous; nevertheless, afterward it yields the peaceable fruit of righteousness to those who have been trained by it.

Heb. 12:11

I am not saying there should not be discipline. To say that would be to contradict the teaching God gives us in the Bible. However, we are not God, and we need to ask for help in all our choices in life. Unhappily, an angry or frustrated and very annoyed parent is not usually in the mood to quietly pray for an idea as to the best punishment for "the deed." We all do make mistakes. Happily, we don't have to pretend to our children that we have always been perfect, and we can take time (a different time) to go back and admit our mistakes.

Be very careful, and remember that the time to prepare to be careful is when you are alone and thinking. It is harder in the midst of chaos! Be careful of what? To consider what is involved. The discipline should be decisive and adequate, but not too much for the misdeed. Differentiate between a genuine mistake and a deliberate deed. Be careful that the reason for the punishment is understood by the child. Make sure love is displayed in the context, and afterwards, in being kind.

We parents are not carbon copies of each other. We could use the same words in discussing discipline but not really behave the same way at all. Another thing is very true: we are not the same parents to our first child that we are to the second, or third, on down to as many as we may have. We grow older; we know more; we have had more experiences in life . . . both good and bad. We have been under the discipline of God longer, if we have been growing as His children. The first child usually has more inexperienced and much less relaxed parents than do subsequent children! It is foolish to act as if you could pick up a list of what to do, and determine to treat each child in exactly the same way.

Children also differ tremendously—even children in the same family. A strong word of disapproval is enough to cause one child to be as shattered as if he had received a physical blow. Another child may receive a spanking and not really be very affected by it at all. A very sensitive person can be shattered in childhood by real cruelty, although it might not look like the cruelty suffered by child abuse victims. The "bruises" are of a different kind.

This is why I personally do not like the "how-to" lists of child rearing. Neither the child nor the parent is personally known by the "how-to" author. God does not treat us like carbon copies. We do not receive from Him a discipline recognized by other people.

I did write in our biography, *The Tapestry*, about the time when a succession of things happened in our little Model-A Ford when we were moving to Wilmington, Delaware, in seminary days. Fran got angrier and angrier as each incident made him feel worse. Then suddenly, our car slipped on a rainy Philadelphia street, and he bumped into another car. He became convinced that that "slip into the car" was the Lord saying to him, "That's enough!" But the Lord didn't tell *me* that that was what happened! I had no business saying anything like, "See? See what the Lord did?"

A similar thing happened to me many years later when my strong determination to go to St. Louis and look for a house (a stubborn plan of mine to arrange our life more conveniently) was stopped just before train time by a steam iron blowing up in my face. I went to the hospital with second-degree burns on my face, instead of to the train station to take the all-night train. That night as I was *not* sleeping in my favorite sleeping car on the train, I spent some of my painful, wakeful hours recognizing God's discipline. After all, it had been a gentle way to pull me back from pushing ahead by "lighting of my own sparks."

But the Lord disciplines us each differently, and He never indicates in His Word that discipline is the explanation for our afflictions and hardships as a whole. We *never* can point the finger at anyone else. And after examining our own heart and intentions we might be reasonably sure that the torn cartilages are not a discipline but only a result of coming down too many mountains. Or we can be reasonably sure that Satan has sent the cancer or the arthritis to try to stop the work we are doing for the Lord, or to try to make us curse God.

Understanding life is not simple!

Can we be fair as a parent? It is hard, but we can pray for help to be fair in our limitedness and finiteness and imperfection. In a boarding school there can be a list of "whacks"—how many for this and that. But I don't think a parent should go by a list for each child, "You are to give three whacks if they do this." "You are to give four whacks if they do that." "You are to make the child sit on a chair in a corner for another thing." It is much more complicated than that, and something to be studied in relationship to the individual child. Study to have a good balance, for there can be a balance.

QUESTION:

A missionary's child told me: "My father left my birthday party to care for the needs of any drunk that came to the door." What can we do to help active Christians not lose their children?

ANSWER:

As in the case of this missionary's child—who was obviously neglected for the needs of others—I have talked to hundreds of such people in their late teens, early twenties, or thirties who have been neglected by parents who are Christian workers of all sorts— missionaries, pastors, or other "full-time workers," as the phrase goes. Let me mention here that we also know many others who have *not* neglected their children and who have carefully and constantly worked out ways to spend more time with their children. *Time* is the precious commodity that can so easily be lost.

Young people have come to us at L'Abri in great bitterness, hating Christianity, in great frustration, with much dark antagonism, or having totally walked away from believing or even searching to find out whether God exists at all. Totally? No, not quite totally, or they wouldn't have come to L'Abri to ask questions or find "something." "You are my last resort. If I don't find truth here, I'm through looking."

To be fair, others have obviously come in answer to the faithful prayers of family or friends. One girl had her pocketbook stolen on a train from Spain to Geneva. Everything was gone! She arrived at the doorstep of Chalet les Melezes with this declaration: "I haven't come to ask any questions or anything like that. I don't want to be here. But I've had my money, traveler's checks, passport, everything stolen, and this was the only place I knew in Switzerland where I could hitchhike and get a free bed and meal. May I stay?"

The answer was yes. Although she didn't know it, that stolen pocketbook was the best thing God had ever done for her! She found more than she had lost. She's one of many you may talk to in heaven because she found truth to be true, and accepted Christ as Savior. When a new passport was issued and money came from the States, she didn't want to leave! So people *do* come without a shred of "wanting to" at all.

Yes, we have had lost sheep who seem to have been neglected for other lost sheep! So often it is not only "career feminists" who discard the influencing of a home and the brand new human beings that are born in a family as not being equal to their career. Unhappily, many Christians whose work or career is the "seeking of the lost" or the "evangelizing of those who have not heard" seem to be completely *blind* to the fact that their own children may be the most important people they are ever going to meet.

That son or that daughter may be one who needs your help in preparation for understanding truth and defending it, because one of your children may far surpass you in being a woman of God, or a man of God. One of your children may speak and make clear the truth in circles you will never reach. It is astounding that "any drunk that came to the door" can loom up as more needy than a little girl who may be shy and not seemingly bothered, but who needs her daddy's expressed love and interest in her. At that time the interest is to be exhibited in blowing up balloons and pinning a tail on the donkey, as well as taking a snapshot of her blowing out candles.

This is something parents need to think about and pray about. If you are missionaries, or a pastor and wife, or Christian workers, or busy doctors and lawyers who are involved in helping people, these few years when children are growing up are important years. (Some may have tried their best and still have at present a very rebellious child. Of course, that happens. We can *not* in any way promise that so many hours equals so much result with your children. It is not a mathematical, precise, always-the-same result. Two or three children from the same family do not all turn out the same and often parents do not know why.)

If your child has to be away at boarding school because you are a missionary or a medical doctor in a mission hospital, determine to spend as much time with them "on paper" as you would day by day if they were at home. Try to see whether it would be possible to have them live with you and study Calvert School courses or other home study, but if in your area this would not be good for the child because of the peculiar form of danger in your district, then spend time "on paper"! Write letters, not to make your child homesick, but in order that no big gap begins to form.

You should not spend your time thinking, "They are away; now I have time to go on with my work without hindrance." No! You use your imagination as you work, in the same way you would if you were planning a surprise for supper and a game afterwards. In your mind, as you are working with your hands, you plan to pick a flower and press it, to draw a picture at the top of your paper, to take some photographs of the patient in the hospital you are caring for. Most important, you write about what the child is doing, as if you were there talking it over. Take yourself into his or her atmosphere and schedule, in your letter, rather than simply dragging the child back in memory. Use your imagination as to what it feels like to have a letter during recess, or in the evening, and see how original you can be. You could tell a short story, if you are good at storytelling, or make up a serial . . . "next installment next time!"

But what about the time it would take? If the child were home, in a normal situation, you'd be up in the night because of a cough, putting the steamer on or giving some medicine or a drink of hot lemonade. I'm talking about treating this period of life as the time you are really with your child, and he or she is with you.

Incidentally, later in life that can work the other way, too. As a grown child I wrote my "Family Letters" to my mother and father and my sisters. I was writing in a descriptive way, to bring my family into the sharing of a life on the other side of the ocean. Letters are not simply a business convenience; they are a part of life. This is a part of life where neglect can take place, or where a balance of the use of time can be put into action!

I still write "Dear Family," although Mother and Father are in heaven. I have sisters, brothers-in-law, nieces and nephews, my own children and grandchildren, *and* what I really think of now as the L'Abri Family . . . people who have come and gone as well as people who have prayed and are an integral part of a work they have never even visited. *Time* can only be spent with so many in "the family" now, by way of letters.

Letter-writing is a very important part of common sense Christian living. Birdie, who used to spend her time talking to people as they came for help in her little chalet, now spends that time writing to people. Letters can cross terrific distances, and can be read and reread. In this answer concerning neglect, we all need to be shaken concerning the part letter-writing has both in "neglect" and in "a balanced use of time to be together."

If your children are at home and a needy person comes to the door, *of course* there are times when emergencies have to take precedence. But try to take that child into the emergency, explaining as much as is advisable by saying, "Look, you and I will talk later, but at this moment there is someone here who needs to be taken to the hospital immediately. I'm sorry we are being interrupted, but that is the way life is, Dear. It isn't simple."

On the other hand, if it is not an emergency or something that needs immediate attention, you say, "I will see you later; right now I am having a half hour (or an hour) with Naomi [or Hannah, or Fiona, or Samantha, or Jessica, or John, or Ranald, or Francis, or Giandi, or Lisby, or Kirsty, or Natasha, or Margaret, or Becky]." I've named my grandchildren in this list! Some of them are pretty grown up by now. The reason I have named my grandchildren is that I want to make this stronger. You should use the name of the person who is asking for time. When you say, "I am talking to Debby," you are stating to yourself as well as to the person, "This is a human being I have an important appointment with."

Don't say apologetically, "I have to talk with *my child*" as if that is rather unimportant but you are caught. Your child is a person, as much a person as the drunk who comes to the door, or the professor from a big university. And children need to grow up knowing they are important to you, that their lives are valuable to you. They should not be expected just to tag along because you preach nine sermons on Sunday and they can choose to come to any one of them. They have to feel a personal personalness!

Time spent alone with your children should be time not simply spent teaching them another Sunday school lesson. Time should be taken to have a meal out together, to go to a place that is a treat for them . . . a park, a beach, a lake boat, a Mississippi riverboat, a walk down a country lane—whatever is available to you where you live. It will be redundant for me to say "concerts" again, but in a year's time something should be included in the area of the arts—concerts, ballets, art museums. You may live near Boston or St. Louis or London or Paris or Zurich or Minneapolis. The possibilities are different depending on where you live. You are getting to know your children, and really treating them as human beings worth sharing good memories with.

When Fran was a pastor in St. Louis, Sunday was his busiest day of the week, with four services at the church. Therefore, Monday was his day off. As soon as the older girls were out of school in the afternoon we'd go with the three girls to the St. Louis Art Museum. This is a good one for children to go from one room to the other, always finding an adequate place to sit and draw in front of a painting or sculpture. They liked that—and looked forward to it.

There was an atmosphere in that museum conducive to children having that privilege. They would walk until they saw something they wanted to try drawing, then sit in front of it and look for a long time. Fran would say, "Sit still and look at that picture. Then tell me what you noticed. You can't really see it when you just walk past." He would teach them to appreciate art.

Then we would go on to a place in the park called "The Jewel Box," a greenhouse full of plants and flowers with a little fountain. We would go and sit in the cool, fragrant, green atmosphere, look at the flowers, talk about them, notice the changes of display as the seasons changed. The greenhouse was a part of our lives, but it was also an important part of the three girls' being *treated* as important. It gave time for some serious answering of questions along the way or for simply enjoying the beauty of God's creativity together.

Christian parents have an imperative, a really urgent need to introduce their children to the kinds of things that will go with them all through life, natural responses to and appreciation of *beauty*. As you introduce them to an enjoyment of beauty of sight and sound, of taste and smell, in this setting your conversation about God is not artificial. You are taking seriously the fact that people are made in the image of the Creator. Creativity is important!

If the little girl you spoke of is grown up now, I have something to say to her, and to others who have had similar experiences. Parents are people, too. Perhaps parents did not have the right care when they were children, and perhaps they did not have anyone teach them some of the things we have been talking about. Remember to feel sorry for the childhood of your parents; pity them for lack of understanding. And ask God to help you to get rid of any bitterness you may have left over, which will only poison you. Lashing out against a memory of a deprived childhood cannot help you who have had neglectful Christian parents, or you who have grown up on the streets.

In any case, you have a family that has God as your Father if you now are one who has found truth to be true. You have a responsibility to do something in these same areas for other human beings. Wallowing in self-pity won't help any of us!

QUESTION:
I wonder how we can possibly be informed about world events when we have to depend on the media for our information?

ANSWER:
It is very hard to know whether we are reading something that is accurate, something that is showing all sides of a question, or something that is simply taking one side. Cameras can focus in a way that tells a different story from cameras focused on the *same* event in another way. The street riot in the film *How Should We Then Live?* showed that very clearly. Just as the focusing of a camera can use one event to report two totally different impressions, so news reporters can also slant a story by what is left out, or by words chosen to influence the reader. Whether the adjective "thoughtful" is used to describe a speaker's face, or whether "confused" is used, certainly will influence the reader's impression. Franky's book *A Time For Anger: The Myth of Neutrality* goes into such things in detail.

As to day-by-day news-gathering for your family, I think I would search for anything that would give further information in another newspaper. If you are reading one you feel is terribly biased, look for another paper and see whether, as you compare the news on one day, you get a better view in the other one.

There is *Newsweek* and *Time*, as you know. Is there much difference between them? Very little, I guess, but at times you get a different slant in one or the other. There is also the *National Review* and *The Wall Street Journal*. You do get different viewpoints.

Debby, our daughter in Switzerland, always reads the Lausanne paper *Twenty-Four Hours, Vingt-quatre Heures* because there is a contributing editor who writes courageously and strongly and has a good viewpoint in general. Prisca has the other paper because her twelve-year-old Giandi wants to read the more full sports section of that paper. O.K., they can compare notes. It is worth comparing notes! We need to keep up on news, and we need to keep each other informed. My husband has felt for years that the Lord really puts it into various people's minds to cut out articles or bits of news to send to him. It is like a "clipping service" because he gets different viewpoints.

Look for ways to find different viewpoints. Don't depend solely on one source for news. The television should not be your only source of news. The impact of the visual is such that *if* it is not accurate, your feeling anyway is too often, "It must have been that way because I *saw* it with my own eyes."

Discuss the news with your family. All of you should try to keep your ears open to find out things that have not been put into the papers. Listen to whatever source of information somebody else has found. Perhaps someone has relatives in Israel or Beirut or Uganda or Poland. News gets through in other ways.

Then—you just have to wait. You also have to say to your children, "We'll wait . . . it's impossible to know the whole story yet." It's a hard problem for us all, no matter what part of the world we live in. None of us knows whether we are getting all of the news. And with some events, no one ever knows the truth of what happened. We really don't. You have to read accounts with the feeling, "I am not going to swallow all of this." You must also be aware of the reader reactions wanted by each author and resist being trapped by such manipulation.

Manipulation *is* going on, and you must overcome it by using a sort of sales resistance. You resist the sales pitch for a thing you do not need to buy at all. You know the person is trying to sell you something you do not need or want. A large percentage of the media is trying to sell you something in the area of ideas and opinions, and actions based on those ideas and opinions. The influence is slanted in one direction; as you read, resist with all that is within you.

Then, as a Christian, you have more you can do. Pray that the Lord will keep you from being manipulated into ideas and actions based on what you read in the newspapers, which really are not a good guide for your actions. This is where you have to come back into the Word of God, comparing what you are being asked to do with what the Bible really does teach. The Bible gives a framework to judge by.

QUESTION:
How can we teach our children to approach the media, especially TV, with a mind of real understanding?

ANSWER:
That also is not something we can have a one, two, three kind of answer for. It is a daily, hourly problem. Naturally, there are going to be different opinions among you—and open discussion is extremely essential.

First, one of the easiest ways of promoting an atmosphere of discussion and reading and music in the household is to prohibit much television watching. Listening to music on the stereo, discussing or reading about the composer and the musicians, and then reading books aloud together is a must as far as I am concerned, if you want to have family life that is conducive to really talking and exchanging ideas. Educating the children to enjoy a great variety of books being read aloud opens the door to reading current events and discussing opinions as a natural part of family life.

The hour of reading by the fireplace, or out in the sunshine, or in a boat . . . educating children to look forward to the family reading aloud together is essential for a great many reasons. As a substitute for TV, it is one of the most important things that can be done. It is hard to include in the day, but it should take precedence over other things.

In our family, not only did I read many hours with each of my children, and together at certain periods of their lives, but they are now reading to their children. At the reading time in Greatham, when Ranald and Susan are busy with L'Abri work—and at reading time in Chalet Gentiana when Debby and Udo are busy with their work—the moment comes when the word is: "Sorry, this is the reading hour for our children." It is not a time of neglecting other people who have come to L'Abri for help. Rather, it is giving the best demonstration they could possibly have of what family life is all about. It is not "putting on a demonstration" like an act! It is simply letting people get a glimpse of the pattern of their family life.

When it comes to news that will be on TV that you want to

look at together, I would say do it together and then discuss it. Have the newspaper read aloud if there is time; or if you have read bits separately, discuss various things. "This is slanted." "Oh really, that was slanted, listen . . ." "There is no truth in this whatsoever; how could they know that, anyway?" "This article is reporting news with editorial opinion trying to change opinion among readers." Then, of course, when you read what you consider good reporting or a good editorial, read it and praise it, and say why it is good.

The way you are introducing your children to international and national news, and helping them to think about it and learning to modify what they are getting, will be valuable to them all their lives. This is a portion of what will make your home an educational supplement to whatever they are getting at school.

QUESTION:

If a family has a handicapped child, do you have any ideas concerning how his siblings can include him in family activities, without spoiling the freedom of the family life? What should be the parents' attitude in this?

ANSWER:

I do believe this is a centrally important question for everyone to think about and consider, because we are being given such a slanted viewpoint in the media on the importance of the life of a person who is born with some handicap. Articles are written concerning the need to do away with babies that do not have a "quality of life" worth preserving, and parents who need help are confused at times.

The Wall Street Journal on July 21, 1982, had a really fair article called "Life or Death Issue: Practice of Neglecting Badly Deformed Babies Stirs Troubled Debate," by W. Stewart Pinkerton, Jr. It was an article well worth reading. However, there is one part of it that seems important to consider in connection with this question.

> Among them [current debates] is the notion that parents have a right to a stable home. Writing in the *British Medical Journal*, Dr. Eliot Slater suggests that the parents' first duty is to preserve the normality of their home, marriage and family life.

This very statement assumes that a "normal" and "stable" home is one where no one has a severe physical affliction! Think about it a moment. In a world that has been abnormal since the

Fall, in a cause-and-effect history in which there have been no perfect human beings (except the Son of God as He became man), we are told that a "normal" or "stable" home is to be made up of a healthy mother and father and children with no difficult hindrances to worry about!

This is a nonsense statement! For a Christian, it is a meaningless concept of life. Common sense Christian living is based on knowing that there is nothing as simple in life as a "stable" home composed of people who have no physical difficulties that would spoil the "quality of life"! It doesn't take much thinking to realize that a "perfect" baby at birth can have an accident at six years old, or have polio or another illness at three, which changes the "perfection." What then?

Every parent has the need to study the basic question of how to raise children to be human beings who are not self-centered, but who are considerate, thoughtful, kind, and sensitive to other people's needs. Selfishness develops easily, with the attention on "me, me, me." To have children turn their imagination and thoughts on someone else's pleasures and needs because their brother or sister is handicapped is to prepare them for a growing unselfishness in their lives ahead, in this world as it really is.

Some months ago Debby and Udo told me of a fellow who was living in Chalet Gentiana with them, as a Farel House student. "We noticed," Debby said, "how very considerate he was. He noticed little things, and jumped up to get things for people, and he was so kind and thoughtful with the children. One day I asked him, 'Could you tell me why you are so different from most young people? You really are so considerate.' "

His answer was one that each parent of a handicapped child should listen to carefully. "I guess it is because we have a Downs Syndrome sister. We other children always thought of what we could do for her so that she wouldn't be left out . . . how we could take care of some need for her and encourage her. You know, we all love her very much, and so it is a genuine interest in her happiness. But, I guess it has made us more aware of other people in general."

A "normal" home, a "stable" home? This boy had been raised in the best kind of a home . . . a home with a handicapped sister whom the parents had carefully taught the brothers to care for and to include. Human beings were growing up in that home with an unselfishness rarely found in the twentieth century.

A lovely black lady talked to me one day about the child she had helped to bring up—an only child in an affluent home with everything money could buy, and the parent's complete attention. "You know," she said wisely, "she had so much of everything that I used to say to her mother, 'She's going to grow up handicapped if you don't watch out.'"

Handicaps are not all physical.

With that as a preface, I would like to answer the question as well as possible. Of course I don't know what the handicap consists of, and so I am unable to be specific. However, first of all I would stress the fact that to care for someone's special need, to use imagination as to what might be done to include that boy or girl in various activities, is *not* a hindrance for the other children but an open door to invention and originality as well as to developing kindness and patience.

If the child is not where the others are mentally, and a game like dominoes is being played, a set of special dominoes for small children, with animals or fruit or flowers to be matched, can be played at one corner of the table with the child. The two games can be going on at once, and turns can be taken as to which game each one is a part of. There are games in which cards are to be matched. There are puzzles that are more simple. This child can be helped to do the puzzle with as much help and enthusiasm as is needed, while a more complicated thousand-piece jigsaw puzzle is being put together by the others.

Scrapbooks can be made by your other children, with pictures that would interest her or him and some pages with textures to feel . . . like velvet, satin, rough wool. Stimulation is always needed.

When the family story is being read, one of the other children can be placing pictures on a felt board or on a magnetic board, much as one would amuse another child at church. The very fact of being together is important for everyone. And stimulating the imagination of your other children as to what might be helpful educationally, or as a pleasure, is a plus in the growth of that personality, not a minus.

When I was in a wheelchair some years ago during a family reunion because of torn cartilages in my knees, my granddaughter Margaret was wheeling me. All of a sudden she said, "Oh Nony, I have an idea. You could hold a mirror right there . . . and then you could see my face as we are talking. Otherwise you have to turn your head, which puts a crick in your neck."

"What an invention!" was my exclamation. That really would

be an addition to a wheelchair, for communication. It is this kind of thing that could be a part of the use of imagination and ingenuity in growing up by any siblings of handicapped children, or by children with ill parents or grandparents.

Where will the kind, thoughtful, caring human beings come from for the next generation of doctors, dentists, pastors, nurses, therapists, teachers if there is no recognition of the value of forgetting oneself in order to put some close relative's needs first, especially during part of the so-called "formative years"?

It is pretty old-fashioned to talk about character building these days. But that is really what it is all about! To be challenged to figure out how someone who is "all locked in" to his handicapped body can have a little more freedom is a challenge that is helpful to character building of the whole family, if the attitude is what it should be. In the second episode of *Whatever Happened to the Human Race?* you meet young people who not only have character, but whose families are more stable than a lot of the ones the British doctor quoted in *The Wall Street Journal* is referring to. Just ask U.S. Surgeon General C. Everett Koop about that, he knows them!

And as we are talking about common sense Christian living, it is a very special contrast to talk to the loving brothers and sisters of the "locked-in" child and to remind them that one day in the future, that body will be perfect in a twinkling of an eye, when Jesus comes back. *Then* there will not be a shred of a handicap, but physical and mental and emotional and spiritual *perfection*! What a contrast. And how great that it is true!

Common sense should tell us to use such contrasts to bring the joy of hope into the normal, everyday conversation of a family.

CHAPTER ELEVEN

The Centrality of Prayer

COMMON SENSE CHRISTIAN LIVING takes place in an atmosphere where prayer is as natural as breathing, as necessary as oxygen, as real as talking to your favorite person with whom there is no strain, as sensible as reaching into the bag of flour for the proper supplies for making bread. To live without prayer being woven into every part of every day is stupid, foolish, senseless, or is an evidence that your belief in the existence of the Creator, who has said we are to call upon Him, is an unsure belief.

People today want advice. People today want strong leadership. *If only,* many people think, *I had someone to ask.* Often in such a moment of crisis, people wildly consider the possibility of looking into astrology, seeking a fortune-teller or a soothsayer or a crystal-gazer, trying to find someone with a reputation of being able to know something of the future upon which to base a decision.

Centuries ago Job called out, "Where can wisdom be found?" Years later another man wrote:

If any of you lacks wisdom, let him ask of God, who gives to all liberally and without reproach, and it will be given to him. But let him ask in faith, with no doubting, for he who doubts is like a wave of the sea driven and tossed by the wind. For let not that man suppose that he will receive anything from the Lord; he is a double-minded man, unstable in all his ways.

Who can pray? The concise answer can be given in a nutshell: *The only one who can pray is one who believes God exists.* It is nonsense to pray to a nonexistent person.

This is what the Bible says in answer to the question, "Who can pray?"

> But without faith it is impossible to please Him, for he who comes to God must believe that He is and that He is a rewarder of those who diligently seek Him.
>
> Heb. 11:6

If we really believe He exists and that we may be admitted into His presence, the reality of diligently, earnestly, sincerely, fervently seeking Him becomes an imperative! This is the child of God coming to the Father, who has extended an invitation to come at any time.

Who else can pray? Can no unbeliever, no confused doubter pray at all? We have covered these passages earlier in this book, but remember again that God has said strongly that if people will seek Him with all their hearts, and search with the earnestness of seeking hidden treasure, they will find Him. Get a record and listen to the music and words of the tenor aria from Part I of Mendelssohn's *Elijah*,[1] taken from Deuteronomy 4:29: "If with all your hearts ye truly seek me, Ye shall ever surely find me . . ." and thank God that the compassion of God is spoken in such beautiful terms to all lost people.

How can people who are not God's children and are in the seeking stage, not sure of His existence, pray? "Oh God, if there is a God, make Yourself known!" or "Please help me to know the truth about Your existence if You are there. I want to know *You*, and bow before You, if indeed You exist."

What is prayer? Prayer first of all is an expression to God, in whatever form of communication you use, of your appreciation of Him as Creator, of the works He has done, of the heavens and the earth, of the amazing complexity of human beings—physically, but also intellectually, emotionally and spiritually. It is praising Him for creating human beings who are so intricate and complicated, and amazing in their creativity.

Hear the description of the appointment of some of the Levites to the task of continual prayer, in 1 Chronicles 16:4–13. Di-

---

[1]There are at least three available recordings of Felix Mendelssohn's *Elijah*: Fruebeck de Burgos English New Philharmonia, Angel 3738-C (three record set); Eugene Ormandy, LSC-6190; and Sir Malcom Sargent: Haddersfield Choral Society, Liverpool Philharmonic, Angel 3558-C (three record set).

gest what is being said here! Do you understand that praise and thanksgiving can be made with music as well as words?

> And he appointed some of the Levites to minister before the ark of the LORD, to commemorate, to thank, and to praise the LORD God of Israel: Asaph the chief, and next to him Zechariah, then Jeiel, Shemiramoth, Jehiel, Mattithiah, Eliab, Benaiah, and Obed-Edom [don't let's skip their names; the fact that God knows each one by name, and cares for His children personally, and hears them either speak or play their flute personally is fantastic. He knows the notes of each person in the whole orchestra! He is a Director with a sensitive, "perfect ear"!]: Jeiel with stringed instruments and harps, but Asaph made music with cymbals; Benaiah and Jahaziel the priests regularly blew the trumpets before the ark of the covenant of God.
> And on that day David first delivered this psalm into the hand of Asaph and his brethren, to thank the LORD:

> > Oh, give thanks to the LORD!
> > Call upon His name;
> > Make known His deeds among the peoples!
> > Sing to Him, sing psalms to Him;
> > Talk of all His wondrous works!
> > Glory in His holy name;
> > Let the hearts of those rejoice who seek the LORD!
> > Seek the LORD and His strength;
> > Seek His face evermore!
> > Remember His marvelous works which He has done,
> > His wonders and the judgments of His mouth,
> > O seed of Israel His servant,
> > You children of Jacob, His chosen ones!
> >   also Ps. 105:1–6

Appreciation can be expressed to God with spoken words in prayer, alone in one's "closet," or sitting on a stone in a field, or walking in the woods or on a city street. Appreciation can be written to God in your handwriting for His eyes alone, written in a private notebook or on the back of an envelope. Praise and thanksgiving can be in the form of a painting if that is a person's best medium of expression, or in song, or with a musical instrument. It doesn't always have to be verbal . . . nor heard by anyone else.

Prose, poetry, or musical instruments can be used by you alone to praise God, with only the sound of the rain adding anything to whatever sound you are making in your communication. A dancer can dance with a heart full of adoration and appreciation being expressed directly to the Lord, as that person dances alone up and down a curving staircase, alone in the house, alone in a room, on the grass or field in the moonlight, with a string trio as the music comes from a record player . . . and no eyes watching except the Lord's.

Prayer *is* praise, worship, adoration, thanksgiving for so very many kinds of things, for what has been done in past history as well as in our own lifetimes—an expression to God of our love. Before anything else, prayer is to consist of all that these verses in Chronicles suggest, and more.

Next, it is right to seek help. Just as it is wrong to go to fortune-tellers, it is right to seek help from God. The reality of our trust is to be shown in our seeking His help in time of real need, when we are out on the end of a limb. We can cry to the Lord in the words of David, and know He will hear us:

> In my distress I called upon the LORD;
> And cried out to my God;
> He heard my voice from His temple,
> And my cry came before Him, even his ears.
>
> Ps. 18:6

God makes very clear that it is wrong for people to "try out" other religions, ways of meditation, false gods. He will not be one among others because He really is the one true God.

It is important, then, to make our communication a two-way communication in an attempt to observe what God is telling us concerning how to be acceptable to Him. By two-way communication I do not mean that we are to hear an audible voice from God or see handwriting on the wall. But reading the Bible and talking to the Lord, making our responses of thanksgiving and our requests in the context of what we have read, will help us concentrate, shutting out hindering things outside or inside our own minds, as well as opening the way to more realistic recognition of the true fact that we are in the presence of God. We are not alone as we talk. He has something to say to us that is written, and that Word is in our hands and is really from Him.

I personally find this method to be a constant help, but since we all differ you may have another way of praying that is special to you.

Let me give you an example of praying in this two-way communication method. As I read 1 Kings 18, and stop to pray, thanking God for the wonder of His giving strong evidence of His existence in answer to Elijah's prayer, thanking Him for the encouragement of those who were convinced as Elijah stood alone with four hundred prophets of Baal against him, it gives me courage to pray for the day we live in. It gives me courage to pray for the many who have been fooled by today's "prophets of Baal," for strength for each of us who are the representatives of the Lord that we might stand firm and be willing for confrontation, in whatever form it comes to us. "Oh God of Elijah," I pray, "You are able to open eyes of understanding today."

As I read of Daniel in the lion's den, there is so much that increases my trust and faith. This is Daniel's God I am praying to! Reread this story and think of your present troubles in the context of Daniel, or of the three young men who were being thrown into the fiery furnace. Remember these important words which the young men said in the face of those who were stronger than they were: "Our God whom we serve is able to deliver us. . . . But if not, . . . we do not serve your gods" (Dan. 3:17–18). They knew God was *able* to bring them out unscathed, but whether He did or not, they were declaring that their faith was far more than a demand that everything would turn out "right" for them.

In your own prayer and in mine, we are encouraged to declare to the Lord with love, "God, You are able to heal my child of polio, but if you do not I still trust You." "God, You are able to take care of my child at college and keep him safe coming home, but if You do not . . . and the news comes of a car crash . . . I still trust You." "I love You, and I trust You. I trust Your Word and I trust Your compassion. I know, God, as I read about David's, Daniel's, Jeremiah's, and Paul's lives, that You see history differently than I do. So I *know* You are able, as I bring You my request . . . but if You do not . . ."

Prayer is also a familiar, growing, deepening communication that gives us a continuity in life. Other things may change, but we still have our prayer life in a (more or less) unbroken line, independent of our geographical location. However, we don't reach a level and then stay on a nice even plateau for the rest of our lives. Life is a mountain climb to the very end! Nothing is simple. We round new corners and come upon patches of thistles and sharp rocks.

We are constantly moving in our prayer life, in our Christian progress, but we are not constantly moving up. That is to say, we are not making a graphline that can be drawn with a ruler at an even slant up across the page. Our graphline is up and down . . . jagged . . . but with a gradual rise! There are days when we feel we could fly. There are times when some of us feel little bubbles

inside us. (Others may not . . . we are all different, remember?)
On those bubbly days we feel so close to the Lord that we can
almost feel His presence in a tangible way. Prayer has been easy
and real, with definiteness and assurance.

At other times, even when we are trying to read and read,
then pray, and do this two-way communication, we feel dry, flat,
uninspired, dull, and we don't feel we are having that closeness at
all. We wonder, "What is wrong? What is wrong? . . . Is something hindering? . . . What is it?"

Be encouraged. God knows our ups and downs. At times
there is a hindrance that needs to be discovered and confessed to
Him, but at other times it is nothing of that sort. You and I are
individuals when it comes to prayer, even as we are when it comes
to human communication. You may have an earache, or a tooth-
ache, or be coming down with a "bug" of some sort, or be un-
usually exhausted. Your "spiritual life" is not separated from your
whole person, or from your whole life.

Your prayer life is a part of your whole life, perhaps more than
anything else because we are plainly told, "Pray continually."
"Pray without ceasing" (see 1 Thess. 5:17). This means we are to
pray at times when we don't feel like it, or don't feel inspired at all.
After all, prayer doesn't have to be long sentences. It is fine to
simply tell the Lord your troubles. "I don't know why, but I can't
form sentences. Do for me what I need, Lord."

How in the world can we possibly "pray without ceasing," or
"pray continually"?

Does this mean you can't read a book or a newspaper because
you have to be praying instead? Does it mean you can do nothing
else at all but pray? To look at it this way would be to make that
command an impossibility. However, I do believe it is something
that *does* have meaning for each one of us. God does not give us
anything that does not have meaning. It seems to me that this
command means that we are to be constantly so conscious of
God's existence and so aware of His presence, that there is a very
short gap between a sudden *need* of speaking to the Lord, and our
actually speaking to Him. I feel it means that we are walking so
close to the reality of His being with us that we naturally talk to
Him (in our minds, of course) when we are in the dentist's chair, in
the waiting room of a doctor's or lawyer's office, out on a tractor,
waiting for a plane or bus, talking to someone who has just had a
shock. Whether it is a brief time of prayer or a long, long one, the

atmosphere of the normality of talking to God is what I feel is meant by the command to "pray continually."

I know a farmer who used to be a L'Abri worker. He writes that he now prays as he works on his tractor. He carries the prayer list with its page of verses and another page of requests on the L'Abri day of prayer each week. In this sense he is still a L'Abri worker. Even as his hours are spent raising quantities of mint, his hours are also being used to affect what is going on thousands of miles away.

My first observation of perfectly natural and conscientious prayer came when I was a very little girl in Shanghai. One morning I went skipping along beside Dr. Hoste, at that time the director of the China Inland Mission (he had followed Hudson Taylor). He didn't turn me away, but simply said, "Edith, I am praying now, but you may come along if you wish."

I walked with him a number of times, holding his hand and being very quiet and impressed as he prayed aloud. It was his custom to walk when he prayed, and he counted it his first responsibility for the mission to pray four hours a day. He prayed for each missionary in the China Inland Mission, and for each of their children by name. He had the list with him, and he went through it. It was not just a recitation of names; he cared about each person and knew something of their needs. He felt this was his work.

"All right, walk with me and pray," he would say in his peculiarly high voice. The impression that penetrates my memory is the respect I received for the *work* of prayer. I know it meant more than any series of lectures in later life could mean.

Whether it is the farmer in his tractor, portioning out time for prayer, or the head of a mission who considers prayer more important than paperwork or talking to a number of people waiting to see him—there is no rule or measuring stick by which you can say, "So much prayer gives so much spiritual result." This is not the way it is; many people could never take four hours every day to pray, nor do they ever have quiet time riding miles on a tractor.

However, in your lifetime there should be some whole days, or blocks of time, that you take to spend alone with the Lord, just as you do with some member of your family or a close friend you haven't seen for a long time. You say, "Let's just not take time eating today! We are going to sit down and have a really uninterrupted conversation together. I haven't seen you for so long; there is a lot of catching up to do."

From time to time we have to do that with the living God, our heavenly Father, the Master of the universe. There is something that cannot take place in snatched moments, and that is an unhindered time of progressive conversation. We talk to each other as human beings for long periods of time in order to get on with things that would never come out in five minutes or even a half hour. If you know you are going to have five hours with another person, you can relax and take your time explaining things, and both of you can take time listening.

I would recommend that you take a longer period of time to communicate with the Lord, to read His word, to carefully bring things to Him concerning yourself and your own need, and to take sufficient time to thank Him for Himself. There is a cumulative freedom of communication as you read and pray for a variety of needs in other people's lives as well as in your own.

As the time goes on, five or six hours or more, there is a sense of quietness, like having been in the home of a very calm person in a location separated from your own pressures. Pressures are removed as the time goes on. Now quickly let me warn you: after such a day the roof can fall in! It is not a guarantee that the calmness will carry over into an easy evening. The time is really like being in a protected country place, and leaving it to go into the chaos of city traffic. Nothing else is like it in my own life. You will have to try such a time to know what I'm talking about.

Why pray? One may well ask that question. And the concise answer is that it will make a difference in history. Another part of that same answer is that God has told us to pray. When Hezekiah was ill, God sent him a message through Isaiah that he should put his house in order because he was going to die. And we are told that Hezekiah turned his face to the wall and prayed to the Lord, weeping bitterly. The reply came back through Isaiah, "Thus says the LORD, the God of David your father: 'I have heard your prayer, I have seen your tears . . . and I will add to your days fifteen years'" (2 Kin. 20:5–6). This was a change in history because of prayer. Hezekiah lived fifteen years longer.

We are given many examples in the Old and New Testaments concerning prayer for oneself. But we are also given examples concerning the responsibility to intercede for other people. Interceding for other people makes a difference in the history of other people's lives, and in many specific incidents in their lives.

In Colossians 4:2–4 Paul asks the Christians specifically for prayer help.

Continue earnestly in prayer, being vigilant in it with thanksgiving; meanwhile praying also for us, that God would open to us a door for the word, to speak the mystery of Christ, for which I am also in chains, that I may make it manifest, as I ought to speak.

We might think that no one could proclaim the truth more vividly and clearly than Paul. Yet Paul is not only admonishing and strongly urging the Colossians to "Continue earnestly in prayer," pointing out that it is a normal part of everyday life for a Christian and a central part of our work, but he is asking them to "pray for me." Why? Is it so that he might get out of the chains more quickly? He doesn't mention desiring to get rid of the chains. He simply states the fact that these chains have been put on him because he is persisting in preaching the truth of the gospel! What he is asking the Christians to pray for is that he may speak more clearly. Paul expects a difference to take place in his ability and power to speak, in answer to prayer. Paul expects history to be different because intercession is taken seriously as an important task. The early Christians prayed for each other in a diversity of need.

In our personal families, as well as in the larger family of believers who are in relationship to each other because of being put in various works together, there is a need at times to drop everything and take the time to intercede seriously while something important is going on. Years ago, when my husband was having a public discussion with Bishop Pike in Chicago before a large audience, we had a night of prayer in Switzerland in two of the chalets, so that we might be praying at the exact time the confrontation was going on. We didn't fast and pray that night; rather, we provided orange juice and rolls for those who came to sit by the fire and pray. Nick Cornelisse led the ones who took that night to pray in Chalet Beau Site, and I led those who came to the Melezes living room. We believed it would make a difference.

Just recently, when Franky had his confrontation on *The Today Show,* Priscilla led Swiss L'Abri people in two hours of prayer during the time of the program. Each branch of L'Abri prayed during those two hours, as did many people of the wider L'Abri family scattered in various places. I stopped my writing of this book for those two hours, and Fran and I sat and prayed together, first one praying aloud, then the other. Why? Because we believe that prayer really is to be considered as basic. God has made that a very clear fact.

As people went off to Australia for meetings and conferences, it was not possible to follow the "time band" for three weeks. But constant prayer for Debby, Udo, Barry, Jerram, and Wim continued to be a part of the responsibility of the L'Abri family during that time.

In this reality of prayer for each other, the small family unit is also meant to portray something of the wonder of the oneness of the entire family of God. And so a little child should be instructed not just by teaching, but by example—at family prayer time, at bedtime, before meals—that prayer is communication with God, in which there is to be included an expression of appreciation for what God has done. It is lovely to hear a small child say "thank you" for all the things on the table, right up to the candles and candlesticks, and the flowers as well as the food. It is also lovely to hear a child very naturally thank God for the dog, as well as for brothers and sisters. Such expression is real, and not just a recited prayer of memorized words.

As you pray, believe that God is able to hear all you are asking and to do it all. But God does not say it is wrong to ask for human help—"horizontal help." We are told to help each other. We are told to comfort one another with the comfort we have received, which in essence is telling us to get together with others who have the same problems we have. If you have a handicapped child, you should come together with others who have children with the same handicaps that you might help each other in practical ways with shared ideas. We need to remember that encouragement is needed and keep our eyes open for new needs.

Courage is given by other human beings coming in at a needy moment and offering, "I'll help you; I understand how important this is." This means an openness to change a schedule at times, rather than being completely absorbed with one little "rut" of life, whether it is an individual "rut" or a church always doing the exact same program and not being interested in looking into some special need in the town. A church could begin a crisis pregnancy center, or help the poor, or distribute hot meals to some elderly people.

As we pray for the needy around us, God may open our eyes to what *we* can do to help in that immediate need. He may use *us* as an answer to our own prayers.

As we pray for the need of education of falsely informed people concerning abortion, one answer may be that, along with others in our church, we do something practical about it such as having an educational series, or purchasing a house to open as a crisis pregnancy center. As we pray for families with older people or handicapped children to care for, we may need to prepare a place where perhaps one day or more a week these children could come to play or to have a special treat such as wheelchair races or whatever your imagination can think up! What skills do you have? A dressmaking class, a woodcarving class, or a jelly-making class would fit some people's needs, perhaps.

The essential thing for each of us to discover is that prayer is *not* an isolationist activity. Prayer involves us in what is going on around us, both locally and in the world. As we pray for Poland, we are also to send off a box to someone we know in Poland. As we pray for Kumar and Ruth in India, we are to buy a rug their community makes or write a letter to Madame Gandhi complaining of the persecution. We are the ones to make truth known, just as the early church was. There is to be a balance among us, as well as balance in each of our lives. We can't each "do everything," but there is "everything to be done" by one or another of us.

We must recognize that prayer alone, prayer together, prayer for ourselves, prayer for each other, continual prayer is an essential portion of our work. But conversely, we must be ready and willing to *do* whatever God shows us we are to do in answer to prayer! As we ask for His will to be made known, for His guidance for the next step, we need to ask with a determination that we will do His will . . . whatever it is. That kind of trust and willingness is what we need as we pray.

Always I feel the need to point out that "answered prayer can be a broken teapot" (or some heirloom). I say that so frequently because it puts a long subject into a nutshell. We prayed earnestly for "the people of God's choice to come up the mountainside to L'Abri." We have prayed this for twenty-seven years, and do still pray that way. All of us involved in the work of L'Abri know that as God answers and sends people, it is His "answers" who break favorite teacups and saucers, irons, teapots, and who burn pans. They also take energy and strength day by day to care for in one way or another, until fatigue screams at us from our bodies.

Are there wonderful results? A million times *yes*. We wouldn't change those twenty-seven years nor keep away any of you who are among that wide, wide scattered L'Abri family. But through the midst of it all, it must be noticed that answered prayer brings affliction—often.

Paul prayed and asked for intercession, that he might speak

with clarity and power. He did. The results were prison, chains, persecution, and eventually martyrdom. Jeremiah asked for help; he said he couldn't speak because he was only a "child." God gave him the words—strong words, powerful words, for Jeremiah's audiences and for centuries since. But Jeremiah's afflictions came as a result of God's answering his prayer for help in speaking!

Asking for God's strength in our weakness to do what He wants us to do does *not* mean we get a kind of permanent feeling of perfect health and happiness. His strength is strong in a diversity of ways.

Why pray? We must remember that God made human beings in the first place with a capacity to converse with Him. Adam and Eve "divorced" that relationship, and the terrible price Jesus paid was not only to give us eternal life but to give us a *present* difference day by day in restoring our relationship with God. We can talk with God! What an overwhelming reality.

What a terrible waste for a Christian *not* to talk to Him. It would be like having a WATS line installed in your home (at some huge price per year you can have unlimited interstate phone calls) and *never* using it to talk to your beloved family, parents, children, brothers and sisters, friends. To waste that "open line," already paid for, and not use it for communication would be to simply waste the ten thousand dollars or whatever it costs.

But the separation in the Trinity when Jesus was alone on the cross, the awful agony of all that death involved, was a price beyond any amount of money. That price was paid to open unlimited communication to each one who would accept the gift of salvation, the substitution of Christ's death in his or her place. To accept that gift, and to only look forward to heaven without using "the unlimited phone" given us to stay in constant communication *now* (which is part of what has been paid for) is, in gentlest terms, foolish! Even a shred of common sense, in the light of what prayer is as a "paid for" open line to God, would tell us that prayer is to be a continual taking the phone off the hook and speaking to the Lord.

QUESTION:
How can we most effectively pray with and for our grandchildren, without interfering with their parents?

ANSWER:
Although I do not know your situation, I am assuming that you mean the parents are not Christians and would not pray with

the children, although you may not mean that. But if this were the case, it would need first of all *great* sensitivity. You have certain responsibilities as grandparents, but you are not the parents. You are responsible, first of all, to pray for your grandchildren. Secondly, you are to pray with them, unless their parents have forbidden you to do so. That period of time only lasts a few years, if it is so. At a certain age a child passes from being a child to being an adult. You want to develop and keep the friendship of that child, so that when that age passes, you are the person the child (now a teen-ager) wants to be with.

If, for instance, the parents have said, "Absolutely you stop this, we don't want the word 'God' mentioned to our child. We will not have the name 'God' mentioned in our child's presence, and we do not want you to pray with our child" (I know grandparents who have had to face that), I would *not* try to kidnap the child and force him or her to listen.

First, I would pray with earnestness, taking special time out of my schedule to do so. Then, in any kind of natural setting—Christmas, Thanksgiving, your anniversary, a birthday dinner—if it is at all possible and especially if it is in your home or you are paying the restaurant bill, you would ask the blessing. It shouldn't be a long one, but you can ask the Lord to give you the words that would penetrate minds with curiosity.

"Thank you, God, that You are there to thank, that it isn't an empty universe with nobody there to thank for this food, and for each other." You would have to try, in the midst of the possibilities of your own situation and as you ask for God's openings, to give most gently and sensitively that which would let the children know as much of the truth as you could possibly let them know. It is basically important that the fact comes across that you believe truth exists. It isn't just "Oh, Grandmother and Grandpa are very religious" that should stick in their minds, but that you believe there is a truth that makes a difference to everything.

As time goes on, they need to know there is an alternative to atheism. Somehow, you want them to realize they have been taught only one theory—that everything has come by chance. "There is an alternative," you want to say. "To be really educated you need to know there is an alternative, and that is that possibly a Creator made everything." Then you can tell something about this Creator, if openings come.

I think it is possible to impart a lot of the needful information about truth without putting it into phraseology that is instantly recognized as being that "taboo Christian stuff." It is set phraseology, set slogans, words that the media make fun of, that would be carried back and be repeated to the parents, who would react immediately: "Oh, your grandparents have been teaching you about Jesus. They want to turn you into religious Jesus freaks." The basic teaching your grandchildren need is to know that *truth* is important and that alternative viewpoints are being taught that need some questions asked about them.

Of equal importance to any openings you get to say a few well-said things along the way is the very important friendship that should be developing. It should be just plain fun to be with you, and your ideas of a fun day or a treat should be more imaginative than anyone's. Whether you are arranging a birthday luncheon, a family reunion, preparing a Christmas package, or having the children for a day with you, your surprises should be really fun surprises. You are making it clear that a Christian is a person who has appreciation of a variety of things, whether you are taking them to a circus, a ballet, a picnic on the beach, or having a treasure hunt in your garden.

As you write letters or send books, or talk to your grandchildren, it should not *always* be about Christian things. Your sympathy and interest in their school problems, their sports, their disappointments, and their special achievements will make you someone to run to with their joys and problems. Naturally, the geographic distance makes a great difference in the kind of things you can do. Wherever they are, much prayer behind the scenes can always be taking place—and part of that prayer is asking for ideas of what to do for them.

This would be the direction I would take: rather than a knock-down-drag-out kind of forceful statement such as, "These are my grandchildren and I am going to do this," take it gently, and pray for a change in the parents.

QUESTION:
Would you please discuss the verse, "If a man considers sin in his heart, the Lord will not hear him"?

ANSWER:
It seems to me that this verse (Ps. 66:18), is a warning to each of us, and one of the very key conditions for prayer. In the New King James Version it reads: "If I regard iniquity in my heart,/The

Lord will not hear." In the NIV it is translated: "If I had cherished sin in my heart,/the Lord would not have listened."

God makes very clear in the Ten Commandments and in all the explanations of those commandments throughout Scripture what sin is, what it consists of. This verse describes a person who deliberately makes the choice to do that which he knows to be sin, and in his heart he decides he is not going to be sorry or ask forgiveness because he definitely wants to continue and to rationalize it all in some way. He will do nothing to change this dichotomy, this hypocritical double standard in his Christian life.

It seems to me this kind of "regarding" or "cherishing" sin in one's heart is a determination to plant a foot firmly in each world, and to keep the two feet separate! "I *will* do this with this foot—and I am going to pray at the same time and ask God to help me with this *other* part of my life. In this part over here—which I will keep separate for myself—I want to do this, and I don't give a hoot whether it is right or wrong. I am deliberately going to do this because I want to."

"I am going to abort my fourth child because I only want three children and I didn't ask to get pregnant. Now I am going to go on and stay in the church, and I'm going to pray. After all, I'm a Christian and lots of people make mistakes, even if it is wrong."

Many people unhappily take this blatant position of doing their own thing in a lot of situations. God has said there are consequences of this attitude. James 4:2–3 is strong:

> You lust and do not have. You murder and covet and cannot obtain. You fight and war. Yet you do not have because you do not ask. You ask and do not receive, because you ask amiss, that you may spend it on your pleasures.

Jesus died that we might be forgiven and cleansed, and the way was to be opened to us for prayer. But that cleansing is not a license to refuse to battle seriously against sin, or to refuse to put it out of our lives. Prayer has conditions that need to be met.

Isaiah 1:15–17 needs to be read in this connection too:

> "When you spread out your hands,
> I will hide My eyes from you;
> Even though you make many prayers,
> I will not hear.
> Your hands are full of blood.
> Wash yourselves, make yourselves clean;

> Put away the evil of your doings
>   from before My eyes.
> Cease to do evil,
> Learn to do good;
> Seek justice,
> Reprove the oppressor;
> Defend the fatherless,
> Plead for the widow."

God says He will not hear prayer under certain conditions. Does that mean He is deaf? No, there is a serious meaning that is very, very deep, and not to be brushed aside because this portion of Scripture is uncomfortable. We need to listen carefully.

God is "not hearing" in the same way that He has spoken of in Isaiah 58, when He says, "I am *not* hearing your cry as you fast and pray, and humble yourselves with sackcloth and ashes. You are exploiting your workers, you are not loving or caring for your own flesh and blood . . . those of your own family. You are doing all these things that are wrong. . . . Away with your religious practices!" (author's paraphrase).

At this point of history in our country, and particularly in our churches, there are those who have one foot in deliberate sin, saying publicly, "I will do this, and I don't care what the Bible says. We are living in a different century now. We have a changed view of things. Because 'everybody does this,' it is O.K." The "this" may be divorce, or it may be abortion. "Everybody has only the number of children they want. If they can't manage it one way, it can be taken care of in another way."

"Everybody looks for happiness in marriage, and a new beginning with a new person is what everybody accepts as all right today."

"Everybody does whatever I have done," is the idea, and so I can keep my foot in that particular thing and keep my other foot in my office in the church or in the Christian world as Sunday school teacher, pastor, leader . . . and as one who is praying.

Yes, that verse you have asked about is one that needs very careful consideration by each of us privately before God, that we may recognize sin, confess it to Him, get it out of our lives, and then go on to thank Him for forgiveness.

QUESTION:
   Do you have any advice for family devotions and prayer when individual schedules are so different?

ANSWER:

Time for family devotions together is difficult to work out when one person has a night shift to work, and one person the day shift, along with whatever the separated times are for the children's school schedules. Some may have to go off on the six o'clock bus and someone else may leave at nine. It isn't easy, but it does need to be worked out during a time when everybody is at home.

If there is absolutely *no* overlapping time when everyone is home, then I would say there might be a possibility of selecting a psalm, or some verses, or something to read that you decide on together. *Each* person will promise to read those verses sometime during the day. Then you would look forward to discussing this at a time when you would be together for a meal.

If this unhappily takes place only once or twice a week, nevertheless you would prepare for it. Even if Sunday is the only day the whole family is together, you ask, "What did you get out of reading Psalm 90?" (or the chapter of a book you decided to read to discuss). "Did you all read it?" As you put the children to bed, or see them at other times, you can talk about the weekly reading. I think there can be a togetherness in reading the same thing even while apart. As you read you wonder what someone else in the family is thinking about it.

"Time blocks" in family life change; our opportunities of being together are not always the same. And so we need to be inventive concerning the important "thinking together" as well as sitting under the teaching of God's Word together.

QUESTION:

What is the value of fasting and praying?

ANSWER:

First of all, the Bible considers fasting and prayer a normal portion of the lives of the children of the living God. God unfolds the value of these practices in various parts of His Word.

I think that there is value in putting aside the good things of life, to put prayer first for a portion of time. The first value would be that of having *time* that could be an unbroken period.

People in different circumstances would be taking a day to fast and pray in different ways. If you are fasting from food—that is, one or two meals—it means that you don't take the time to prepare food, nor the time to eat, nor the time to do the cleaning up afterwards. You do not have conversation with each other; you are also fasting from "horizontal" conversation in order to concentrate on conversation with the Lord.

In 1 Corinthians 7:5, putting aside of the sexual relationship between husband and wife for a time is only for the reason of prayer. The emphasis here is vital. Sexual fasting must be the result of mutual agreement to give prayer first priority, and is not in any sense "bribing the Lord" with our abstinence. It is rather that some special need has arisen, perhaps a child with a life-threatening illness or a relative's marriage in great difficulty, that demands a special indication from us of the extreme importance of this particular period of prayer. Any fasting, whether from conversation, food, or sexual intercourse, should serve to heighten the intensity of special prayer times and underscore their seriousness.

It seems to me this is a very strong admonition—that in fasting we are not to deprive other people of our normal responsibility toward them. It is *not* a spiritual act to fast and pray and push a husband or wife into temptation sexually. It seems to me also that it is not a spiritual thing to deprive a family of food, insisting that you are fasting to pray and therefore will not cook. Nor can a nurse "fast" from answering her bell calling her to a patient, or a doctor "fast" from his beeper. The arrangement has to be one that fits in. And "fitting in" a time of fasting and praying is harder for some than for others.

You ask what the value of fasting and prayer is. In human conversations, we feel a freedom to explain things more clearly when we are not pressed by time. There is the same freedom in conversation with the Lord when there is time to express appreciation for details of His creation and the many things for which we are thankful. As we have time to read the Bible and meditate upon what we have read and then to pray in a two-way kind of conversation alone with the Lord, there is a growing closeness to Him with none of the usual interruptions to conversation, even the good things of the usual daily schedule, breaking into that communication.

To plan a period of uninterrupted time, and to be in a place where one is cut off from the usual intrusions of telephone or people, is to really *underline* the importance of prayer, or intercession, or talking to the living God. It also helps make known to the Lord how serious and true our belief is that He is God indeed, and that we are filled with wonder that we are accepted into His presence because of the victory of Christ's death. The action of taking

*******FRIDAY JULY 30, 1982
L'ABRI's 28th ANNUAL DAY
OF FASTING AND PRAYER ********

Oh how I love your law! I meditate on it all day long........
Your word is a lamp to my feet and a light for my path........
My eyes stay open through the watches of the night,
that I may meditate on your promises.................
I rise before dawn and cry for help; I have put my hope in your
word.   Psalm 119:97,105,148,147

The Lord is my light and my salvation; whom shall I fear?
the Lord is the strength of my life: of whom shall I be afraid?
                                                    Ps. 27:1

Unto thee will I cry, O Lord my rock; be not silent to me; lest,
if thou be silent to me, I become like them that go down into the pit.
Hear the voice of my supplications, when I cry unto thee, when I lift
up my hands toward thy holy oracle.............
The Lord is my strength and my shield; my heart trusted in him, and I
am helped; therefore my heart greatly rejoiceth; and with my (voice)
song will I praise him.   Psalm 28:1,2,7

As we look back over 27 years of L'Abri, and look around at the great
temptations in this terrible time of history to one or another kind of
falseness in our uncluttered reality of closeness to God in the work of
L'Abri, and in our lives, let us read DANIEL 9, entirely, inaddition to:
" So I turned to the Lord God and pleaded with him in prayer and petition,
in fasting, and in sackcloth and ashes.   I prayed to the Lord my God and
confessed: ' O Lord, the great and awesome God, who keeps his covenant
of love with all who love him and obey his commands, we have sinned and
done wrong. . . . . . Now, O Lord, our God, ...hear the prayers and
petitions of your servant. For your sake, O Lord, look with favor....Give
ear, O God and hear; open your eyes and see the desolation of the city
that bears your name. We do not make requests of you because we are righteous
but because of your great mercy. Oh Lord, listen! O Lord forgive!
O Lord, hear and act! For your sake, O my God, do not delay, because your
city and your people bear your Name!"   Daniel 9:3,4,17,18,19
May we plead for forgiveness for any pride that has crept in in any way.
May we plead for the fulfillment of our spiritual needs as well as all the
need of guidance and material provision ONLY ON THE BASIS OF THE LORD's
mercy, His promises, and our desire to see Him glorified ....not because
of any feeling that " we have arrived" ...not "because we are righteous".

(Abraham) staggered not at the promise of God through unbelief; but was
strong in the faith, giving glory to God; And being fully persuaded that
what he had promised he was able to perform.   ROMANS 4:20,21

As we who are members, workers, helpers, students, donors, faithful people
of The Praying Family of L'Abri, interceed for the needs of the work, we
must be faithful in interceeding for each other.
2 TIMOTHY 1:3,11,12,14,   2:3
I thank God, whom I serve, as my forefathers did, with a clear conscience,
as night and day I constantly remember you in my prayers.............
And of this gospel I was appointed a herald and an apostle and a teacher.
That is why I am suffering as I am.   Yet I am not ashamed, because I know
whom I have believed, and am convinced that he is able to guard what I
have entrusted to him for that day...GUARD.the good deposit that was entrusted to you - GUARD it with the Holy Spirit who lives in us. ('the pattern
of sound teaching, with faith and love in Christ Jesus')   Endure
hardship with us like a good soldier of Christ Jesus. "

Page - 2 -

As we pray together in this special day of fasting and prayer, and continue
through the month of AUGUST with this same prayer list....as the wars rage
in the world and terror fills many people's hearts, as we become confused at
times as to when we might be tempted with pride,in looking at the falseness
or sin among various "bodies" of people naming the name of Christ,-- yet have
the other danger of being silent when we should speak out.   Let us pray....
each of us for ourselves, each of us for each other...as ones who have been
"entrusted with God's work".   PAUL speaks to TITUS giving him that which
we need: " Rather be hospitable, one who loves what is good, who is self-con‐
trolled, upright, holy and disciplined. He must hold firmly to the trustworthy message as it has been taught, so that he can encourage others by
sound doctirne and refute those who oppose it."   Titus 1: 8,9

"I always thank my God as I remember you in my prayers...............And one
thing more: Prepare a guest room for me, because I hope to be restored to you
in answer to your prayers."   Philemon 4,22

We really do need to PREPARE IN PRACTICAL WAYS FOR ANSWERS TO PRAYER!
Praying with expectation of His answers:...of sufficient grace to go on under
difficult and unchanging circumstances, or....changes in direct answer also.

1. Pray for each BRANCH of L'Abri, and for each MEMBER, WORKER, STUDENT,
GUEST, PRAYING FAMILY, DONORS, and all who are bound together in the wider
L'Abri Family.   Please pray with the added list enclosed.
2. PRAY for the children of L'Abri, of all ages from babies to college
students, for spiritual and physical health, for education, recreation, family
life, vacations, and the Lord's help in all the diversity of choices ahead.
3. PRAY for PROTECTION for each of the L'Abri Workers and families and for
all the wider L'Abri family...protection in the midst of evil, of disasters
of so many kinds, of wars and rumors of wars, of riots and terrorist's sudden
attacks etc. protection from accidents amidst so much travel, protection
from attacks of a diverse sort, from epidemics of diverse germs!!!!! and
from false ideas and philosophies in insidious forms.
4. PRAY for the CONTENT of all the messages L'Abri people will be giving in
this month ahead, the months ahead, and the year ahead...whether in one to
one conversations, Bible classes, lectures, sermons, articles, books, seminars
and conferences. Pray that the Holy Spirit may open the truth and treasures
of the Bible to each of us in study, and give a clear clarion voice to us as
we communicate in any form...tapes, films, phone conversations etc. etc.
5. PRAY FOR THE MINI CONFERENCES in September, October, November, as people
are registering in the 20 cities now, as the 20 committees prepare all the
details, as L'Abri people prepare their messages, PRAY FOR THE PEOPLE OF
GOD's CHOICE TO COME TO EACH ONE OF THESE, and pray for the blend of people
to be a help in discussions, and future contacts with each other also.
Pray for all the material needs to be met, for the physical work to be shared,
for the auditoriums and rooms to be theright ones. Pray for "eyes of understanding to be opened", and for minds and hearts to be prepared ahead of
time.
6: PLEASE PRAY FOR ALL THESE SAME THINGS FOR EACH BRANCH OF L'ABRI IN AUGUST
..the people of God's choice to come to each branch, the content of all the
lectures and conversations, and eyes of understanding to be opened. PRAY
also for preparation for Sept.Oct.Nov. in each branch when Workers are away.
7. PRAY for PREPARATION for all other conferences ahead in L'Abri in this
coming year, for the L'Abri Ensemble, for Scandanavian conferences and
speaking engagements, for English speaking etc., for Holland, and any other
countries or conferences where L'Abri Members and Workers will be speaking.
8. PRAY FOR THE WRITING OF BOOKS....that whoever is meant to write, may be
given strength to do so, and the content the Lord would have. For books
already written to be placed where the Lord would have them, for the films
to be distributed where God would have them.
9. PRAY FOR THE FINANCIAL NEEDS OF L'Abri to be supplied in each branch of
the work, and for properties and furnishings where needed.

time to pray in this way is a "doing" of our faith, rather than simply talking about it.

At L'Abri we have an annual day of fasting and prayer each July 30. In addition to that, we call a day of fasting and prayer when the Members and Workers feel such a day of prayer is needed because someone has gone to speak in Poland or Sweden or Australia or Germany or Canada or the United States. Or a day of prayer is called when there is a financial need, or a special need of wisdom for decisions that must be made by the Members concerning some area of the work, or the need of some student facing a difficulty, or a serious illness or accident. For such a day we put aside the noon meal, which frees people from meal preparation and washing dishes, as well as freeing people from conversation with each other, to have hours for prayer. No one is made to feel compelled to fast, and food is placed where someone who has a physical need for food may come and have it, then go back to the woods or fields to be alone.

You know when you feel a heavy need of help, and you alone can work out a way of having unbroken hours by putting aside things that will not harm some other person.

The prayer list shown on pages 223 and 224 might be helpful as an example of one of our L'Abri lists for a day of prayer. As you read a verse and stop to pray before reading the next one, you will find your own petitions and requests coming quite naturally in the context of some of these passages.

QUESTION:
In praying for God's will, how do we know we have received answers to prayer for our families?

ANSWER:
In praying for God's will, His direction and guidance, we are always in a moment-by-moment situation. Constantly there can be a bend in the path ahead, with a new vista ahead of which we are unaware. God doesn't give blueprints to any of us for the entire span of life ahead. This is one of the things concerning prayer that causes me to realize day by day, and year after year in my own life, that God has given something very priceless in *not* giving blueprints and in *not* giving outlined answers that cover a long time ahead. He has kept us and keeps us now, in a postition in which we need that communication day after day to know one step at a time.

Today I know I must continue to write this book rather than going for a "day-off walk"! How do I know? It's complicated, but the moment came when I was sure it was right to agree to a contract as to a time to be finished, and, God willing, I intend to finish it with His strength. There is integrity in carrying out something you have promised to do and meeting a deadline. It is part of the whole work ethic. It isn't mystical. It is practical honesty.

God has made very clear that His children are not to be hypocritical, to promise things they don't intend to carry out. God's will is clear in His word on many everyday things. So today, I fulfill what I have promised to do today, even if other things clamor to be done within my own desires, or even if others try to turn me aside.

With that said, I would say that in my own pictorial view of seeking God's will I see a rushing stream in the mountains or fields, with stones big enough to put a foot on to cross. I picture God showing me one stone big enough to start across on, and then one stone on which to put my foot next. And then the waters whirl around, and I am to stay where I am, on that particular stone, until *He* shows me the next step. To rush ahead on my own would be disastrous.

The Bible verses I would refer to for this kind of "waiting" are Isaiah 50:10–11. They are verses that have been a part of our prayer lists for L'Abri through the years. The contrast is a sharp reminder, time after time: "Watch out and don't light your own sparks."

> "Who among you fears the LORD?
> Who obeys the voice of His Servant?
> Who walks in darkness
> And has no light?
> Let him trust in the name of the LORD
> And rely upon his God.
> Look, all you who kindle a fire,
> Who encircle yourselves with sparks:
> Walk in the light of your fire and in the sparks you have
>   kindled—
> This you shall have from My hand:
> You shall lie down in torment."

It is a warning to watch out for impatience in wanting to "get on with it," whatever "it" happens to be. God tells us that to be in a fog, a dark place, to have no clue of what comes next, is to be in a place where we *need* to trust Him and keep our hand in His hand, waiting for Him to show us where to go or what to do next. The foolish choice is to turn away from the common sense realization that God means us to wait, and to insist on lighting our own flares.

We are where we are today, each of us. You are a doctor today in one particular town, or you are a bookstore seller today; you are a dentist today, or you are a grocer at this time; you are a grandmother today. Today you and I are involved in a great number of things, fulfilling the purposes for which God has us where we are, doing the combination of routine or imaginative things we are doing. All right—you and I often want to know, "What comes next?" God is saying, "Trust Me." He is saying, "Stay in the place where you are until I show you [in a variety of ways, usually not mystical at all] what comes next." He is saying, "Blessed is the person who waits in the dark, holding My hand."

The contrast is the whole thing of choice again. There are those who don't want to wait for God, but who push that off in order to have their own choices. God's word to them is, "All right, choose to light your own sparks and walk in that self-made flare of light. You are free to make your own choice to do your thing. But, you will have this from My hand: you will lie down in sorrow." It is the negative promise again, fairly and clearly.

As life continues, this thing of knowing the Lord's will is a matter of asking a day at a time, waiting for Him and waiting upon Him in prayer. Sometimes we find that He leads to a second stone that we think is to be permanent, but that turns out only to lead to another one in a year of two. That does *not* mean you did not know God's will for that time when you found a certain house, only to discover after fixing it up that your work was to be somewhere else and that house had to go! Now up goes a "for sale" sign, or a "for rent" sign on the place you felt would be your place of continuity!

You are not necessarily outside of the Lord's will if you get to Africa and find that you can't learn the language easily, or that you need to be in the hospital with malaria right away. He does not promise us that everything is going to go smoothly. The smoothness of the next step is not the criterion of your having found the Lord's will. Satan would like us to be confused on that point! May we never forget it.

As you look back over the answers to your prayer through various open doors, a house being found and a "job" opening up, you are sure that God answered your prayers and took you to whatever it is you are in now. Then suddenly the roof falls in, water pipes burst, rats are found in the cellar, your children are ill one after another, a burglar breaks in, a fire bursts forth, a string of difficulties hits you. That does *not* prove you are not in the Lord's will.

Don't stop praying for your basic work and for all the individual difficulties you face one after another. Pray for a supply of the needs, physical, intellectual, emotional, and material—and for courage and strength to go on. Perhaps the school for the children is to be a different one next year. That does not mean that this year you were "out of the Lord's will" to have them in their present school.

Was Paul not in the Lord's will when that "thorn in the flesh" bothered him so much? Paul put it this way:

> And lest I should be exalted above measure by the abundance of the revelations, a thorn in the flesh was given to me, a messenger of Satan to buffet me, lest I be exalted above measure. Concerning this thing I pleaded with the Lord three times that it might depart from me. And He said to me, "My grace is sufficient for you, for My strength is made perfect in weakness." Therefore most gladly I will rather boast in my infirmities, that the power of Christ may rest upon me. Therefore I take pleasure in infirmities, in reproaches, in needs, in persecutions, in distresses, for Christ's sake. For when I am weak, then I am strong.
>
> 2 Cor. 12:7–10

I want to point out two things here. Paul prayed three times. Is that an indication we cannot repeat the same plea oftener? Not at all. Jesus made clear that we are to be like the importunate widow, who bothered the judge so frequently. We should "always . . . pray and not lose heart" (Luke 18:1).

However, there are two kinds of answers.

It would have been possible for God to remove Paul's thorn in the flesh, whatever it was. Many times answers to prayer are recognizable because they are so vividly exactly what we asked for. Naturally, this kind of an answer brings joy, recognition, encouragement, and an assurance that the Lord has heard and that He is with us supplying the need in our present place in His will.

On the other hand, there is the other kind of answer, which is the answer God gave Paul concerning that "thorn." Why did Paul stop asking for the removal of the thorn? I don't believe it was with a sense of giving up—not at all. Paul accepted the Lord's answer. He was excited about the *answer!* It's like being able to say, "I've been doing more work with this cancer than I could have done without it." It is recognizing in some small measure the wonder of what God is doing. It is recognizing that it couldn't be human strength.

Paul says, "I will rather boast in my infirmities, that the power of Christ may rest upon me" (2 Cor. 12:9). He is excited about the reality of having experienced the answer to prayer which was a very literal receiving of God's power in His weakness. "My strength is made perfect in weakness" is God speaking truth, and Paul had tested in one instance after another the reality of that truth taking place.

He goes on to say, "Therefore I take pleasure in infirmities, in reproaches, in needs, in persecutions, in distresses." He isn't being sadistic; he really is amazed and delighted at the reality of what God is doing in answer to prayer—enabling Paul to do what he could not possibly have done himself in the midst of his human weakness and suffering. Paul accepted God's answer with joy!

Now what we need to recognize, each of us in our own prayer lives and in our prayer for God's will, is that we will also have both kinds of answers.

CHAPTER TWELVE

---~~~---

Sensible Balance in Building and Battle

WHAT A FORLORN SIGHT the broken walls of Jerusalem must have been to those who had known a different day when the city was bustling with life and the gates were intact. It was Hanai, one of the brothers of Nehemiah, who brought the crushing news to him from Judah, something like what you might see in your papers today about some part of the world that is home to someone! The story is told in the Book of Nehemiah in the Old Testament.

> And they said to me, "The survivors who are left from the captivity in the province are there in great distress and reproach. The wall of Jerusalem is also broken down, and its gates are burned with fire."
>
> 1:3

Nehemiah's reaction was that which is the common sense reaction of anyone in time of crisis who really belongs to God and trusts Him: "So it was, when I heard these words, that I sat down and wept, and mourned for many days; I was fasting and praying before the God of heaven" (1:4).

Nehemiah determined to ask King Artaxerxes for permission to rebuild the wall. The beauty of the "order" of his asking is that when the king says, "What do you request?" Nehemiah prays (obviously silently) to God, and *then* answers the king: "If it pleases the king . . . , I ask that you send me to Judah, to the city of my fathers' tombs, that I may rebuild it" (2:5).

Nehemiah gives God the credit for answering his prayer when he reports, "And the king granted them to me according to the good hand of my God upon me" (2:8).

Can't you feel it? This is far from mechanical. It is real. Nehemiah is really crushed by the situation in Jerusalem. He weeps. His tears and emotions are real, not an act. But as he mourns he turns to God with faith and trust, pouring out his prayer with fasting, spending time telling God about it and asking for help. He determines to take the next step and speak to the king. But in this action he depends on the Lord's power to help him. Is he sure then of the following step?

Listen again to what he says as he inspects the walls of Jerusalem: "Then I arose in the night, I and a few men with me; I told no one what my God had put in my heart to do at Jerusalem" (2:12). Yes, he is sure. He is sure God put the idea and determination within him to *do* something.

When he comes to the moment of speaking to those who would be doing the practical work of the rebuilding, he says with firm conviction:

> "You see the distress that we are in, how Jerusalem lies waste, and its gates are burned with fire. Come and let us build the wall of Jerusalem, that we may no longer be a reproach." And I told them of the hand of my God which had been good upon me, and also of the king's words that he had spoken to me.
>
> 2:17–18

Their response was immediate: "Then they set their hands to do this good work."

Today we live in a time when walls have indeed been broken down all around us, and gates burned with fire! If your imagination is vivid, please picture the stones in this imaginary wall as "ideas," "ideals," "standards," "principles." In a rubble such as we see pictured after a bombing lie stones and dust, stones consisting of broken families, broken understanding of what human beings are, shifting morals, lack of any unchanging base for law or justice, shifting standards, lopsided humanistic teaching in schools, a low view of moral life, inconsistent reasons for supporting life or death, instability tumbling in clouds of dust rather than firm assurance coming from any area in the humanistic media. Ideas pour forth like broken stones lying about a ruined wall. A wall that once gave some form of protection as it outlined the "city" is now a shambles.

We who believe that truth exists, that there is stability, solidity, an unchanging standard, a steadfast pattern for life, a comforting continuity of morals, need to dust off the stones and start rebuilding. I find that Nehemiah's rebuilding of the walls is a pattern meant for us today.

As we read the Book of Nehemiah and recognize what is around us and before us, we learn something of what the sensible balance is in both building and in battle for our own Christian living.

As you read Nehemiah 2, you will find that as soon as the building began, opposition took place. Life is never simple! Not only does Satan attack anything that is constructive, but people do, too.

> But when Sanballat the Horonite, Tobiah the Ammonite official, and Geshem the Arab heard of it, they laughed us to scorn and despised us, and said, "What is this thing that you are doing? Will you rebel against the king?"
>
> 2:19

Note the mocking, the ridicule, and then a directly false accusation. They were not rebelling against the king; as you know, they had permission. That did not stop bystanders from believing the false words. Nehemiah simply answered at that time, "The God of heaven Himself will prosper us; therefore we His servants will arise and build. . . ." (2:20). An honest answer . . . and a determination to go on doing the physical, practical work with expectation of God's help.

The third chapter is fascinating in its account of the various families assigned to rebuild different parts of the wall, and different gates. "The sons of Hassenaah built the Fish Gate; they laid its beams and hung its doors with its bolts and bars" (3:3). It is really thrilling to me that God mentions the bolts and bars, as well as the names of the people who faithfully did their share of the work of rebuilding. Don't ever forget they did it by families. The working together of families to rebuild the shattered walls is central in importance. How we should pray for whole families today to be involved in the rebuilding that is needed!

As you continue to read this third chapter, don't skip over Shallum (v. 12). "Shallum the son of Hallohesh, leader of half the district of Jerusalem; he and his daughters made repairs." Note carefully, please: he is an official, but he is dirtying his hands and getting in on the practical work, the hard work of rebuilding, with the help of his daughters. Daughters! It seems to me people purposely skip over the involvement of the women, the daughters, the little girls and the big sisters, as part not only of the family but of the wider work . . . the togetherness of reclaiming or rebuilding what has been demolished by the enemy.

As you read you'll notice the Levites are involved, too, and also the goldsmiths and merchants. The picture is of a togetherness. Nobody is too big or too little. No little people. No big people. All at this moment are working together to build something.

If you wanted to paint this scene, you would be in danger of painting a false representation of what is going on if you read only these first three chapters, got out your canvas, and furiously proceeded to picture a happy, peaceful, joyous scene of a cross section of people with a cross section of talents and personalities joining together in a positive work. You would be in danger of painting too idealistically, too romantically. It was *not* like that. You haven't seen anything yet. If you were painting this story you would need other colors and a lot more space on your canvas because a lot is going on at one time.

This is a battle you need to paint, not just a building. It is a balance of building and battling!

The fourth chapter is something you need to read frequently for your own life in this century. I need to read it frequently for my life. We need to remember it in a great variety of situations if we are to understand the balance of a common sense Christian life.

> But it so happened, when Sanballat heard that we were rebuilding the wall, that he was furious and very indignant, and mocked the Jews. And he spoke before his brethren and the army of Samaria, and said, "What are these feeble Jews doing? Will they fortify themselves? Will they offer sacrifices? Will they complete it in a day? Will they revive the stones from the heaps of rubbish—stones that are burned?"
>
> 4:1–2

What a parallel to the attacks of humanistic, unbelieving people today when efforts are being made to "rebuild" from the rubble. "Those ideas are antiquated. Will they bring back to life such words as *purity* and *scrupulous*? How can they bring back such talk of an absolute when truth no longer exists, when such ideas are a heap of rubble?" The attack is very similar and is accompanied by similiar scorn.

Now as we read on we find Tobiah the Ammonite trying to comfort and reassure Sanballat by saying, "Whatever they build, if even a fox goes up on it, he will break down their stone wall" (4:3).

The sarcasm is biting and the point is clear: no stronger attack is needed to finish off the building than the weight of a fox. A fox could tumble all their efforts in a minute.

Now prayer is the first response of Nehemiah and the people. "Hear, O our God, for we are despised." They pray for help against the enemy. The fabulous balance that we must watch for, and keep watching for in our own lives, is demonstrated here as they finished praying, and they went straight on with their building.

"So we built the wall, and the entire wall was joined together up to half its height, for the people had a mind to work" (4:6). You may be sure they prayed with all their hearts, but this did not clash with their working with all their hearts. They kept on in the face of insults and threats, while praying for help.

> Now it happened, when Sanballat, Tobiah, the Arabs, the Ammonites, and the Ashdodites heard that the walls of Jerusalem were being restored and the gaps were beginning to be closed, that they became very angry, and all of them conspired together to come and attack Jerusalem and create confusion.
>
> 4:7–8

Please notice that when the walls began to look as though something was really succeeding, and the stones were neatly placed one upon another so that it began to be recognizably a wall, then the tune of the scornful "other side" changed. No more was the talk of sending a fox to spoil the wall; now the entire mixture of Arabs and Ammonites and all the rest of them forgot their own differences and banded together to plot an attack!

The similarity of this account to what is actually taking place right now is astounding. I might say it is incredible . . . except as we read Nehemiah it is not surprising and it is credible indeed. As long as challenges to prevailing attitudes stay harmlessly in the midst of rubble, as long as people who believe God's Word to be true and who attempt to live by it and teach it can be ignored, all is quiet. But when the Judeo-Christian position on the existence of God, the existence of an absolute base for law and morals, the rebuilding of family life, the need for righteousness and honesty and integrity and virtue are again becoming recognized, then there will be a plotting together to "attack Jerusalem and create confusion." What was the reaction of Nehemiah as he led the people? "But we prayed to our God and posted a guard day and night to meet this threat" (4:9 NIV).

Practical! Common sense believers! They prayed believing that God was able to do something, all right. They prayed believing that God existed and would reward those who diligently seek Him. This is not speaking of a cursory, artificial, hypocritical, formal kind of mumbling a few words. They really prayed—and then they really posted a guard to meet the threat of the oncoming army. They armed themselves and prepared for battle. Two things happened next.

First came a discouraged and despondent reaction on the part of the people in Judah as they said, "The strength of the laborers is failing, and there is so much rubbish that we are not able to build the wall" (4:10).

Can't you just feel their dejection? They feel weary and hopeless. Somebody has said a gloomy thing and others have caught the morose pessimism. "It's impossible . . . we can't do anything . . . it's all gone too far. How can we change what has happened? It is really hopeless. There are too many of them and too few of us. We can't scrounge around in the midst of all the dirt any longer. We're too tired. Let's just take a bath and forget it! Whose idea was this, anyway?" Can you, can I, relate to this kind of feeling time after time in today's battles? Satan may be trying to discourage us, but we can often discourage ourselves or one another! We are in danger of being in that same condition just before the enemy comes at us with a concentrated attack.

While the people of Judah were saying this, the second thing came from the enemy's side: "And our adversaries said, 'They will neither know nor see anything, till we come into their midst and kill them and cause the work to cease'" (4:11). This threat, this frightening plan was overheard by Jews who lived near them. These Jews then came and "told us ten times, 'From whatever place you turn, they will be upon us'" (4:12).

A great help!

Not once, but ten times over and over and over, these who should have been helping the work and preparing to fight were gloomily saying, "Just quit. We're going to get killed . . . wait and see. They'll be everywhere."

What a picture of history! So often those who should be helping as friends and part of the family are helping the enemy. People jump too quickly, fearing man more than they trust God.

Nehemiah was a tremendous leader in this moment. He got busy doing what needed to be done, most efficiently. "Therefore I positioned men behind the lower parts of the wall, at the openings; and I set the people according to their families, with their swords, their spears, and their bows" (4:13).

He wasted no time in equipping the people who were rebuilding with the equipment needed to ward off the attack that was on its way. They were also posted strategically for both building and fighting, some behind the lowest points at the exposed places . . . all by families. This was a together defense. There was something worth defending. Never forget that: there is something worth defending when you are one of God's people under His direction in the moment of history that is your moment. We are not there to see how brave and faithful we would have been. But we are here now, and *now* is our moment for whatever God would have us do.

Nehemiah goes on: "And I looked, and arose and said to the nobles, to the leaders, and to the rest of the people, 'Do not be afraid of them. Remember the Lord, great and awesome, and fight for your brethren, your sons, your daughters, your wives, and your houses'" (4:14).

Are you excited? Does that paragraph make you proud of Nehemiah as someone whose hand you want to shake someday? What he has said applies to us so thoroughly. We are to remember the Lord in our battle; in the midst of fears and tremblings and weariness we are to remember the Lord. He is great and awesome. How can we do less than trust Him and stand for His truth, which He has given us to make known in our time of history?

But as we remember the Lord we are also to fight for our families . . . our brothers and sisters, our sons and daughters, our wives, our homes. We are to fight for the very existence of the family, as well as for each individual from the youngest to the oldest. There is something worth fighting for, says Nehemiah. Remember the Lord and remember your families. Don't stop. Endure to the end. Don't give up!

The next sentence is really fantastic. The enemy's reaction is amazing. "And it happened, when our enemies heard that it was known to us, and that God had brought their counsel to nothing, that all of us returned to the wall, everyone to his work" (4:15).

This communication, passed on or overheard, convinced the enemies not only that their secret plot had been discovered, but that the God of the Israelites had frustrated their plan. They gave some kind of indication that they had been "foiled" by the God so alien to them.

It reminds me a bit of the kind of remarks that are made today about such things as herpes, as if "perhaps, there is a reason for the old order of things." Whether it is as definite as that or not, certainly there is a different attitude on the part of liberals and humanists today in recognizing that they have been "foiled" in some measure, and that their walking in to stop any replacing of stones in the wall is not going to be as easy a takeover as had been imagined. The communication has been passed on or overheard that their plot for a complete takeover has been discovered, and that fear has *not* turned the persistent workers in the rebuilding away from their resolution to go on. It is going to be harder than they thought.

Back to Nehemiah:

> So it was, from that time on, that half of my servants worked at construction, while the other half held the spears, the shields, the bows and wore armor; and the leaders were behind all the house of Judah. Those who built the wall, and those who carried burdens, loaded themselves so that with one hand they worked at construction, and with the other held a weapon. Every one of the builders had his sword girded at his side as he built. And the one who sounded the trumpet was beside me.
>
> 4:16–18

That painting that is being painted on the huge canvas now needs to show half the men working away at the walls, with women and children too . . . a colorful sight. Then there have to be spears, shields, bows, and armor painted on the other half . . . in their hands, slung over their shoulders. This is a military protection for the workers who are giving themselves to the rising wall. Those who carried the materials held what was necessary for the work in one hand and a weapon in the other. And the builders wore a sword on their sides as they worked. The daughters, too? I imagine so.

It is interesting that when the great preacher Spurgeon started a Christian magazine that went out from London, he called it *The Sword and the Trowel*, since he felt that the Christian's life should be lived in that way . . . with a trowel to build and a sword to fight the enemy—equal equipment. We have a positive work to do in making truth known, in helping people to have patterns for family life, in caring for unborn babies, for elderly people, for handicapped people, for orphans needing adoption, in answering the questions of honest, confused people seeking truth . . . a very wide variety and a tremendous amount of positive work. But we are also to be fighting evil and fighting the enemies of truth who would "tear down the stones" the minute we put them in place. It is a matter of praying constantly for God's help in the balance of building and battling.

And what about the man who sounded the trumpet? Read on.

> Then I said to the nobles, the rulers, and the rest of the people, "The work is great and extensive, and we are separated far from one another on the wall. Therefore, wherever you hear the sound of the trumpet, rally to us there. Our God will fight for us."
>
> 4:19–20

Where are you geographically? Where am I? Where are all the others in this battle for truth in this particular moment of history? Amazingly we are scattered along "the wall." We are indeed scattered, and we have various tasks to be doing. The enemy comes at different points, and each of us is suddenly exposed and in danger of being "shot down." We need help.

There is a truly wonderful balance of what the common sense reality is as to what we are to do when we need help. Yes, we pray and call out to God. But what was done in Nehemiah's time is also to be done by us. We are to "blow the trumpet" when we see a need on some area of the wall. We are to "blow the trumpet" for horizontal help—the help of other Christians.

"There is going to be a vote in Congress on the abortion bill. Send a letter to your congressman, please, if you care about righting this wrong." That might be one trumpet blow.

"A professor is going to be giving a lecture in his university that is particularly difficult and will be challenged because he is giving it from the Christian base. Pray for him on Wednesday, the eighth, please." That's another kind of trumpet.

There are meant to be blasts of the trumpet for a gathering, whether it is to be a gathering in person or a helping from the distance by prayer. We need each other's help and as we see this vivid rebuilding of the wall and visualize the men blowing the trumpets, we can realize perhaps more realistically that we need to be ready and willing to respond to the call for "help, help . . . over there . . . on that part of the wall."

The need may be on the part of a doctor who is taking a firm stand against abortion, or a lawyer, or a businesswoman who is fighting a wrong attack by the IRS. There are great diversities of sudden attacks in this complicated battle for truth we are in while we are trying to rebuild the brokenness.

What would we think of anyone in Nehemiah's time who heard that trumpet call but did not respond and come?

But over and over again comes the assurance, "Our God will fight for us!" God does not sleep. He does not have days that are different in different time zones. He is with us all the time and cares for our needs. Yet this is *His Word*, not just a story about a man named Nehemiah. It is God teaching us the balance of what is expected of *us*, even though He will never leave us nor forsake us and even though He is always available for us to talk to. He expects us to really work. Do listen to the next paragraph to see what I mean.

> So we labored in the work, and half of the men held the spears from daybreak until the stars appeared. At the same time I also said to the people, "Let each man and his servant stay at night in Jerusalem, that they may be our guard by night and a working party by day." So neither I, my brethren, my servants, nor the men of the guard who followed me took off our clothes, except that everyone took them off for washing.
>
> 4:21–23

This was a singlemindness and determination to accomplish the work which did not punch time clocks or count the hours. There are times in our lives when this kind of intensive push is needed. This is not a picture of everyday life month after month, year after year. It is an occasional task that takes precedence over other things. In its own way, this kind of work is like fasting and prayer. One puts aside the "good things" for the hours to be spent in concentrated prayer. In this period, the "good things" such as family life and work in the fields are put aside for the emergency work on the wall.

In the midst of our constant search for balance, this picture does not tell us we are to do one project after another that takes us away from the normal things that make up life. It is a picture of the fact that such a time does arrive. For each of us it will arrive in different forms. Suddenly there is an emergency we are faced with, during which we work and battle. Perhaps it is on a seminar tour, a conference tour, a speaking trip in a far country, a trip to visit orphanages in India and Kenya, a trip to Cambodia to find out what can be done for refugees, a trip to see what can be done for the Siberian Six in Moscow in the American Embassy, or a trip to Washington, D.C., to register approval or disapproval over an important issue.

Whatever it is, there are times when we need to work from dawn to starlight and to not take off our clothing, except for washing, because we need to be on call like a doctor or a nurse. The emergency may be an epidemic or a famine or a flood, during which our help is needed physically and spiritually. When the emergency comes, we must realize we actually are "putting stones in the wall." The humanness we show to other human beings is a strategic part of demonstrating that our lives are different and that on our base, with God as our helper, we do care about people.

We are to be the ones whom people would feel free to call on with trumpet blows because of an urgency involved with the particular aspect of rebuilding that is the emergency need at the moment.

Unhappily, as the Old Testament records the history of God's people, we see that the time when they are doing what is beautiful and right doesn't last long. Too soon there is a turning away. We who have the Holy Spirit dwelling in us have more help than they had, and we are strongly cautioned not to become *weary* in doing good. In Galatians we have a call to attention that should be like the roll of a drum, to make us really listen:

> But the fruit of the Spirit is love, joy, peace, longsuffering, kindness, goodness, faithfulness, gentleness, self-control. . . . If we live in the Spirit, . . . let us not become conceited, provoking one another, envying one another. Brethren, if a man is overtaken in any trespass, you who are spiritual restore such a one in a spirit of gentleness, considering yourself lest you also be tempted. Bear one another's burdens, and so fulfill the law of Christ. For if anyone thinks himself to be something, when he is nothing, he deceives himself. But let each one examine his own work, and then he will have rejoicing in himself alone, and not in another. For each one shall bear his own load. . . . Do not be deceived, God is not mocked; for whatever a man sows, that he will also reap. For he who sows to his flesh will of the flesh reap corruption, but he who sows to the Spirit will of the Spirit reap everlasting life. And let us not grow weary while doing good, for in due season we shall reap if we do not lose heart. Therefore, as we have opportunity, let us do good to all, especially to those who are of the household of faith.
>
> Gal. 5:22–23,25—6:5,7–10

If we read and reread this Scripture and ask God for help to live so that we will be sensitive to whatever trumpet blast applies to us, in bearing someone's personal burden, or in helping to rebuild the broken-down standards, the tumbling-down principles, the lost norms, for our brothers and sisters, our parents, our wives and husbands, our children and grandchildren . . . and for the generations descended from those who have died for the freedoms to live under these standards . . . if we do not give up, it will affect a lot more people than simply those in our own family.

The "walls" we are concerned about, that are crumbling now, have to do with real education being available; with the possibility of the next generation having choice based on knowledge; with having truth somewhere within earshot or eyesight so that it can be compared with that which is false. You and I were not born two hundred years ago; we were not born in Nehemiah's time, either. We can't daydream ourselves into another period of history. This is our history; this is our moment of responsibility. What are we doing in the area of the battle and in the area of rebuilding? We are not meant to live in a protected little ghetto and let the enemy spread lies without giving the people that hear or read an alternative. This is a part of our responsibility, to "do good to all people".

We can't just nod satisfyingly to each other when we read Isaiah 32:6:

> For the foolish person will speak foolishness,
> And his heart will work iniquity:
> To practice ungodliness,
> To utter error against the LORD.

We have to do something about the "error" that is being spread. We are not to be fools in ignoring the destruction of such lies. We who are the children of light are meant to speak truth as we have the opportunity.

Chapter 5 of Nehemiah tells of what Nehemiah did for the poor, whose lands and possessions had been taken away unfairly. The response of the Jews was wonderful at that point. Oh, that God's people might always be consistent in doing His compassionate will! When Nehemiah described just what should be given back and how the nobles and officials were not to lord it over the people, the response was, "'Amen!' . . . Then the people did according to this promise" (v. 13). And on went the work of the wall until it was finished!

Then again Sanballat, Tobiah, and Geshem the Arab, and the rest of the enemies tried to scheme ways of wrecking the whole project before the end. Each time Nehemiah was given wisdom to see through the schemes, and to realize that they were trying to intimidate him by giving him false messages supposedly from the Lord. Nehemiah kept on in a straight line, doing his job of rebuilding without deviation. The enemies of truth and the enemies of believers have always kept on trying to break down the Word of God itself, as well as the people of God. This battle will go on to the end.

Remember that Satan is accusing each believer before God day and night. He also wants to destroy the projects of whatever "rebuilding" is taking place. We can't let down. We need always to go on, with the same prayer Nehemiah prayed in that stage of his project: "For they all were trying to make us afraid, saying, 'Their hands will be weakened in the work, and it will not be done.' Now therefore, O God, strengthen my hands" (6:9).

There are a lot of people who are hoping our hands will get too weak for the work. A lot of people are trying to discourage you and me, trying to frighten us one way or another. Our resource for strength is the same as Nehemiah's. "Now strengthen my hands," we may pray again and again.

Then comes that glorious conclusion to this particular fifty-two-day project.

> So the wall was finished on the twenty-fifth day of the month of Elul, in fifty-two days. And it happened, when all our enemies heard of it, and all the nations around us saw these things, that they were very disheartened in their own eyes; for they perceived that this work was done by our God.
>
> 6:15–16

Marvelous! Wonderful! The mighty God had done a work, through His faithful people, and for that moment the enemies lost their self-confidence. For that moment they realized the work had been done with the help of God. I have a record player here, and I want to hear the "Hallelujah Chorus" from Handel's *Messiah* once more . . . right now! The Everlasting Father, the Prince of Peace whom Handel knew, was known to Nehemiah, too. I wonder what he sang that day? The trumpets would have blown a note of triumph, of victory. The task was completed. A victory won.

Oh, that we might reach a point where we could rejoice that the enemies of truth have lost their self-confidence, that they have realized that we have had the help of our God. Our prayer must always be that this recognition would mean, for some, a turning *to* the true God and crying out, "The Lord, He is God. Why didn't someone tell me this before?"

Let me quickly say that this verse and its note of victory does not end the Bible. Nor does it even end the Book of Nehemiah! The Bible is a realistic Book, true to what happened, true to the recounting of the weakness of God's people. But the victory did happen, and we can treasure it as something God meant us to know about. He also is able to help us in the rebuilding that is before us, and to bring victory along the way.

When we come to a similar experience of having fantastic answers to prayer while continuing in the face of attacks from the enemy on every hand, of completing a task that was seemingly impossible, of bringing about at least some measure of respect from our enemies for the God whom we state has helped us, are we then to close the book of our lives and say, "O.K., I did it with the help of God. Now the story is finished, and I can go fishing for the rest of my life"?

Anything wrong with fishing? Or golf? Or vacations? Or walks in the woods? Or swimming laps in a pool? Or walking on a beach? Or collecting shells or stamps or paintings? Anything wrong with heaving a sigh of relief, and taking a break with your family, or alone? No. A comforting assurance from the Lord in Psalm 127:1–2 points out that there certainly are times when sleep is a gift, when we are not meant to push on.

> Unless the LORD builds the house,
> They labor in vain who build it;
> Unless the LORD guards the city,
> The watchman stays awake in vain.
> It is vain for you to rise up early,
> To sit up late,
> To eat the bread of sorrows;
> For so He gives His beloved sleep.

There is meant to be a common sense balance in our battles and in our building. In the midst of all life, there are to be times of sleep, rest, refreshment given by the Lord. Psalm 23 so beautifully reminds us of this, over and over in life:

He maketh me to lie down in green pastures: he leadeth me beside the still waters. He restoreth my soul: he leadeth me in the paths of righteousness for his name's sake. . . . Thou preparest a table before me in the presence of mine enemies: thou anointest my head with oil; my cup runneth over. Surely goodness and mercy shall follow me all the days of my life: and I will dwell in the house of the LORD for ever.

vv. 2–3,5–6KJV

David knew a life of constant battles, yet he could write this with truthfulness. Our battles will never end until the Lord comes back, or until we die and go to be in the house of the Lord to await His second coming and our resurrected bodies. But however long we have of battle, we are not to feel guilty when the Lord gives us suddenly a table spread "in the presence of mine enemies." Whether that table is in New York, Chicago, London, or Hong Kong, we can be very conscious that in the middle of a tense time of confrontation for the Lord, we are unexpectedly enjoying the refreshment of good food and congenial conversation while surrounded by all that is involved in the battle. At other times we are separated from everything by actually being in a place of "green pastures," a place that is refreshing to body and spirit, a place where sleep and relaxation are possible away from the noise of battle and the heat of the day.

Balance. God's words to us are balanced. He constantly reminds us He knows our frailness and our weaknesses. We are to ask for the refreshment needed. If only a cup of water is possible in the midst of things, with no other let up, then we ask for the needed strength to be given us as a transfusion. However, He does the giving to enable us to go on. At other times, He plainly opens a door to a "break"—another geographic spot, a place away from the telephone, the doorbell. *He* is always accessible, but He knows we need to be tucked away in a green pasture at times, because in our finiteness *we* cannot go on being always accessible!

Ask for wisdom and balance, for yourself and for your loved ones.

We need constant balance in the building and in the battling! Ephesians 6:10–20 gives us the direct command of the Lord not only to be strong in the Lord and in His mighty power, but to be sure we have put on all the equipment, which we are meant to *use*.

> Put on the whole armor of God, that you may be able to stand against the wiles of the devil. [Note that the devil has schemes, and that you and I individually are to put on the armor and to stand. Someone else cannot take my place, or yours.] For we do not wrestle against flesh and blood, but against principalities, against powers, against the rulers of the darkness of this age, against spiritual hosts of wickedness in the heavenly places.
>
> v. 11–12

The forces against which we are pitted are so far beyond our strength that the giant Goliath would be a midget by comparison.

How can we begin such a struggle? How can we stand with such strength against us to knock us down?

> Stand therefore, having girded your waist with truth, having put on the breastplate of righteousness, and having shod your feet with the preparation of the gospel of peace.
>
> vv. 14–15

Note that truth is the first piece of equipment. That ought to be sufficient to arrest our attention and cause us to gasp. Truth matters. Truth comes first. Truth is something you discover with your mind, and then it permeates your whole person. Truth exists, and it is so true that it is the first effective piece of equipment for the battle. If what God asks us to defend is not *true*, then there is nothing further to talk about. We are not to take our stand, or plunge into danger to defend one religion among many religions. This is *truth* we are being given. Buckle it around your waist. Put your hand on that belt and feel the tangibility of that solid, pure leather . . . no flimsy, gaudy, falling-apart sash of destructible material, but solid truth!

That breastplate of righteousness is made up of Christ's perfect righteousness in our place, as we are so prone to fall into temptations or make mistakes. But we must not overlook the fact that we are not then to "sin that grace may bound"; we are not to shrug our shoulders and say, "I'm O.K.; I don't need to look into the Ten Commandments. I don't need to struggle against temptations." We are meant to change and grow and in the Lord's strength have a reality of growing righteousness, which sets apart our lives as different from the culture around us.

Then our feet are to be "shod" that we may run, as carriers of good news run. We have the only good news that exists in the world today, a message of peace. It is not a foolish manmade peace that is so temporary that the announcements are drowned out by the rumble of the next war in the world, but an everlasting peace. It is a message worth running to spread.

> Above all, taking the shield of faith with which you will be able to quench all the fiery darts of the wicked one.
>
> v. 16

There are darts! They do fly, and flame, and are dangerous—not simply a piece of theater! We need to actively recognize that the darts are a threat, and pray with faith that God is able to divert their direction and keep us safe. Faith, James tells us, is demonstrated by action based on that faith. This is something that, incident by incident in our own history, we are to recognize. Time after time we find we have taken a step out on the end of a limb because we have faith that God is there and will hear our cry for help as we take that particularly vulnerable spot out there within view of the one releasing the darts!

> And take the helmet of salvation, and the sword of the Spirit, which is the word of God.
>
> v. 17

You really need to have that helmet; it is of basic necessity to be saved, converted, born again, to be a believer, a child of God, a sheep of the Shepherd's flock, before you have that helmet of protection.

And then the two-edged sword for penetrating attack is none other than the Bible, the Word of God, His clear communication that has been applicable to every century of history. The Word of God has a power of penetration that time does not dull. That sword does not become rusty, no matter what its critics say. This is our weapon, and when it is given as less than "true" or has had something added or removed, it is an unwieldy sword indeed. We are carefully warned not to take away or add anything to the Word of God. Seen in the light of its being our "sword," that warning becomes most vivid.

If the painter I imagined painting Nehemiah's rebuilding the walls were to paint the difference between a sword, whole and as it was made to be, and two others—one with lumps of additional metal on it, rendering it uselessly spoiled with bumpy awkwardness taking away the sleek efficiency, and a second one with bites taken out of it, giving dull jagged sides to the blade, and a cracked and uncomfortable handle—the youngest child could see the contrast. How different would be the perfectly unspoiled, gleaming sword, perfectly balanced in contrast to the two spoiled ones.

> [Pray] always with all prayer and supplication in the Spirit, being watchful to this end with all perseverance and supplication for all the saints—and for me, that utterance may be given to me, that I may open my mouth boldly to make known the mystery of the gospel, for which I am an ambassador in chains; that in it I may speak boldly, as I ought to speak.
>
> vv. 18–20

Neither the battle nor the building can go on without prayer. Help is needed, and it must be asked for. Over and over again the central need is prayer. The Spirit will help and Jesus Christ is also helping as our mediator. The Father is ready to hear and answer. We are not to neglect prayer on any occasion. "All prayer and supplication" implies a terrific diversity, originality, and naturalness at the same time. We need to be alert, wide awake, sensitive to each other's needs, ears open for the sound of a distant trumpet.

Paul then makes it very personal in asking prayer for himself. He is not sitting outside the circle of need. He includes himself in the need of having others pray for words to be given by the Lord when he speaks. He also asks that along with the right words, he may have a calmness rather than a fear. He asks prayer that he may make the truth known fearlessly. Why? Because the attack is sure to come! In fact, he is already in chains for speaking truth. He expects to continue the battle *and* the building in that moment of history, in spite of the chains. He was *not* indicating that it would be a matter of common sense to run away and be accepted by the majority! No, Paul's word to Timothy and to us is, "Endure hardship as a good soldier of Jesus Christ" (2 Tim. 2:3).

What is common sense Christian living? It encompasses the whole of life, from childhood to old age. It includes the whole person, giving freedom for creativity and commanding us to rejoice and be glad. It makes a place for reality of sorrow because of the results of the Fall. It is a life wherein we are to be responsible for a certain portion of history and geography during our own lifetime in whatever God has for us to say or do. It is a life of battle as we live among many who have turned away from God and would fiercely oppose our message. It is a life of unity with the people of God, but a life of diversity in our tremendously different sensitivities, talents, and understandings. It is a life during which we are meant to seek wisdom and understanding, as well as to oppose that which is false and opposed to truth. It is a life during which we look to each other for help and comfort, but it is also a life during which only God our Father, Jesus our Savior and Advocate and the Holy Spirit our Comforter can be counted on always, without fail or without being hindered by lack of time.

Common sense Christian living is not a "group living," a "group effort," a matter of always being able to count on other people's complete understanding and their running to our aid. We need to be sure of what God would have us do or say, and then do it without a pat on the back or the approval of everyone else. There are times when each of us needs to be willing to stand alone, as a kind of David, with our own particular slingshot and our own kind of smooth stones, advancing toward our own particular Goliath.

Paul warns Timothy of the very kind of thing I mean. This should bring us to our knees before the Lord. Paul warns Timothy of the man Alexander the metal worker, or "coppersmith" as he is called in the King James Version. Alexander, Paul warns, is a dangerous man, because he is against the message of truth. But note what Paul says in recounting his own experience. Evidently a confrontation took place, and no one came to Paul's aid.

If this is so for Paul, what about Timothy? What about you? What about me? We too are being warned that at times no one, or very few people, will be on our side, but we are also being encouraged that if God be with us then who can be against us? Use your sense! Isn't God enough help?

> Alexander the coppersmith did me much harm. May the Lord repay him according to his works. You also must beware of him, for he has greatly resisted our words. At my first defense no one stood with me, but all forsook me. May it not be charged against them. But the Lord stood with me and strengthened me, so that the message might be preached fully through me, and that all the Gentiles might hear. And I was delivered out of the mouth of the lion. And the Lord will deliver me from every evil work and preserve me for His heavenly kingdom. To Him be glory forever and ever. Amen!
>
> 2 Tim. 4:14–18

One day the trumpet will sound to announce that our need of balance in building and battle will be over!

That trumpet blast will bring *all* of the Lord's family together . . . from every tribe and nation and kindred and language . . . from every time band and from every moment in history. There will be a complete response to that trumpet note, as the dead will arise and those who are alive will be changed. The meeting place will be the air. No one will be left out who has responded to God's invitation, "Come." That trumpet call will announce the end of our need to endure hardship of any kind, and the beginning of our discovery of perfection for eternity.

We are allowed to pray, "Even so, come, Lord Jesus."

The grace of our Lord Jesus Christ be with us all.